Boston Confronts Jim Crow

BOSTON CONFRONTS JIM CROW

1890–1920

Mark R. Schneider

Northeastern University Press
BOSTON

Northeastern University Press 1997

Library of Congress Cataloging-in-Publication Data

Schneider, Mark, 1946–
 Boston confronts Jim Crow, 1890–1920 / Mark R. Schneider.
  p. cm.
 Includes bibliographical references and index.
 ISBN 1-55553-296-9 (cloth). — ISBN 1-55553-295-0 (pbk.)
  1. Boston (Mass.)—Race relations. 2. Afro-Americans—
 Segregation—Massachusetts—Boston. 3. Afro-Americans—
 History—1877–1964. 4. Boston (Mass.)—Biography. I. Title.
 F73.9.N4S36 1997
 974.4′6100496073—dc20   96–32144

Designed by Milenda Nan Ok Lee

Composed in Adobe Caslon by Coghill Composition in Richmond, Virginia. Printed and bound by Thomson-Shore, Inc., in Dexter, Michigan. The paper is Glatfelter Supple Opaque Recycled, an acid-free sheet.

MANUFACTURED IN THE UNITED STATES OF AMERICA
00 99 98 97   4 3 2 1

For Judith

Contents

Preface

"The problem of the Twentieth Century is the problem of the color line," W. E. B. Du Bois wrote in the forethought to *The Souls of Black Folk* in 1903.[1] Nowhere was that crucial American dilemma more earnestly addressed between 1890 and 1920 than in Boston. During these thirty years, white supremacists of varying stripes denied African-Americans their civil and political rights, segregated them socially, exploited them economically, and enforced the new order by means of increasingly public violence. This study discusses what Bostonians did as the white South drew a rigid color line through its society, and the white North greeted its African-American migrants with paternalism at best and violence at worst. It seeks to discover the sources of their ideas and actions in the unique antislavery tradition of the city.

Boston remained a singular place in its attitude toward race relations during this period, producing important national leaders for the reform movement. Although I have not attempted to compare Boston to New York, Chicago, Philadelphia, or other northern cities, the special role of Bostonians in the country as a whole should become obvious.[2] In a general sense, the city did follow the pattern of increasing hostility toward new black residents and indifference to the new order in the South. Boston, however, as the home of abolition, had too great an investment in its past to follow the national trend entirely. African-Americans and antiracist whites were proud of their city throughout this period, and between 1890 and 1920 they urged their fellow Americans to live up to Boston's best traditions.

On the national level, the question of the endurance of the abolitionist legacy has been most thoughtfully addressed by James M. McPherson, author of two outstanding books on this subject.[3] In the introduction to the second volume, *The Abolitionist Legacy,* he wrote that he "challenge[d] the prevailing assumption that most abolitionists abandoned the battle for Negro rights after 1870." He compiled a table of 284 first-, second-, and third-generation abolitionists and traced their responses to the erosion of civil rights between 1870 and 1909, the year the National Association for the Advancement of Colored People was founded. Even those who backed away from the full civil rights program maintained their long-term perspective by contributing to the education of the freedpeople. The present study affirms McPherson's conclusion that on the whole, the dwindling group of race reformers backed full citizenship rights for African-Americans.

The interracial minority that carried forward the antislavery heritage was small but significant.[4] Boston's compact African-American community was particularly militant. It produced national leadership in the person of William Monroe Trotter and his outspoken *Guardian* newspaper; Mrs. Josephine St. Pierre Ruffin of the African-American women's club movement; and Butler and Mary Wilson of the National Association for the Advancement of Colored People. White activists such as civil rights attorney Moorfield Storey, Irish revolutionary and poet John Boyle O'Reilly, and NAACP leader Francis Jackson Garrison, youngest son of abolitionist William Lloyd Garrison, anchored themselves in the reform tradition that began in the 1830s. These people drew their inspiration in part from Boston's intellectual and political heritage.

Of course, not all Bostonians of this era who acted upon American race relations consistently defended notions of equality for African-Americans. Republican politicians like Henry Cabot Lodge and George Frisbie Hoar led the congressional fight for the Federal Elections bill of 1890 that would protect black voters, but shortly afterward Lodge especially became disillusioned with the possibility for progress. Attorney William Henry Lewis, a supporter of Booker T. Washington, kept silent in the face of injustice, hoping to win political advancement. Women's suffrage advocate Henry Blackwell did not uphold the views of his wife Lucy Stone, when he proposed that the votes of "respectable" women would counterbalance the votes of blacks and immigrants. Nor could Irish-American leaders like Patrick J. Maguire or Cardinal William Henry O'Connell remain true to the legacy of John Boyle O'Reilly. On the U.S. Supreme Court, the rulings of Oliver Wendell Holmes were decidedly tepid on questions of civil rights. These people embraced Boston's antislavery tradition with varying degrees of ambivalence, at different moments in their careers.

That tradition was itself created by Bostonians of the Gilded Age and Progressive Era. In the aftermath of the Civil War, they built statues and sang odes to those who championed the rights of the slaves and freedpeople. William Lloyd Garrison, Wendell Phillips, Charles Sumner and the African-American veterans of the Massachusetts 54th and 55th Regiments were celebrated by Boston mayors, state governors, and schoolchildren. From our more distant perspective we can appreciate that Boston's legacy included conservatives who feared to antagonize the South or cared nothing about the slaves, as well as reformers. The Boston of our period, however, constructed a myth of itself, and a not entirely fictitious one either, as a bastion of freedom. All socially conscious Bostonians had to reckon with the meaning of that myth as they confronted Jim Crow.

We follow the narrative by examining the work of leaders who left a paper trail. It is therefore a political and intellectual history that relies upon traditional historical source material: newspapers, books, correspondence, judicial and legislative debate. As all historians of race relations know, this trail is more difficult to follow through the African-American community. Boston's black community newspapers—the *Courant* (1890s, virtually disappeared), the *Chronicle* (begun 1916 but unavailable in early years), and the *Guardian* (begun 1901, and available only in random numbers)—provide a very spotty record for this period. The journal of the Woman's Era Club is not available in its entirety. Manuscript collections scarcely exist and those that do are incomplete. There is a complete set of the *Colored American Magazine* and *Alexander's Magazine*, both literary and political monthlies that together span the years from 1900 to 1909. For the white activists, much more has been preserved.

The actors here are grouped together in part by profession, in part by political orientation, and in part by chronology. While this makes for a certain amount of repetition—both Trotter and the NAACP, for example, fought separately to ban the movie *The Birth of a Nation*—I hope it has facilitated thematic clarity. In this form of organization I have been influenced by Arthur Mann's *Yankee Reformers in the Urban Age*, which discusses various groups of Boston reformers.[5]

A selective discussion inevitably raises a question in the mind of the reader, Why is this person included, but not that? Indeed, a case could be made that such important local figures as ward boss Martin Lomasney, Harvard professor William James, and Supreme Court Justice Louis Brandeis deserve to be considered in a study such as this. My guideline was to find representative types who acted on the race problem in this period, rather than to attempt a comprehensive summary. For better or worse, Irish Democrat John F. Fitzgerald stands in for Lomasney, Harvard president Charles W. Eliot for

James, and Oliver Wendell Holmes for Brandeis. Further, I have included state residents from nearby cities, especially Cambridge.

In his introduction to *The Black Image in the White Mind: The Debate on Afro-American Character and Destiny, 1817–1914*, George M. Fredrickson urges future historians to avoid introducing the color line into their own discourse and organization of text.[6] I have tried to follow his advice. This study discusses politicians, lawyers, suffragists, Irish-Americans, and supporters of Booker Washington, Monroe Trotter, and the NAACP. In each case I have tried to "integrate" the discussion racially. Most of these groupings included people of both races; even in discussing Irish leaders of Boston's Democratic Party, Catholic Church, or trade union movement, I have tried not to neglect African-American Democratic voters, Catholic parishioners, or workers.

Periodizations for historical studies are necessarily arbitrary; a case may always be made for moving one's dates backward or forward in the stream of events. Nevertheless, 1890 marks an important turning point in American race relations. In that year, Massachusetts Congressman Henry Cabot Lodge and Senator George Frisbie Hoar led a fight to protect African-American voting rights in the South. The defeat of that campaign in January 1891 marked the collapse of northern Republican concern for civil rights. In 1890, Mississippi effectively disfranchised its African-American voters at a constitutional convention that heralded a southern trend. That year, too, a divided woman's suffrage movement reunited, and New England suffragists argued that votes for women could help assure white supremacy in the South. In August 1890, John Boyle O'Reilly died, silencing the voice of the nation's outstanding Irish-born supporter of African-American rights. Thirty years later, segregation and disfranchisement were firmly established throughout the South. African-Americans had endured persecution by Presidents Theodore Roosevelt and Woodrow Wilson, and had been mobbed by racists in the North and lynched in the South. Nevertheless, the experience of the World War and the Great Migration northward contributed to the appearance of a "New Negro" by 1920. The NAACP leadership that year passed into the hands of James Weldon Johnson, an African-American; thousands of Marcus Garvey supporters demonstrated their Negro nationalism in the North; and in 1919 African-American citizens fought back when attacked by white mobs. A new self confidence marked the appearance of the New Negro, soon to be celebrated in the arts by the Harlem Renaissance.

A few words on terminology. This book is about the antislavery tradition in the broad sense. First, I have made no attempt to distinguish between abolitionists, who advocated the immediate end to slavery, and antislavery people who may have desired this, but publicly advocated only its containment.[7] By 1890, the distinction had lost its force; the antiracists of our period were faced with a new set of questions. Second, when narrating, I use the contemporary terms "African-American" and "black" in the text. However, when summarizing the words of others, I have remained faithful to the historical context and employed the terms that the speakers or writers would have used: often that term is "colored American"; sometimes it is "Negro." Finally, I have used the term "Jim Crow" generically to stand for the varying aspects of race discrimination, rather than to denote segregation.

The people in this story grappled with the knot of American race relations at a time when white supremacists were pulling the ropes ever more tightly about the entire society. Probably the most significant accomplishment of the Bostonians was to build the NAACP, the sword that ultimately cleaved the legal tangle. Along with those who never joined it, but contributed in their own fashion to the undoing of racial inequality, the heirs of Boston's best traditions provided a vital link to the modern civil rights movement. Those who confront our contemporary form of Jim Crow society may recognize something of themselves in these characters from the nadir of African-American history.

This study is rooted in the history of Boston and its African-American community, but it does not purport to recount those stories. In particular, much is left out here that pertains to Boston's African-American history in this period: the life of its institutions such as churches and fraternal lodges, and much of the social history of its average citizens. The focus is on the political and intellectual lives of activists as they looked outward at the race relations of the nation as a whole, and how they relied upon their sense of the past.

Acknowledgments

THIS BOOK would not have been possible without the counsel and unfailingly good cheer of Andrew Buni, who supported it in its earliest stages. Karen Miller and Alan Lawson questioned various assumptions I made and contributed constructive criticism in good measure. Stephen R. Fox generously corrected substantive and stylistic errors in the chapter on Monroe Trotter. Those errors that remain throughout the text, of course, are all mine.

At Northeastern University Press, John Weingartner patiently steered the manuscript through the maze of the publishing process. My close friend, Seth Wigderson of the University of Maine at Augusta, offered encouragement and advice along the way. Judith Periale provided indispensable assistance with the final manuscript preparation.

Thanks are also due to the staffs of the various libraries and historical societies listed in the bibliography. Virginia H. Smith of the Massachusetts Historical Society, Esme Bhan of the Moorland-Spingarn Research Center of Howard University, and the workers at the microfilm department at the Boston Public Library were particularly helpful.

Most of all, Judith Beth Cohen reminded me to enjoy myself throughout this project, and provided the love and happiness that helped me to complete it.

Boston Confronts Jim Crow

Phillips School, Boston, Massachusetts, ca. 1897. Courtesy of the Society for the Preservation of New England Antiquities.

❧❧❧❧❧❧❧

What Kept Abolition
Alive in Boston?

BEFORE BOSTON WAS BORN, it existed in the human imagination as a dream of purity. Its founder, John Winthrop, wrote that "we shall be as a City upon a Hill," a New England, even before the first settlers abandoned the old. Just as the original Puritans hoped to purge England of sin, so did their spiritual heirs, two hundred years later, hope to purify America by purging it of slavery. Beginning as a small and despised band, the abolitionists lived to see their goal accomplished within little more than a generation, but at the cost of a terrible war. This book tells the story of how their spiritual descendants, both African-American and white, continued their legacy.

This small group of Bostonians played a unique role in American life between 1890 and 1920 as national leaders in the fight against Jim Crow. While there were other activists like them throughout the country, they alone felt a special responsibility because of their own city's history. To understand why this was so, we must address three broad questions. First, who were Boston's African-Americans, and what made their community different from others in the North? Second, what was the connection between the city's history and its race reformers of the day, and what was Boston like between 1890 and 1920? Third, what were the national trends that encouraged the establishment of the Jim Crow system, and what did that system entail?[1]

AFRICAN-AMERICAN BOSTON, 1890–1920

African-American Bostonians tended to be more politically radical than their contemporaries for a variety of reasons. The demographics of the black community there help explain this radicalism. Although Boston was largely unaffected by the Great Migration to the North during World War I, half the city's black people were southern migrants for much of this period. These new arrivals were well suited to urban life and eager to advance economically, but, like second- or third-generation residents, they found their way forward blocked by race discrimination. At the same time, they felt themselves to be more free than other African-Americans. The small size of the black community insulated it from the more blatant forms of racism that afflicted other urban centers. In addition, a divided and exclusive upper class, the class that provided the basis for accommodation in other northern centers, was too weak to dominate the political life of the community. Finally, black Bostonians developed their own community institutions, enjoyed a favorable political climate, and had a proud history of resistance to oppression. These factors combined to make Boston a hotbed of African-American militance.

Boston's black population grew from 8,125 in 1890 to 16,350 in 1920, doubling in size over thirty years. Nevertheless, in 1890 Boston's African-Americans comprised only 1.8 percent of the total population, and only 2.2 percent by 1920. Across the Charles River, Cambridge in 1920 was 4.9 percent black with 5,334 residents. Together the two cities contributed about half the state's total African-American population of 45,466. The next largest community in Massachusetts was New Bedford, with 4,998 African-Americans, followed by Springfield (2,650), Worcester (1,258), and a remainder spread around the state. In the Boston metropolitan area Chelsea, West Medford, Everett and a few other towns had small black communities as well.[2]

Statistically, Boston's black population was insignificant in relation to the national African-American population. The vast majority of African-Americans between 1890 and 1920 lived in the South. In 1920, roughly 8,911,000 of America's 10,463,131 total African-American population could be found in the South and West South Central states. Only 79,051 lived in all of New England, less than 1 percent of the total nationally. While black people comprised 9.9 percent of the population nationally, they were only 2.2 percent in Boston.[3]

Boston's black population was small in total numbers relative even to other northern cities. Boston as a whole was the fifth-largest city in 1890 and seventh nationally in 1920, with 748,060 residents in the latter year. Boston ranked twenty-seventh in black population that year. By contrast, 152,467 African-Americans lived in New York, nearly ten times Boston's figure. Philadelphia was home to 134,229 black people and Chicago and Washington, D.C., had more than 109,000. Nevertheless, Boston's 2.2 percent black population figure in 1920 was not far behind New York's 2.7 percent or Chicago's 4.1 percent, but significantly behind Philadelphia's 7.4 percent.[4]

This population inhabited the new African-American community that

formed in the South End and Lower Roxbury districts from about 1890 onward. The earliest black community in Boston centered in the Copp's Hill
area of the North End along the waterfront where the men worked as steve-
dores, laborers, and sailors. As Boston merchants built their fortunes in the
carrying trade, they moved to Beacon Hill, and African-Americans followed,
occupying the north and west slopes. There they worked as house servants,
waiters, laborers, or artisans. By 1900, an increasing Jewish migration to this
area, now called the West End, caused many residents to move toward the
South End, where southern black migrants were locating. Between 1900 and
1910 the older neighborhood decreased in size by 50 percent. In 1920 7,319
African-Americans, about half the city's total, inhabited the South End's
Ward 13. In two adjoining wards lived another 4,899 African-Americans.
Cambridgeport, not far from the South End, became the center of Cambridge's community of color. By 1920 the South End formed the core of a
growing metropolitan African-American community.[5]

While Boston's black population was increasingly grouped in one geo-
graphic area, that neighborhood was racially integrated. New immigrants,
especially from czarist Russia and southern Europe, also located in the South
End. Ward 13, in which 45 percent of the city's blacks lived in 1920, was only
28 percent black and Ward 7, with 22 percent, was only 9.9 percent African-
American. Thus two-thirds of Boston's black citizens resided in an integrated
setting, and the remainder dwelled in overwhelmingly white neighborhoods.
There were particular clusters of black neighborhoods within the South
End—for example the area around Back Bay station where many Pullman
porters lived—and there were places in which blacks shared tenement buildings with Jews, Germans, or Irish. African-American children attended integrated schools, usually constituting less than 10 percent of the student body.
Black Bostonians lived in a core neighborhood that was a community, not a
ghetto.[6]

The small size of this community, both in population and geography,
probably encouraged its political militance. The black population offered no
serious economic competition to whites, who fought among themselves along
ethnic lines for jobs. Nor did issues regarding use of physical space arise in
this period, as we shall next observe. The small scale meant that activist
leaders could easily know and communicate with one another. At the same
time, the community was large enough so that meetings of protest or celebration could fill Faneuil Hall or the Twelfth Baptist Church, and the participants could feel the strength of their numbers.[7]

Compared to other African-Americans nationally, even to other northerners, Bostonians probably worried less about white violence. They moved

about the city without fear of attack. They had a proud and officially celebrated history. Politically they were well represented in city and state government until the turn of the century. Gradually, however, these advantages slowly eroded, as race relations deteriorated nationally. Nevertheless, black Bostonians remained proud of their city, probably until at least 1915, when they failed to prevent the showing of the film, *The Birth of a Nation*.

Between 1890 and 1920, many northern cities or their environs were the scenes of violence against African-Americans, especially after the Great Migration. These included New York and Akron, Ohio, in 1900; Springfield, Illinois, in 1908; Coatesville, Pennsylvania, in 1911; East St. Louis in 1917; and Chicago and Washington, D.C., in 1919. Boston's African-Americans were never victims of racial violence during this time.[8]

In 1910, the prize fight between African-American Jack Johnson and the "Great White Hope" Jim Jeffries provided a litmus test of race relations nationally. Men gathered in huge downtown crowds to hear announcers read blow-by-blow descriptions of the fight from a ticker tape. When Johnson defeated Jeffries, cities throughout the country erupted in racial violence, producing thousands of injuries and eight deaths. Gangs of hoodlums beat up black people in New York, and in the nation's capital hundreds of African-Americans were arrested. Nothing of this sort transpired in Boston. The fight took place on 4 July, when for the first time in the city's history, an African-American, James H. Wolff, delivered Boston's official Independence Day oration. While black Bostonians basked in Wolff's reflected glory, a mostly white crowd of 10,000 gathered in increasing gloom to hear of Johnson's victory. Only one minor racial confrontation occurred.[9]

Central public space was not circumscribed by race hatred. Bostonians had a long tradition of using Faneuil Hall as a meeting place for protest gatherings. This symbolic downtown structure was located between the West and South Ends, and black people showed their self-confidence by appropriating this race-neutral space without fear. On one occasion, activists organized marches from both neighborhoods to Faneuil Hall. During the 1915 protests against the film *The Birth of a Nation*, black people picketed the movie theater, and massed at the State House and on Boston Common.[10]

Time and again, prominent African-American Bostonians testified to the favorable racial climate of the city. When Josephine St. Pierre Ruffin organized a national conference of African-American women in 1895, she declared that only Boston had a suitable "atmosphere" for such a meeting. Susie King Taylor, a slave from Savannah, escaped to Union lines during the Civil War and made her way to Boston. In 1902 she recalled her experiences: "I have been in many states and cities, and in each I have looked for liberty and justice, equal for the black as for the white, but it was not until I was within the borders of New England, and reached old Massachusetts, that I found it." In May 1904, the *Colored American Magazine* reprinted a Boston Sunday *Herald* article titled "Boston as the Paradise of the Negro," in which several prominent black Bostonians testified to this sanguine view of the city's racial climate. Editor William Monroe Trotter concurred when he invited his supporters to attend the 1911 convention of his National Independent Political League convention. "Welcome to the Home of Abolition," his *Guardian* newspaper enthused, "where it is no crime to be black."[11]

Once a southern politician expressed the same idea, but with opposite sentiments. When an Arkansas African-American was convicted of assault with intent to kill in 1902, he was sentenced to three years in prison. Arkansas Governor Jefferson Davis, returning home after a sojourn in Massachusetts, pardoned the convict under the condition that he relocate to the Bay State. The governor heard "many expressions of sympathy by the citizens of Massachusetts for what they were pleased to call the poor oppressed negro of the south," and he now would give the Bostonians "the opportunity to reform one."[12]

If this favorable racial climate surpassed that of other cities, contemporary observers and most later students of the period agree that racial feeling was nontheless increasing in Boston. Ray Stannard Baker, the celebrated progressive journalist, noticed Boston's shift in sentiment in his 1908 account of national race relations. John Daniels, a white social worker at the South End's settlement for southern black migrants, the Robert Gould Shaw House, published the most comprehensive account of the issue in 1914, after working nine years on his manuscript. He set the date of decline at about 1895, citing the passage of a state civil rights bill two years earlier as the high point, and the redistricting of the city in 1895 to the disadvantage of black voters as the turning point. Adelaide Cromwell Hill, writing in 1952, placed the beginning of the period of decline at about 1910–15, associating the problem with changing power relations among the whites and the failure of black leaders to integrate southern migrants into the community. Richard A. Ballou surveyed the existing literature in 1984 and concluded that Boston and Cleveland had the best racial climate nationally, but that around the turn of the century white attitudes began to harden.[13]

At the top of Boston's African-American community was an upper class that, according to Willard B. Gatewood, "had a reputation for exclusiveness that went even beyond that of those in Washington or Philadelphia." Wealthy men such as the merchant tailor John H. Lewis and the baker Joseph Lee, distinguished old-line families of less means like the Ruffins, Ridleys,

Duprees, Haydens, and others formed part of this circle. Professionals like doctor Samuel Courtney, editor William Monroe Trotter, and lawyers Clement Morgan, William Henry Lewis, or Butler Wilson also counted. They established a genteel way of life complete with white servants, vacations on Martha's Vineyard, musical training for children, and membership in select clubs that were modeled on those of white society.[14]

However, this upper class could not lead the community, as we shall see in greater detail when we examine Booker T. Washington's support. Some of its members were socially conservative businessmen who believed that hard work and market forces would bring their own rewards. These people joined the National Negro Business League, which was nonpolitical. They had more links to white society than similar groups in other cities. While they established social clubs of their own, they also patronized the Boston Symphony Orchestra or similar institutions; some even depended economically on white clients. Comprising perhaps 2 percent of the community, the more conservative among them held aloof from the popular classes, and they had no real political base.

The vast majority of Boston and Cambridge's 22,000 African-Americans in 1920 were unskilled laborers, working as janitors, domestic servants, porters, or laundresses. This was true both of people whose ancestors were Bostonians, and of recent arrivals from the South. Very few were able to escape from poverty by obtaining better-paying jobs as factory operatives, entering the professions, or starting their own business. In contrast, Irish-Americans and new immigrants from czarist Russia or southern Europe did advance economically in this period and afterward.[15]

Using sophisticated statistical techniques, Stephan Thernstrom has argued persuasively that second-generation black Bostonians fared no better than recent arrivals, and that they fell behind second-generation Irish workers during the period we are considering. "Probably the most significant feature of the economic plight of blacks in Boston," Thernstrom concluded, "was their lack of access to blue-collar jobs above the most menial level." By 1890 the Irish were well advanced in the construction trades, and proportionate to their population were four times better represented there than African-Americans. Semiskilled jobs in public transportation or even the shoe industry were relatively closed to black Bostonians regardless of longevity in Boston.[16]

Elizabeth Pleck showed that race discrimination was the cause of this economic failure. Theoretically, white employers should have hired blacks as the cheapest labor available, but the labor market did not function in a race-neutral manner to provide equal access to jobs for African-Americans. Pleck writes: "Urban employers, workers, and unions helped to perpetuate [black poverty] by erecting two major, distinct racial barriers, exclusion and unsuccessful competition." Employers excluded black workers for fear that white workers would refuse to work alongside them. White workers also combined to keep African-Americans out of skilled crafts and wrote exclusionary agreements into union bylaws. Blacks suffered "unsuccessful competition" when white consumers and business competitors forced them out of some semi-skilled trades, such as barbering, by combining in a race-conscious way to compete against them. Some artisans who were second-generation black Bostonians lost their workshops or trades in this manner to European immigrant artisans.[17]

Boston African-Americans were not able to escape the working class by establishing their own businesses. Pleck identified 197 black business concerns in 1900, but 107 of these were in the personal service category, which involved very small amounts of start-up capital. Moreover, 63 percent of African-American enterprises failed between 1880 and 1890, and 53 percent between 1890 and 1900. By contrast, only 27 percent of Irish-owned businesses failed in Boston during the earlier period. Pleck attributes the disparity to the greater access to capital that the Irish had. Contrasting the high rate of African-American business failure to the lower rate suffered by Chinese immigrants, she suggested that the Chinese organized revolving credit pools and regulated competition among themselves, while African-Americans did not. Why this organization occurred is beyond the scope of this discussion; what matters is that black Bostonians rarely moved out of the working class.[18]

A remarkably high percentage of Boston's black population were migrants from the South. In 1890, they constituted 46 percent of the total population; in 1900, 53 percent; and in 1930 (the next date for which figures are available), 37 percent. John Daniels argued that these southern migrants, unlike long-term Boston residents, gave offense to white Bostonians by their rural manners and uncouth behavior. There may have been some truth to this observation by a contemporary but paternalist reporter. However, as Daniels himself recorded, many of these newcomers came with lofty ambitions, hoping to educate themselves and their children, and many did.[19]

Pleck showed that these migrants were actually a select group who were well prepared for northern urban life. They came largely from Tidewater cities, especially in Virginia. Motivated in part by declining economic opportunities, they came to Boston hoping to rise financially and educationally. They followed a pattern of chain migration and maintenance of kinship ties that pulled them to Boston. Most Virginia out-migrants traveled only the shorter distance to Philadelphia or New York, which offered similar job opportunities. This suggests that the smaller number who came to Boston had a specific reason for bypassing the other seacoast cities; they probably had relatives already there or some other specific reason for choosing Boston. Pleck found them to be more urban, literate, mulatto and Upper South in origin than most southern blacks. Those who had been slaves also might have had some industrial experience, unlike most former plantation workers. Peter Randolph, born a slave in the Virginia Tidewater in 1825, and later minister of Boston's Ebenezer Baptist Church, was a key leader of the migrant community in the South End. Randolph discouraged emotional southern religious practices and helped acculturate new arrivals to the more reserved behavior of Boston. Pleck's portrait of the southern migrants is of "a clannish culture" that had the potential and desire to advance socially and economically, but was blocked by discrimination.[20]

Boston's African-American community also included a small West Indian population. In 1910 they numbered 566 people; by 1920 the prospect of better jobs had swelled their numbers to 2,877, or about 19 percent of the total black population. Most of these were working-class people with middle-class aspirations. By 1916, they launched their own newspaper, the *Boston Chronicle*. Many were Catholics or Episcopalians; although they maintained their island culture, they did not form a distinct neighborhood within the South End. Many men had been construction workers in the West Indies, but were barred from their trade by lily-white unions in Boston, and found themselves downwardly mobile. There is little evidence that they flocked to the message of Marcus Garvey, the New York–based leader of the nationalist Universal Negro Improvement Association.[21]

Progressive Era observers John Daniels and Frederic Bushee showed that black Bostonians endured more hardship than whites in the areas of death and disease, housing, education, and criminality. Historian Peter C. Holloran examined social services for destitute children over the century from 1830 to 1930. Taken as a whole, they present a mixed picture of paternalist reformers addressing complex social problems with varying degrees of success.

Boston's African-Americans died more often from fatal infectious diseases than their white fellow citizens. Tuberculosis in particular afflicted black Bostonians more relentlessly than whites. Between 1900 and 1910 the black birth and death rate was balanced at 25.4 per thousand, but while the white birth rate equaled the black, whites died at a rate of only 18.7 per thousand. The increase in the black population in these years was due to migration rather than natural increase.

Housing was worse for black people. Although their population density was not worse than that of whites throughout the city, African-Americans more frequently inhabited tenement housing or alley buildings with poor light and ventilation. Bushee ascribed this situation to defects in African-American character. Daniels's picture of limited economic possibilities suggests, rather, that poverty forced the poor into poor housing, and he also saw a trend toward improvement in this area.

Joined to this advance was the positive use that black Bostonians made of the public schools. Daniels introduced as a "typical instance" the case of a Georgia migrant family who arrived in Boston between 1897 and 1899 specifically so the six children could attend school, which they did successfully. African-American children performed as well as their fellow students, but poverty forced more black children to quit school to take up employment. Some of those who stayed in school achieved honors, and six African-Americans taught in the schools. The less sanguine Bushee, without presenting evidence, thought African-Americans paid less heed to education than white ethnic groups. Neither used comparative statistics for other cities. In 1920, 2.6 percent of black Bostonians over the age of twenty-one were illiterate in a city with 5 percent illiteracy as a whole. This figure is deceptive by itself, for only .1 percent of native-born white adults were illiterate, but 10.5 percent of foreign-born whites were illiterate. In New York, 2.3 percent of all black people were illiterate; in Philadelphia, 5.4 percent; Chicago, 4.5 percent; and Washington, 10.7 percent. Black Bostonians, therefore, were less literate than native-born whites but more literate than the foreign-born; compared to other northern African-Americans they were more literate than most.

Boston's African-Americans were not more inclined to pauperism or reliance upon charity than whites. Daniels noted the limited use of public and private charity by black people. Historian Peter Holloran, writing seventy years later, uncovered a spotty record of service for black orphans. He found that African-Americans maintained their own social services through kinship networks. When these failed, orphans were served by white church-based services, some of which were integrated and some segregated. Bushee agreed that there were few African-American paupers, but thought the statistics masked more cases of semi-dependency. In 1900, Daniels wrote, 76 percent of African-American Bostonians were gainfully employed and 65 percent of white men; 40 percent of black women worked and 24 percent of white women. This higher employment rate, which included children, showed that African-Americans had to leave school earlier to find work.

In the area of crime, Daniels found that 3.3 percent of all state penitentiary inmates were black when the state was only 1.1 percent African-American. Given the legacy of slavery and employment discrimination, Daniels interpreted this figure to be low. Bushee used city jail figures from the 1890s to argue that African-Americans were inclined toward criminality and drunkenness.[22]

Despite these economic and social disabilities, African-American Bostonians possessed an impressive array of community institutions at the turn of the century, and they would continue to build new ones to meet future needs. The most important of these was the church. The First African Baptist Church dates to 1805, and was followed by a separate Methodist Church in 1818, two African Methodist Episcopal churches (1833 and 1838), and another Baptist church in 1840. After the Civil War, African-Americans founded important Congregational and Episcopal churches. Black Bostonians started the first separate Masonic Lodge, the Prince Hall chapter, in 1787, when they were refused admission to the Grand Lodge along with whites. African-American women in Boston had several community-based clubs, the most important of which was the Woman's Era Club founded in 1893 by Josephine St. Pierre Ruffin. In 1900, Booker Washington launched his National Negro Business League in Boston. Professional African-Americans formed two separate literary societies, one in the West End and one in the South End. During the period under consideration, black Bostonians published at least four newspapers—the *Courant*, *Woman's Era*, *Guardian*, and *Chronicle*—and two magazines, the *Colored American Magazine* and *Alexander's*. These institutions provided a framework in which people could construct their lives, and fight for their rights.[23]

Moreover, these institutions were rooted in the collective memory of an heroic past. The antislavery traditions of white Boston contributed to the self-confidence of Boston's African-Americans. In defense of their rights, they could appeal to their special heritage as Bostonians and argue that the denial of equality to African-Americans contradicted the city's rhetorical commitment to equal rights. Black Bostonians in the antebellum period won a remarkable degree of political freedom and racial integration. Massachusetts African-Americans more rapidly than others eradicated slavery, won the right to vote, integrated the public schools and accommodations, defended fugitive slaves, and contributed troops during the Civil War.

While the Massachusetts Constitution of 1780 laid the groundwork for the abolition of slavery within the state, it was an African-American's lawsuit that definitively ended the practice. Quock Walker, arguing that his deceased master had freed him in his will, won his case in the state Supreme Judicial Court in 1783, dealing slavery a mortal blow. The Constitution made no mention of race, and black men could vote.[24]

In the pre–William Lloyd Garrison era, when interracial social mixing or political fraternization was taboo, black Bostonians built their own social institutions. David Walker and John Hilton founded the General Colored Association of Massachusetts in 1826 to oppose slavery. Walker, a North Carolina freedman, distributed the country's first African-American newspaper, *Freedom's Journal*, published in New York. He worshiped at Samuel Snowden's African-Methodist Episcopal Church, and made his living selling secondhand clothes in the community. Walker probably lived his life completely among African-Americans. His pamphlet, the "Appeal," justified slave rebellion, condemned white religious and educational leaders for keeping blacks in ignorance, and attacked the American Colonization Society for seeking to deport them to Africa.[25]

The abolitionist movement led by William Lloyd Garrison greatly expanded the possibilities for African-American political action. Its newspaper, The *Liberator*, had a mostly black subscription base during the 1830s, and also functioned as a community journal. For the first time, the races worked together in the New England Anti-Slavery Society, and African-American Garrisonians such as Boston's William Cooper Nell and Salem's John Lenox Remond achieved great authority in their community. When Frederick Douglass lived in Lynn, Massachusetts, in the early 1840s, he inaugurated a successful campaign to desegregate the railroads. Encouraged by white allies, black activists in Massachusetts eradicated legal segregation and thus weakened racist attitudes.[26]

The movement to desegregate the public schools struck a powerful blow against Negrophobia. If schoolchildren could be educated together, that would show that African-Americans were human beings entitled to equal rights, and worthy of being treated as social equals. School integration would cast slavery in a more harsh light than any propaganda, because it would demonstrate in life that the slaves were fully human. William Cooper Nell, whose father had worked with David Walker, set out to achieve this goal as a youth. He joined with the Garrisonians, and led a long crusade through the school boards and courts to desegregate the schools. This campaign included a boycott of the African school that a minority of the community endorsed. Nell triumphed in 1855 when the state legislature outlawed segregated education. That year he published *Colored Patriots of the Revolution*, which showed the contributions of African-Americans to the struggle against Great Britain. Nell's career, and the defeat of segregation, gave lasting impetus to the notion that African-Americans deserved full equality to whites.[27]

The struggle for integration and the close alliance of Boston's black activists with Garrison at once encouraged and retarded the development of separate institutions. Unlike black New Yorkers or Philadelphians, Bostonians held back from the convention movement of the antebellum period, but some black Garrisonians supported the movement. While they opposed separate institutions such as manual training schools or separate public schools, they did encourage separate self-improvement societies such as the Boston Minors Exhibition Society and the Boston Female Benevolent and Intelligence Society. Nevertheless, the prevailing Garrisonian view was that separate institutions were a concession to racism.[28]

On the other hand, by the 1850s many black Garrisonians broke with their leader's precepts regarding political action and nonresistance. The climate that Garrison created by socializing with the outcast minority and asserting their fundamental human rights encouraged self-organization by African-Americans. One expression of this self-confidence was the initiative they showed in rescuing escaped slaves from would-be slave catchers. In 1836, a contingent of African-American women freed fugitives Eliza Small and Polly Ann Bates from a courtroom where they were about to be returned to slavery. Lewis Hayden, one of the central leaders of the antebellum black community, threatened to blow up the slave hunters who had come for Ellen and William Crafts with dynamite in 1850. The next year Hayden and attorney Robert Morris engineered the daring rescue of Fred Wilkins ("Shadrach") from a courtroom. Like David Walker, Hayden too operated a clothing store, and exercised his leadership more assertively within the African-American community than in collaboration with whites. African-Americans also participated in rescue attempts in which whites took the lead. These highly dramatic episodes were in large measure the result of black self-organization and were facilitated by the climate brought about by Garrisonian abolitionism.[29]

The Civil War deepened the sense of African-American Bostonians that they were the authors of their own liberation. The Massachusetts 54th Regiment was the first black unit of northern free volunteers, and the 55th followed soon after. Soldiers were recruited around the state and nation for the regiments. In Boston, Wendell Phillips and attorney Robert C. Morris addressed a February meeting at the Joy Street Church, the oldest black community meeting-house in the city. In all, 3,967 African-Americans served in Massachusetts regiments. Their heroic assault on Fort Wagner disproved white assumptions about the fighting abilities of African-American soldiers. After the war, many of the veterans settled in Boston, bringing with them a new confidence and expectation of equal rights. Among them were James Monroe Trotter, father of the militant editor, and James H. Wolff, an attorney who headed an integrated Grand Army of the Republic post. At least one white officer of a black regiment, Norwood P. Hallowell, became a prominent civil rights activist in later years. In 1890, Luis F. Emilio published a

popular account of the regiment's exploits, and in 1897 the city officially celebrated the African-American veterans by dedicating the Augustus Saint-
Gaudens sculpture that stands across from the statehouse. Between 1890 and
1920, these African-American veterans and their descendants were a powerful
force for civil rights.[30]

In the thirty years following the end of the Civil War, African-Americans
in Boston enjoyed a political preferment that was unusual in the North. Black
people held seats in the state legislature from 1866, when Charles L. Mitchell,
an abolitionist and Civil War veteran, and Edwin G. Walker, son of David
Walker, were elected. These were the first two African-Americans elected to
any state legislature. Off and on, African-Americans served in the legislature
until 1902–03, when William Henry Lewis served his last term. Democratic
Governor Benjamin F. Butler appointed George L. Ruffin judge of the
Charleston Court in 1883; he was the first African-American jurist in the
North. An African-American representative from the heavily Republican
West End served on the Boston City Council until the 1895 redistricting.
Prominent federal appointees of the late nineteenth century included James
Monroe Trotter, William H. Dupree, Charles L. Mitchell, John M. Lenox,
and Archibald Grimké. These civil servants all performed their duties respon-
sibly. The next generation, however, was blocked from political office.[31]

The socioeconomic setting and political-cultural history of African-American Boston explains its militance between 1890 and 1920. The black community was small enough in size and geography to be insulated from white
depredation, yet large and growing enough to feel self-confident. Black Bostonians enjoyed a unique personal freedom and regarded their city as a haven
from oppression. At the same time, long-term residents and migrants were
frustrated economically and endured harsher lives than their white neighbors.
They had a proud abolitionist tradition, and the institutions through which
to express themselves. The social basis for political accommodation, a business class, was weaker in Boston than in other cities. As the South began to
codify Jim Crow practices, and as white northerners regarded this process
with indifference, African-American Bostonians, many of whom were recent
migrants from the South, responded with anger and protest.

BOSTON'S ANTISLAVERY TRADITION IN A
RAPIDLY CHANGING CITY

Bostonians who opposed racism between 1890 and 1920 were heirs to several
traditions of antislavery action. African-American Bostonians had the models
of David Walker, Frederick Douglass, Lewis Hayden, and William Cooper

Nell, among others. Irish-Americans could consider the antislavery stance of
Daniel O'Connell, whose legacy was revived in Boston by John Boyle
O'Reilly. The most celebrated history was the diverse tradition of the Yankee
New Englanders. Antislavery sentiment and its particularly Boston variant,
abolitionism, were deeply rooted in the entire project that began with the
arrival at Shawmut of John Winthrop and his Puritan followers in 1630. Boston's Revolutionary experience and its religious and intellectual achievements
also provided inspiration for a later generation. The abolitionist beliefs of
William Lloyd Garrison and Wendell Phillips, the political antislavery approach of the Conscience Whigs who helped found the Republican Party,
and the Reconstruction Era fight of Charles Sumner to guarantee civil and
political equality to the freedpeople, were living legacies to the activists of
1890 to 1920.

Yet, these "New Abolitionists," as they sometimes called themselves, were
a tiny minority in a rapidly changing Boston that honored its abolitionist past
in words rather than deeds. The overwhelming public issue for politically
minded Bostonians of the day was not the race question, but the gradually
polarizing struggle between Yankee and British-American Protestant on one
side, and Irish-American Catholic on the other. Both groups alternately
courted and resisted the "new immigrants" who arrived from Russia and
southern Europe as well. The small number of activists kept the antislavery
tradition alive by struggling against the emerging Jim Crow system; to understand their actions we must reprise their heritage and describe their city.

Regardless of their religion, Boston's civil rights activists owed much to
the original Puritan settlers. While the expressed Puritan view of slavery was
ambivalent, its deep structure of belief conflicted with slaveholding. On the
one hand slavery and the slave trade were practiced in Massachusetts, and
during the seventeenth and eighteenth centuries Boston's religious leaders
showed little hostility to them. Puritan divine Cotton Mather even accepted
a slave as a gift. On the other hand, judge Samuel Sewall issued a pamphlet
condemning slavery in newly secular Massachusetts in 1700. The Puritan
equating of virtue with independence, its emphasis upon the redemptive
qualities of hard work and thrift, and the freedom of its congregations from
hierarchy—all contributed to a worldview inimical to slavery. As the slavocracy bred an aristocratic society that devalued individual labor, imposed rigid
thought control on the South, and sought to extend that control to American
institutions, those who subscribed to the constellation of values evoked by
Puritanism recoiled.[32]

The liberating forces unleashed by the American Revolution further undermined the institution of slavery. The Revolutionary rhetoric of Bostonians

about liberty and independence drew their attention to the contradiction posed by slavery to a free democratic society. Among Boston's first Revolutionary martyrs was the African-American Crispus Attucks. When the men of Massachusetts met to ratify the Constitution, most agreed with the anti-Federalist argument that slavery was indeed a wicked institution, but Federalists convinced the majority that slavery was best opposed by means of strong government and Union. Boston's Revolutionary tradition was also part of the heritage of antiracist activists.[33]

The development of Unitarianism from Congregationalism in the early nineteenth century furthered spiritual antipathy to slavery in New England. This more benign religion envisioned a world in which man was not born a sinner, condemned—except for an elect few—to eternal hellfire. Man's deeds on earth therefore assumed greater importance. One historian, at least, argues a direct link between the Unitarianism of William Ellery Channing and the broad antislavery movement championed by preachers like Theodore Dwight Weld. Transcendentalism, the secular correlate of Unitarianism, argued for values of self-reliance, personal moral responsibility for the plight of others, and the possibility of saintliness within each individual. Ralph Waldo Emerson, Henry David Thoreau, and Harriet Beecher Stowe all contributed to an enduring Boston-based New England legacy. The ideas of Unitarianism and Transcendentalism advanced the multifaceted movement to reform schools, prisons, and treatment of the handicapped, and to effect temperance and secure women's rights. While these reform movements were not unique to Boston, their expression was particularly strong in the city that gave birth to these twinned humanist philosophies.[34]

Massachusetts politicians, including Bostonians, contributed to the antislavery tradition that emphasized free labor, free soil, and free men. Distinct from abolitionism, which called for immediate emancipation and vilified slaveholders as sinners, antislavery sought to contain the peculiar institution within the South, where it would expire of its inner contradictions. This sentiment led Congressman and former President John Quincy Adams to oppose the ban on presentation of antislavery petitions to Congress between 1836 and 1844. A Conscience Whig grouping that included Charles Francis Adams, Stephen C. Phillips, John G. Palfrey, Henry Wilson, Richard Henry Dana, Charles Sumner, and others opposed the annexation of Texas. They triumphed in state politics in the 1860 election that brought John Andrew to the governorship and carried the state for Abraham Lincoln. The Republican Party, which dominated state politics for most of the period under our consideration, looked to these antislavery politicians as their political forebears.[35]

However, Boston was not simply a hotbed of antislavery. The postwar generation, seeking to ratify in public memory the outcome of the war, celebrated its antislavery partisans. The reality was more complex. Throughout the antebellum period, the "lords of the loom," textile manufacturing barons such as the brothers Amos and Abott Lawrence, forged significant social and economic ties to the planter aristocracy that supplied them with cotton. Daniel Webster, Robert C. Winthrop, and Edward Everett represented the "Cotton Whigs" in government, as Chief Justice of the Supreme Judicial Court Lemuel Shaw or United States Associate Justice Benjamin C. Robbins did on the bench. When southern governors demanded the extirpation of David Walker's "Appeal" or Garrison's *Liberator*, Boston Mayor Harrison Gray Otis correctly reassured his southern inquisitors that no man of property paid either any heed. The well-heeled "broadcloth mob" that nearly lynched Garrison in 1835 never entirely disappeared. However, even the Cotton Whigs were radicalized by the dramatic chain of events leading to the Civil War.[36]

For the generation that confronted Jim Crow between 1890 and 1920, the central actors in the antebellum drama were the abolitionists William Lloyd Garrison, Frederick Douglass, Wendell Phillips, and Charles Sumner. As early as 1837, Massachusetts was home to 145 abolition societies, more than one-tenth of the nation's total, exceeded only by New York and Ohio. These thousands of activists included many other prominent local and national leaders, such as Samuel E. Sewall, Samuel J. May, Maria Weston Chapman, Bronson Alcott, David and Lydia Maria Child, the poet John Greenleaf Whittier, Sarah and Angelina Grimké and countless others. Their three decades of endeavor left a particularly powerful legacy in Boston. Descendants of these activists, both literal and figurative offspring, had to grapple with their heritage. Ancient veterans had to come to terms with their own pasts in the face of new challenges.[37]

This legacy was extremely complex and contained within it conflicting tendencies. If there was one common theme, it was simply the moral imperative to "make the world better" as suffragist and former abolitionist Lucy Stone whispered on her deathbed to her daughter Alice Stone Blackwell. History had left few clear lessons for the next generation, except that virtue might be rewarded by actual victory in the real world: slavery was dead and would never come back. Some questions that had vexed the antebellum reformers were now closed or moot. The Constitution, which by 1870 guaranteed the rights of African-Americans, could now be safely looked to as a bedrock of freedom rather than a "covenant with death and an agreement with hell," as Garrison once called it. There was no longer a question of abstaining from politics or "coming out" of immoral churches. How the abolitionists had handled these problems were now historical questions for the antiracists of the 1890s.

The many real questions that confronted the New Abolitionists could not be solved by appeals to authority. How should antiracists organize? Should blacks and whites maintain separate organizations? What relation should women's rights bear to African-American rights? What was the relation of broader socioeconomic questions to the civil rights agenda? What should civil rights activists do in politics? What balance should they strike between federal authority and the states' rights argument advanced by the South? These and other questions could not be answered simply by studying the actions of earlier leaders; they had differed widely among themselves, as a vast historiography now attests.[38] Still, the men and women of 1890 to 1920 measured their opinions by the legacy of their antecedents, hoping to find clues to the questions of their day in the answers given in the past.

Although the abolitionists left no textbooks, their inspiration was real and played a special role in Boston. Every village and town in the country had its Civil War memorial, but Boston erected monuments to its African-American Revolutionary martyrs and Civil War veterans, and officially celebrated the most radical of the abolitionists, the Garrisonians. Participants in the antislavery crusade lived on throughout this epoch and served as living reminders of the work of the past, even if they retreated from former positions. Frederick Douglass had lived a few years in New Bedford and Lynn, Massachusetts, and his spirit hovered over the civil rights community even after his death in 1895. Josephine St. Pierre Ruffin was the widow of Douglass's friend George Ruffin; she founded Boston's Woman's Era Club. Thomas Wentworth Higginson, Unitarian minister and backer of John Brown, devoted himself to literature and an occasional political foray. William Lloyd Garrison II, eldest son of the great abolitionist, was the conscience of the women's suffrage movement. Youngest son Francis Jackson Garrison served as the first president of Boston's National Association for the Advancement of Colored People until his death in 1916. Editor William Monroe Trotter's father was a Civil War veteran who refused to accept less pay than white soldiers. Charles Sumner's secretary, Moorfield Storey, was the national president of the NAACP and a key association legal strategist until his death in 1929. Albert E. Pillsbury, another Boston NAACP leader, was the nephew of abolitionist Parker Pillsbury. The African-American attorney, diplomat, and later NAACP leader Archibald Grimké was a protégé of his famous abolitionist aunts Sarah and Angelina Grimké; as a young man he strolled with the elderly Wendell Phillips. These people who fought for equal rights between 1890 and 1920 knew the heroes and heroines of the past intimately. Unlike the previous generation, who lived to see the abolition of slavery, the second-generation Trotters and Garrisons lived to see the triumph of institutionalized racism. Perhaps more painfully, none of them lived to see a new generation follow in their footsteps.

The foremost question facing the city in the years 1890–1920 was the relation between the Brahmin aristocracy and Protestant population on the one hand, and the rapidly growing Irish-Catholic population on the other. While this relation was marked by cooperation as well as conflict, the mayoral victories of John F. Fitzgerald in 1905 and James Michael Curley in 1913 exacerbated the tensions. Old and new immigrants fought with both sides, and with each other. Shared Catholicity was sometimes a source of friction, rather than cohesion, as ethnic groups vied for power within the church. In the North End, Italian- and Irish-American workers competed for jobs. Labor struggles punctuated this generally prosperous era, especially in the wake of the 1893 depression and the post–World War I economic uncertainty. To regulate the authority of the emerging Irish-led political majority in the city, Yankee elitists turned to Progressive governmental reforms that sparked intense controversy. Some among the same elite encouraged restrictions on foreign immigration, and became increasingly attracted to racialist theories of human character. White Bostonians turned inward, leaving the South to settle "its own" race problem. A new mood of anxiety and disillusion affected even those who had participated in the earlier movement. Those who fought on now bucked the tide of a new era, sometimes seeming to be aged people agitating the questions of a bygone day.[39]

Although Irish-Americans had often opposed antislavery activity in the antebellum period, the experience of the Civil War and the radicalism of the Irish national struggle encouraged some sympathy for the postwar plight of African-Americans. This sentiment was best expressed by the poet and nationalist John Boyle O'Reilly, editor of the Boston *Pilot* until his death in 1890. When an American-born son of Irish immigrants secured the mayoralty for the first time in 1905, John F. Fitzgerald appealed with some success for African-American votes. In office, Fitzgerald spoke at meetings sponsored by William Monroe Trotter and the NAACP, expressing the solidarity of Irish-Americans with their fellow victims of discrimination. Generally, Irish-Americans and African-Americans tended to be divided politically; the former were largely Democrats and the latter Republicans. During the dispute over the 1890 Federal Elections bill, the Irish-American regular Democratic weekly, the *Republic*, bitterly attacked a bill that would guarantee black voting rights.[40]

The Irish-Yankee struggle affected black Bostonians in unforeseen ways.

As the Irish gained political ascendancy in Boston, bankers and financiers lost confidence in the city's investment climate. Fearing that their profits would be taxed to provide social services to the lower classes, they increasingly invested abroad and created conservative trust funds. Financially conservative Boston was bypassed by other metropolitan centers in the East and Midwest. The failure of the local capitalist class to spur economic growth made it difficult for African-Americans to advance in a stagnant economy, and limited the growth of black entrepreneurship.[41]

In addition, the polarized situation in Boston had short and long-term political consequences for black Bostonians. In the short term, Boston's ethnic and class conflicts diverted attention from the worsening racial oppression in the South. Especially after the failure of the Federal Elections bill in 1890, Brahmin Republican politicians gave up trying to build an alliance with African-American southerners as a lost cause. In that year, Massachusetts Republicans lost the state house to a coalition of Democrats and Republican independents, or Mugwumps. Among them were former Republicans like Moorfield Storey, once Charles Sumner's secretary and later a leader of the NAACP. Some black voters even declared for the Democrats as Republicans disappointed them. William Monroe Trotter hoped that African-Americans would hold an electoral balance of power, but as their already small vote split they were increasingly disregarded. In 1895, a redistricting of the city's wards diluted black voting strength, and African-Americans disappeared from the City Council until the 1960s. In the longer term, the ethnic nationalism inspired by politicians like James Michael Curley encouraged race chauvinism that decades later would turn against a larger and resurgent black community.

A new wave of immigration to America and Boston from czarist Russia, Italy, and the Balkans caused a rethinking of the notion of race by a significant part of the Brahmin elite. Some members of the upper class who once believed in the ability of America to assimilate its immigrants now began to argue that in fact, "races" had distinct hereditary traits, and therefore immigration of inferior races should be limited. They regarded northern Europeans—Britons, Germans, Scandinavians—as superior, and all else as inferior. The campaign of the Boston-based Immigration Restriction League succeeded in passing national restrictive legislation in 1922 and 1924. Despite the fact that the league's actions were not directed at African-Americans, the ideological apparatus that underlay the campaign was easily directed against them. Many leaders whose forebears had upheld the malleability of humankind now showed a devolution of values: the striking example was the Adams family, whose earlier generations were antislavery people and whose later generations became racists. Henry Cabot Lodge began his political career under the influence of Charles Sumner, but he developed into an immigration restrictionist. Lodge in turn was the power behind the appointment of Oliver Wendell Holmes to the Supreme Court, and Holmes, despite his friendship with prominent Jewish legal scholars, proved a disappointment to civil rights supporters. The immigration to Boston of Jews, Italians, Balts, and Slavs in general encouraged conservative notions about race among Bostonians who legislated on or wrote about the matter.[42]

Even among the best elements of the aristocracy, a certain retrogression could be seen from the end of the heroic era of the Civil War and the early Reconstruction period. Abolitionist leaders such as minister Theodore Parker died in 1860, Sumner in 1874, Garrison in 1879, Phillips in 1884, and Douglass in 1895. The death of these leaders left a void that the new generation could not fill, not because of personal failings but because of wider shifts in public sentiment. The closest to these men in stature and heroism was Thomas Wentworth Higginson, mastermind of attempted rescues of fugitive slaves, staunch ally of John Brown, and commander of the First South Carolina Volunteers, a regiment of freedmen. If Higginson exhibited a paternalistic attitude toward his troops in his book about their exploits, he was still far in advance of other whites in his racial sensibilities. Higginson, however, in the postwar period devoted himself to civic and literary affairs, retreating from defense of the freedmen's rights. Lucy Stone and Henry Blackwell, Garrisonian abolitionists in the antebellum period, argued later that women's suffrage would guarantee white supremacy in the South. Some former abolitionists did retreat on questions of racial equality under the pressure of evolving national opinion.[43]

Within this context, however, various small and sometimes overlapping groups of activists, influenced by the earlier humanitarian traditions, fought a defensive battle to preserve the gains registered by the Fourteenth and Fifteenth Amendments. Sometimes isolated, sometimes able to rally thousands of supporters and more conservative thinkers to their side, they cried out against the drift toward racism that characterized the period. The group around William Monroe Trotter, the NAACP, and diverse individual activists such as John Boyle O'Reilly, Josephine St. Pierre Ruffin, and briefly even Republican Congressman Henry Cabot Lodge, exerted a unique national influence for civil rights.

THE NATIONAL RISE OF RACISM

A complex interaction of factors framed the debate on race relations during the Gilded Age and Progressive Era. Antidemocratic tendencies toward the consolidation of capital fueled racist sentiment in the North as well as the South, and when southern African-Americans fled to the North in the Great Migration during the World War, they were met by mobs in many northern cities. Economic unrest, imperial expansion with its accompanying ideological justification, negative presidential action, the appearance of new reform issues, and the turmoil that followed in the wake of World War I all contributed to the national rise of racism. While this phenomenon was general to the country as a whole, a qualitatively different and more virulent form of race hatred gathered strength in the South and expressed itself with increasing violence and crudity between 1890 and 1920. White supremacists gradually disfranchised African-American voters, segregated them socially, forced millions into poverty or debt peonage, and lynched them publicly to enforce the new order with terror. Since this study examines the response of Bostonians to this process, we need briefly to reprise its salient developments.

The Gilded Age was above all a period of capital consolidation that gave birth to powerful trusts and spectacularly wealthy individuals whose economic decisions controlled the lives of millions. A profound economic depression sparked labor upsurges in the early 1890s, and although the economy rebounded by the time of the Spanish-American War, the next twenty years were also punctuated by labor unrest, culminating in the strike wave of 1919 that affected much of America's basic industry. As workers formed themselves into an American Federation of Labor, they infused the organization with their racial attitudes and generally excluded African-American laborers. White workers conceived of blacks as potential strikebreakers; they in turn resented being excluded from jobs for which they were qualified. The economic tensions of the period encouraged white chauvinism nationally.[44]

America's acquisition of foreign colonies inhabited by people of color further exacerbated domestic race problems. The American empire was born during the golden era of world imperialism, when the European powers dominated Africa and Asia, taking up Rudyard Kipling's "white man's burden." As Americans made themselves masters of the Caribbean, Hawaii, and the Philippines, they justified their dominance over foreign peoples by asserting their racial superiority. Although the foreign wars marked an expansion of federal power that southerners often wished to check, they joined enthusiastically in the war effort. The United States conquered Cuba, Puerto Rico, Hawaii, and the Philippines as a white supremacist power.[45]

Presidential leadership both followed and molded popular national trends. After the failure of the Federal Elections bill in 1890 during the administration of Benjamin Harrison, Republican presidents increasingly ceded the South to Democratic control and abandoned the project of building up an

African-American–based Republican Party. Like his predecessor, Democratic President Grover Cleveland looked on silently as lynching soared throughout the South. William McKinley, the last Civil War veteran to serve in the White House, studiously avoided comment upon southern outrages like the Wilmington, North Carolina, massacre of 1898. Theodore Roosevelt shocked southern sensibilities by inviting Booker T. Washington to dinner at the White House, but learned never to repeat that indiscretion. When he discharged without due process a large number of African-American troops in the wake of the Brownsville incident of 1906, African-Americans grew increasingly disenchanted with the Republican Party. In this case, black soldiers were accused of shooting up a town that had been hostile to them, but recent scholarship suggests that the men were innocent. William Howard Taft, the cabinet member responsible for the dismissal, deeply offended African-Americans by his action. Woodrow Wilson's two terms marked the very bottom for African-Americans. Wilson's segregation of the federal departments made Jim Crow national and integration local. This triumph of southern policy stood firm until the Franklin Roosevelt administration.[46]

Even the appearance of Progressivism paradoxically played into the hands of racists. At the simplest level, northern reformers were diverted from the race question, viewing it as an old and intractable problem, the failed project of an older generation. In the South, Progressive reform of industry and politics was inextricably connected with white supremacy. When southern Progressives directed economic reform agitation against Big Business, they railed against northern control and whipped up sectional and racial pride. When primary elections replaced boss control in the South, these were white primaries. Charles B. Aycock of North Carolina, James K. Vardaman of Mississippi, and Hoke Smith of Georgia were all white supremacists who won gubernatorial office with promises of Progressive reform.[47]

World War I and the participation of black troops sharpened racial conflict. As American industry strove to meet Allied war needs, and European immigration was cut off, African-Americans were pulled to the North by the promise of industrial jobs and pushed from the South by crop failures and Jim Crow practices. Between 1910 and 1920, about 323,000 African-Americans, 4.9 percent of the 1910 southern black population, left the region. In the North, they were greeted with suspicion and sometimes violence by white workers, but many found jobs and a new independence. When the United States entered the war, African-American troops fought bravely despite suffering indignities. As they returned home, these veterans expected white Americans to live up to Woodrow Wilson's promise that victory would make the world safe for democracy. Having received the gratitude of white French citizens, they were all the more disillusioned by the explosion of violence in 1919. The Great Migration and World War I made Negrophobia more a national than a strictly southern problem.[48]

Despite the prevalence of northern racism, the southern variety was qualitatively different. African-Americans suffered discrimination of all sorts in the North, but the South between 1890 and 1920 codified legal caste relations between the races. The South built a different kind of society in this period, an undemocratic order founded upon race-based social engineering. This new caste society was in one sense more terrifying than slave society, in that the popular masses felt vested in white supremacy. Even the paternalism of the slave master, now expressed in support for Booker Washington's policy of accommodation and racial uplift, came under attack. Political disfranchisement, social segregation, and economic oppression defined the new order, and public lynching, a secular ritual, consecrated it in blood.

The southern populist revolt of the early 1890s at first sought to unite black and white farmers against railroads, banks, and politicians in their service. Alarmed at the success of southern Alliance candidates, regular Democrats broke the populist racial coalition by invoking white supremacy. The failure of the Alliance to withstand this attack greatly encouraged sentiment to disfranchise black voters. Throughout the region, disfranchisement had been accomplished by fraud until 1890, but fraud offended northern sensibilities and was, obviously, illegal. Henry Cabot Lodge's Federal Elections bill threatened to send United States election commissioners to supervise elections where fraud was alleged, but the bill was defeated in the Senate in 1891. Mississippi inaugurated the trend toward official disfranchisement in 1890 by calling a constitutional convention that established a literacy test for voting, which could be avoided by means of an "understanding" clause: illiterates who "understood" the constitution could vote. This project of Black Belt plantation aristocrats threatened also to disfranchise poor whites, and the new constitution, like all that followed save one, was not even submitted to popular ratification. In other states, property requirements or poll taxes were added, and some opted for "grandfather" clauses that permitted descendants of 1867 voters (all white) or veterans to vote. By means of convention or amendment, South Carolina in 1895, Louisiana in 1898, North Carolina in 1900, Alabama in 1901, Georgia in 1908, and all the other southern states rid themselves of millions of potential African-American voters. The movement was encouraged by the 1898 decision of the Supreme Court in *Williams v. Mississippi* that upheld the state's voting procedure.[49]

Racial segregation was spottily enforced until the late 1880s and coincided with the economic fluctuations that brought on populism. In the late 1880s and early 1890s, southern states began passing laws to segregate public transportation. This new arrangement was ratified by the *Plessy v. Ferguson* Supreme Court ruling on a Louisiana case in 1896. In the first decade of the new century ten southern states expanded transportation segregation legislation, and in the next decade many cities established residential segregation ordinances. Schools had never been integrated. Bostonians who confronted Jim Crow were thus disputing a new system with roots in the past, not a long-established "folkway" that had always existed.[50]

The violence and terror that enforced this new arrangement was similarly rooted in the legacy of slavery and the overthrow of Reconstruction. Nevertheless, the phenomenon of lynching reached new depths in the early 1890s. As the numbers of lynchings decreased in the new century, the spectacles became increasingly public and barbaric. The most dramatic of these ceremonies included the extrajudicial executions of Sam Hose near Atlanta in 1899; Leo Frank, a Jew, also near Atlanta in 1915; and that of a retarded man in Waco, Texas, in 1916. Southern whites often charged that their victims had outraged white women, but sometimes, as in the 1892 Memphis case that set Ida B. Wells on her antilynching crusade, the victims were merely successful business competitors. During the 1890s there were 187.5 lynchings annually, 82 percent of which were committed in the South; in the following decade that percentage rose to 92 percent. In addition to these depredations launched upon individually targeted citizens, white mobs sometimes invaded black districts and indiscriminately killed and terrorized African-Americans at random. These riots had diverse causes but a common goal of enforcing white supremacy. The most spectacular of these incidents took place in Wilmington, North Carolina, in 1898; Atlanta in 1906; Elaine, Arkansas, in 1919; and Tulsa, Oklahoma, in 1921. Fittingly, it was the spread of mob violence to the North, in the Springfield, Illinois, attack of 1908, that sparked the founding of the NAACP.[51]

Nineteen years before that reform organization was launched, Boston's Republican politicians sought to ensure their party's hegemony by protecting the right of African-American men to vote. The next chapter examines how the city's political and journalistic leaders fought in the halls of Congress, the columns of the newspapers, and the meeting-halls of Boston to sway public opinion.

Congressman Henry Cabot Lodge painted by John S. Sargent. Photograph taken by Edward Moore, published in Boston *Herald*, August 15, 1963. Courtesy of the Boston Public Library.

ONE

❦❦❦❦❦

The Federal Elections Bill of 1890 and Boston's Upper Class

BY 1890, THE BOSTON BRAHMINS constituted a highly self-conscious yet heterogeneous leadership class. The term "Brahmin" was coined by the city's unofficial poet laureate Oliver Wendell Holmes, and referred to families with "four or five generations of gentlemen and gentlewomen"; that is, it described a cultural-intellectual aristocracy rather than nouveau owners of railroads or paper mills.[1] The analogy to India's leading caste was apt, for membership in Boston's upper class was granted more by inheritance than by striving. The Cabots and Lowells may well have been deeply involved in the commercial spirit of the age, but they retained a sense of distaste for mere covetousness, ostentation, or lust for power. To one degree or another, to be a "proper Bostonian" in 1890 was to be still concerned with building John Winthrop's city on a hill, or at least a representative institution of that model for all humanity.

At the same time, to be a Brahmin in 1890 was also to feel threatened from without, and to share a sense of the decline of one's values. New financial empires based in New York or industrial conglomerates in Pennsylvania and Ohio dwarfed the conservative investment houses of State Street. Midwestern farmers revolted against eastern bankers and railroad men. Southern politicians, both Bourbon and Populist, defended their racial mores against perceived northern encroachments. Nationally, the dominance of the Republican Party could no longer be taken for granted, and by 1884 many Brahmins had become Independents. In Boston itself, Hugh O'Brien, a Democratic Irishman, won the mayoralty that year.

Massachusetts Republicans resolved to reestablish party hegemony by passing a Federal Elections bill that would protect black voters in the South. In 1890, Representative Henry Cabot Lodge and Senator George Frisbie

Hoar led the last congressional battle for civil rights legislation until the 1920s, when an antilynching bill failed. Black Bostonians rallied in a united show of support, as Republican Julius C. Chappelle and Democrat Edwin Garrison Walker recognized the import of the initiative. White Boston Democrats argued against the "Force Bill," as they called it, dismissing the right of southern African-Americans to vote. Democrat William Eustis Russell, of prominent Cambridge lineage, won the gubernatorial election that year. The Independents, or Mugwumps, took a cautiously negative approach toward the bill. This camp, which included many former civil rights advocates, had wearied of efforts to defend African-American rights; they were motivated primarily by a desire for civil service reform. Thomas Wentworth Higginson, an occasional politician, typified this group. Each faction also was represented by at least one newspaper that discussed the issue of voting rights at length.

None of these politicians or newspapers, of course, was concerned solely with civil rights matters. The Federal Elections bill emerged in the context of national debate about the tariff, currency, civil service reform, and other issues. Nevertheless, the question of the African-American's place in society surfaced with special force after the Republican electoral victory of 1888 which brought Benjamin Harrison to the presidency and Republican majorities to both houses of Congress. The politics of the post–Reconstruction Era was marked above all by parity between an increasingly "solid" Republican North and Democratic South so that neither party dominated two branches of government for long. Republicans now sensed an opportunity to break the Solid South, but to do that, black men would have to vote. Convinced that southern Democrats were employing fraud and intimidation to control the ballot, Republicans sought to craft a putatively nonpartisan and nonsectional law that would mandate federal supervision of contested elections. The bill passed the House in July 1890 but failed in the Senate the following January. Silver state Republicans and northern machine politicians kept the bill from the floor when southerners threatened an economic boycott and filibuster.[2]

The failure of the bill marked the end of an era in American race relations, and the beginning of the nadir of African-American history. Mississippi disfranchised its black voters during the course of that very year, followed by South Carolina in 1895, and Louisiana in 1898. Lynching reached an all-time high in 1892. While the increasing tensions brought on by the Populist movement and the depression of 1893 were the main factors behind these developments, the failure of the Federal Elections bill also contributed to the South's sense that the North would no longer interfere with its race relations policies.

It is a significant testimony to the primacy of Massachusetts in the civil rights crusade that the fight for the election bill was led by Bay State Brahmins Lodge and Hoar. These politicians were both descendants of Boston's political antislavery movement and the tradition of Charles Sumner and John Quincy Adams. This, however, was the last fight of powerful Bostonians for civil rights in Congress. Their retreat greatly facilitated the national advance of racism.

REPUBLICAN VICTORY IN THE HOUSE

Between 1877 and 1890, Republican political strategists oscillated between two policies. Sometimes they felt that the antebellum Whig coalition could be rebuilt as the South industrialized and modernized. The Compromise of 1877, which removed federal troops from the South and gave the White House to Rutherford B. Hayes, was the classic example of this policy. Northern Republicans hoped that one part of the arrangement, construction of a railroad linking the South with the Pacific Coast, would stimulate a "New Departure" in which northern commercial values would triumph over southern provincialism. These hopes were repeatedly disappointed. Presidents Hayes, James A. Garfield, Chester A. Arthur, and Benjamin Harrison could not find a successful formula to build a viable Republican Party in the South. Confronted with race-baiting, the southern white Republicans could not be swayed to build a biracial political party. Repeated attacks on African-American voters drove northern Republicans to "wave the bloody shirt" to create an equally solid North. The party that led the Civil War victory was not about to surrender to an unregenerate South after Reconstruction. At stake was northern industry and commerce itself. In Republican eyes, Democratic victory meant unprotected industry, a debased currency, and weaker control of rebellious workers, farmers, and Irish immigrants.[3]

Northern Republicans had ample reason to believe they were being cheated. Using the 1880 census figures, they calculated that in 1888, thirty-three congressional districts in the former slave states had black population majorities. At a time when the overwhelming majority of African-Americans voted Republican, only three of these districts returned Republican congressmen. A mere 697,425 men voted in these districts, but thirty-three New York districts polled 1,206,304 votes. Intimidation of black voters thus accounted for at least thirty stolen seats, of the 123 districts in the old slave states. Beyond this, Republicans tallied another eleven southern districts in which there was a small majority of whites, enough of whom were Republicans, to produce a majority, all of which went Democrat in 1888. To the Democratic claim that the southern Republicans were an isolated minority, their opponents pointed to the seventeen southern Republicans returned to the 51st Congress. Furthermore, the Republicans estimated that these stolen districts would produce Republican presidential victories in Virginia, the Carolinas, Tennessee, Georgia, Alabama, Mississippi, Louisiana, and Florida.[4]

Henry Cabot Lodge was serving only his second term in the U.S. Congress, representing the state's North Shore, when he began to formulate a bill to address this problem. Lodge had already helped to elect his ally Thomas Reed of Maine as Speaker of the House. Reed in turn saw that Lodge was named chairman of a special committee on elections.[5]

Lodge was a proper Bostonian to the marrow of his bones. He descended from old merchant families on both sides of his lineage, trained at the fashionable Mr. Dixwell's School as a boy, and studied at Harvard and its law school. Later he earned a Ph.D. in history, and taught at Harvard. Senator Charles Sumner was a visitor at his boyhood home, and Lodge, born in 1850, was powerfully influenced by the Senator during the Civil War and Reconstruction. With his friends Henry and Brooks Adams, and Moorfield Storey, he opposed President Ulysses S. Grant as a Liberal Republican. Lodge also harbored his own political ambitions, and by 1883 he became chairman of the party's state committee. Lodge encountered the defining moment of his career when the following year he backed the controversial party presidential nominee James G. Blaine, whose opponents charged him with corruption. Lodge's former friends in the Liberal camp cut off personal relations with him. Men like Charles R. Codman, Harvard President Charles W. Eliot, Moorfield Storey, and Thomas Wentworth Higginson repudiated him. They argued that gentlemen of honor should not support opportunists like Blaine, even though he was the party candidate.[6]

Stung by their attacks, Lodge felt that the principles of the party were more important than the morality of the candidate. Two years later he won a close battle for U.S. Congress by a few hundred votes, and was reelected in 1888 by a wide margin. Newly elected President Benjamin Harrison had barely won, and so sought to broaden his base by conciliating the South. West Virginia had voted Republican, and for the first time several other southern states returned impressive Republican minorities. Encouraged, Harrison appointed many southerners to office. But when Democrats counterattacked by race-baiting their rivals, the southern Republicans adopted the same tactics. Alabama led the way by forming an all-white Republican Party. African-American Republicans protested to Harrison unsuccessfully. Barred from the Republican Party, enough Alabama African-Americans voted Democratic so that the Republicans lost the next election. Nevertheless, Harrison and other leading Republicans backed lily-whites again in Louisiana and Virginia with the same results. With nothing to vote for, fearful of violence or economic reprisal, African-Americans did not vote, and Democrats triumphed. Northern Republican newpapers, including Liberal Republican journals like the *New York Times*, called for a reexamination of political strategy.[7]

The question of African-American rights now assumed new importance in northern Republican eyes. In the spring of 1890 New Hampshire Senator Henry W. Blair proposed an education bill that would for the first time award federal dollars rather than land grants to the states. The grants would be based on the percent of adult illiterates in a state; thus the money would flow disproportionately to the South. The bill did not mandate desegregation, but states could not discriminate in apportioning the funds. Blair's stated motivation was to educate the southern African-American and prepare him for full citizenship. Despite President Harrison's support, the bill succumbed to a diverse coalition that foreshadowed the fate of the Lodge bill. Southern Democrats opposed the bill as unwarranted federal interference in state affairs, arguing that the cost would be used to justify an increased revenue tariff. Some northern Republicans feared the bill gave the South too much leeway; others opposed any federal control over education. Like the Lodge bill, it represented an attempt by northern Republicans to modernize the South by crafting nominally nonsectional legislation.[8]

When the lily-white Republican faction in Virginia lost the governor's race, in 1889, President Harrison began to cast about for a formula to rebuild a Republican Party in the South that included black voters. In April 1890 the party leaders instructed Lodge to craft an appropriate measure. As chairman of the Elections Committee, Lodge was already holding hearings on the subject. The congressmen heard ample testimony that black and white Republicans were defrauded in congressional elections. Lodge's bill provided that one hundred voters in a congressional district, or fifty in a county, could demand an investigation into alleged irregularities. Bipartisan panels were to be appointed by U.S. District Court judges to investigate. These supervisors were granted broad powers to inspect registration books. In the context of the times, this was a strong measure. Nevertheless, the bill was narrow in scope in that it addressed only elections to national office. Moreover, it said nothing about guaranteeing a secret ballot, a measure Massachusetts had passed in 1886 and about which Lodge cared passionately. The proposal was consonant with the Fourteenth Amendment, which gave Congress limited powers to regulate the election of its members.[9]

Lodge was probably guided by mixed motives in framing the bill. Certainly political expediency was one concern. He was a party loyalist and fierce partisan against Democrats and Mugwumps. However, he was also the heir of dovetailing Boston political traditions that informed the bill. As a Harvard historian particularly concerned with federalism and his own family heritage, Lodge believed in a strong national government and fair ballot. As a follower of Sumner, he also believed in the Fourteenth Amendment and the principle of equal protection under the law. Lodge's advocacy of this measure was heartfelt and genuine. If he downplayed the particular injustice against African-Americans in motivating the bill, he did not ignore the issue. His speeches reflected a blend of idealism and realism in appraising the temper of the Congress and later the electorate.

Lodge also showed little regard for the political consequences of his advocacy. When a friend warned that the bill might prove deleterious to his political health, the congressman was undaunted. "I supposed that you proposed the bill as a party measure," attorney Sigourney Butler wrote. "But your letter shows an intensity of conviction on the subject that I did not guess." The Federal Elections bill was part of the nationalist framework that made him also a protectionist, opponent of immigration, and later an imperialist. "If it is important to protect American industries, it is vastly more important to protect American voters in their right to vote," he argued. He denied there was anything sectional about the matter, criticizing crooked elections in New Jersey and calling for secret ballot laws North and South. "To demand honest elections," he asserted, "is neither to raise a 'war issue' nor is it 'waving the bloody shirt.' "[10]

Southern Republicans, black and white, testified to the urgency of passage. "The elections—both state and Federal—as held in South Carolina under its present management are a perfect farce," wrote a white Republican. After detailing a long list of fraudulent practices that effectively disfranchised all Republicans in the Camden, South Carolina, area, the writer concluded, "The colored people are now *really* in a worse condition than they were as slaves. They have no protection whatever for life or property." When the bill was tabled in the Senate, South Carolina Republicans were stymied in the election of 1890. "The failure to pass the Lodge Election bill has knocked us completely out in this state," wrote a Charleston African-American in a letter forwarded to Lodge. He mournfully concluded that now "we will have trouble to carry the black district" when before four districts might have gone Republican. From Scottsboro, Alabama, an unlettered white Republican showing no particular concern for African-American rights advised that "white men are a lone [sic] nominated on the Republican state ticket in Alabama. Yet they are as regularly counted out as if they were Negroes." Albion W. Tourgee, Ohio novelist and one-time carpetbagger in North Carolina, wrote Lodge regarding the high stakes for southerners concerned with the democratic process.[11]

Southern Republican congressmen did not necessarily see the matter in the same light. In the party caucus southern and western representatives argued that it was an obstacle to passage of pro-silver laws. The southerners claimed that the bill would merely inflame sectional tensions, which ought to be cooled. The measure squeaked through the caucus by only one vote, but strict party discipline enforced by Speaker Reed would guarantee victory if the ranks turned out to vote when the bill reached the floor.[12]

Lodge made a gallant appeal for his bill in a speech to the House on 26 June. According to the *Boston Globe*, a vociferous Lodge opponent, "A great many Democrats expressed surprise that he should have been so temperate in what he said and complimented him by saying that it was the speech of a statesman holding mistaken views." The purpose of the bill, Lodge argued, was "to secure complete publicity at every stage of a congressional election." Far from being a partisan measure, the ultimate enforcement agency would be the neutral judiciary that would appoint the election officers. The bill was simply a fair ballot measure to secure every voter his rights. Nevertheless, because many Americans believed that in some southern districts the elections were fraudulent, the bill would dispel that notion if the allegations were false. No party would benefit by the law if in fact there was no fraud. Nor did Lodge shrink from the real issue. Citing fraud at the North first, he reminded the congressmen that "as to the South, it was largely a question of race." He recalled the loyalty of the Negro both to his master under slavery and to his nation during the war, and vowed that the Negro "deserved a better reward from the country, North and South," than to be cheated of his rights.[13]

After the bill passed, disgruntled Mugwump opponents defeated Lodge's bid for election as overseer at Harvard. Loyal Republicans rallied to his side. Curtis Guild Jr., later the governor but then working with his father on the *Commercial Bulletin*, condemned the "little knot of Mugwumps bitter in defeat [at the House passage of the election bill] indulging in puerile revenge." Curtis Guild Sr. assured Lodge that he was following in the footsteps of former Massachusetts congressmen later elevated to the Senate. Albert Bushnell Hart of the Harvard history department affirmed that the bill was constitutional and deserved to pass in the Senate. In the fall, Benjamin R. Curtis, a descendant of the moderate former Supreme Court Justice who dissented in the Dred Scott decision, assured Lodge of his backing.[14]

Throughout the spring, the Republican press campaigned for the bill as well. The *Boston Advertiser*, which had been purchased by a group of party men headed by Lodge, was edited by William E. Barrett and functioned as a party organ. Virtually Lodge's personal mouthpiece, it reprinted the entire oration, which was "the talk of the capital." That same day it editorialized against a Georgia white supremacist who opposed Negro education. The following day it disputed the Mugwump-oriented *Boston Herald*, which lamented that nothing could be done about election fraud. To drive home the point that something must be done about conditions in the South, the *Advertiser* ran a page-one story about a Louisiana black man killed by a mob of two hundred whites when it was alleged that he was storing guns.[15] The *Boston Journal*, edited by W. W. Clapp, oriented more to the "Half-Breed" camp of Senator Hoar, falling between the Stalwarts and the Mugwump Liberals. The *Journal* saw the Lodge bill as an extension of the secret ballot. "It is in effect an application to Congressional elections of the principle of genuine ballot reform which are embodied in the legislation of this and several other states."[16]

After a hot debate on the floor, the Lodge bill passed by a strict party vote of 155 to 149 with 24 abstentions. One southern Union Laborite voted in favor and two Republicans defected. In the Senate, however, there were no rules to keep the Republican caucus in line and no equivalent to "Czar" Reed. Senator Hoar had to confront a more formidable opposition than did Congressman Lodge.[17]

AFRICAN-AMERICAN POLITICS

Well aware of the difficulties the bill would face in the Senate, Boston's African-Americans rallied to the bill's support in the summer of 1890. As we have earlier noted, this community had a proud political heritage that dated back to the colonial period. After the Civil War, at least one African-American always served in the General Court (the state legislature) or the City Council. In addition, black Bostonians received some small political patronage in the form of appointive office. African-Americans generally voted overwhelmingly Republican, although a handful of leaders espoused political independence and could be found, to varying degrees, within the Democratic camp.

Political divisions in Boston reflected differing strategies within the national African-American polity. Frederick Douglass remained the most authoritative national leader until his death in 1895, and his antebellum sojourn in Massachusetts probably increased his influence in Boston. Douglass urged African-Americans to stay with the Republican Party and served in appointive office, but he criticized Republican backsliding. Other leaders, such as Timothy Thomas Fortune, editor of the *New York Age*, advocated political independence and a divided vote. During the struggle for the Lodge bill, however, Fortune joined Douglass in the Republican camp.[18]

In January 1890, Fortune called the first convention of the National Afro-American League, which 141 delegates attended in Chicago. This meeting announced a strong civil rights perspective, naming as its first priority the defense of black voting rights in the South, and affirming a nonpartisan political stance. The only Massachusetts man to sign the convention call was J. Gordon Street, future editor of Boston's soon-to-appear race weekly, the *Courant*, and the only state delegate was Joshua A. Brockett of Cambridge's St. Paul African Methodist Episcopal Church. Brockett became chairperson of the Cambridge Colored National League and Edwin G. Walker, son of abolitionist David Walker and a key leader of the community despite his Democratic sympathies, led the Boston group.[19]

A second convention, held in Washington, D.C., in February, seemed more important to Boston leaders. They held a conference of their own to elect eighteen delegates to this meeting, at which was founded the Citizens' Equal Rights Association. While most of these delegates did not actually attend the Washington convention, two Bostonians played prominent roles there: W. H. Dupree served as convention vice president, and Julius C. Chappelle, a former state legislator, chaired the resolutions committee. More than four hundred delegates attended this meeting, which was older in composition than the Chicago gathering, had more politicians in attendance, and was apparently somewhat more conservative. These delegates too declared for civil rights, but also spoke of the need for economic progress and self-help. Despite some obscure controversy in Boston about the convention's work, Butler Wilson, reporting the meeting in the *New York Age*, approved the Washington group's commitment to the Blair education bill and congressional efforts to defend southern black voting rights. The fact that Boston elected Edwin Walker a delegate to the meeting, and that J. C. Price, president of Fortune's League, chaired the Washington gathering, suggests that no fundamental principles divided the two organizations. In Boston, they cooperated during the following year.[20]

Around the same time, *Atlanta Constitution* editor Henry Grady spoke in Boston before prominent businessmen, arguing that the issues of the Civil War were now definitively over. The black community and its neo-abolitionist allies brought a thousand people to a Tremont Temple meeting to rebut Grady's portrayal of southern racial harmony and progress. The Reverends A. A. Miner, Alexander Crummell, and Joshua A. Brockett insisted that Grady had painted over the real problems. William Lloyd Garrison II sent a letter to the meeting, arguing that Grady's death immediately after the speech had softened reaction against his white supremacist views. In the *New York Age*, Butler Wilson contrasted the elevation of Maria Baldwin, an African-American teacher, to school principal in a mostly white school, to Grady's presentation of blacks as best fit for menial jobs. Fortune, in the editorial column, called Grady the legitimate heir to the former president of the Confederacy, Jefferson Davis.[21]

This all-out attack on a representative of the Democrats did not preclude displeasure with local Republicans. In the 1889 local elections, the Republicans had swept aside the Democrats, and two African-Americans—Charles E. Harris of the West End's Ward Nine and Paul C. Brooks from a South End ward that in 1890 was less than 5 percent black—were elected to the city council. However, according to Butler Wilson, neither Republican Mayor Thomas Hart nor Governor John Quincy Adams Brackett sufficiently rewarded black voters with patronage appointments. Democratic Mayor Hugh O'Brien and Democratic Governor Benjamin Butler had equal or better records. Republican failure to appoint a colored man was "stupid and dangerous"; now that white Republicans were bolting the party, so might colored men.[22]

In the summer, both black community groups turned their attention to the elections bill pending in the Senate. The Colored National League invited Captain Nathan Appleton, a white Brahmin veteran, to their conference, who declared that a fair ballot at the South should be "enforced by gunpoint if necessary." Meanwhile, a state meeting of the Massachusetts Citizens' Equal Rights Association held at Worcester resolved its solidarity with the Colored National League and hoped for a merger. Together they called a Faneuil Hall rally for 1 August.[23]

Five hundred people responded eagerly to the summons. Chairman Julius C. Chappelle of the Equal Rights Association declared that colored Americans should have been guaranteed voting rights at the end of the war. Edwin G. Walker, probably the leading African-American Democrat in the state, said that "the best men of today are found in the Republican party and because there are in that party men who are dishonest, I do not censure the whole party." Three black politicians presented a resolution endorsing the Lodge bill, which the meeting adopted. African-American attorney Edward Everett Brown, *Courant* editor J. Gordon Street, and others spoke as well.

White neo-abolitionists delivered stirring orations also. Norwood P. Hallowell, a "fighting Quaker" officer in the Massachusetts 54th Regiment, arraigned the various northern opponents of the bill. He castigated merchants who feared the threatened southern economic boycott and tariff reformers who placed their business interests above civil rights. The civil service reformers (here he meant the Mugwumps) failed to see that a free ballot would encourage honest government, not retard it. The veteran's kinsman Richard P. Hallowell pointed to the Wendell Phillips portrait on the wall and dramatically declared that if Phillips could speak, he would denounce the Mugwumps as latter-day doughfaces. He later sent a journalistic account of the meeting to Senator Hoar, along with a petition backing the bill.[24] The meeting showed the ability of black and white activists to work together, and the independence of African-American politicians from strict party politics. Walker's presence and the choice of the nonpolitician Hallowells showed that this was not simply a Republican rally.

Chappelle was a South Carolina migrant who had worked as a barber by day and studied by night to earn a high school degree. Elected to the Boston City Council and the state Republican committee, he served in the legislature from 1883 to 1886. There he sponsored Progressive legislation to eliminate the Massachusetts poll tax, regulate child and female labor, and provide free textbooks in the public schools and free evening high schools. He was the prime legislative mover on the Boston Massacre/Crispus Attucks statue. Chappelle worked within the main line of African-American politics, in the spirit of Frederick Douglass, and certainly best represented the community's sentiments at the meeting.[25]

By contrast, Walker was a native Bostonian, the son of the fiery abolitionist David Walker. As a young man he owned a leather shop that employed fifteen workers. Through participation in the antebellum freedom struggle he developed an interest in the law and won prominence as an attorney. In 1866 he became the first African-American to be elected to a state legislature. Although he won office as a Republican, he soon switched allegiance to the Democrats. Perhaps his mainly Irish clientele as an attorney influenced his decision. Walker admired Irish revolutionary leaders, was the only African-American to speak at the memorial to poet John Boyle O'Reilly, and was even admitted to an Irish lodge. He campaigned for Yankee Democrat Benjamin Butler, who appointed him a municipal judge, but Republicans blocked his nomination. About sixty years old at the time of the 1890 meeting, Walker's Democratic loyalties reflected the peculiarities of Boston racial politics. His vigorous support of the Lodge bill showed him to be no Democratic pawn either. In 1896, five years before his death, he almost ran for president as an independent candidate.[26]

This enthusiastic rally combined with two other events in August that marked a high point of good feeling in a community whose state leaders were at the head of the congressional civil rights battle. For the first time, the Grand Army of the Republic held its annual encampment in a festive and elaborately decorated Boston. Soldiers paraded in the streets and ships passed in review in the harbor. About twenty African-American veterans' posts marched in the parade, including two from Massachusetts. The men of the 54th and 55th Regiments staged their own campfire, led by William H. Dupree, James Monroe Trotter, Charles L. Mitchell, and Charles Lenox. The celebration clearly encouraged the sense that racial harmony prevailed in the city. Then came an unrelated court ruling in the case of a black man who assaulted a white man, after the latter had racially taunted him. The law, the judge found, compelled a guilty verdict, but justice was on the defendant's side. The black man was fined one penny. "This is justice meted out in Massachusetts," exulted the *New York Age*. "We hope to see the time when the colored man will be treated as well elsewhere."[27]

As the November election neared, African-American leaders urged the ranks to turn out for the Republicans. Frederick Douglass, speaking in Boston at an abolitionist reunion, led the way. With him on the platform was George T. Downing of Newport, Rhode Island, a leading Independent. In New York, Fortune urged the Republicans to run a straight-out ticket and defeat the foe. Bostonians urged a vote for congressional candidate Edward L. Pierce, a Civil War veteran and friend of Sumner's, who had donated a library to Sea Island freedpeople.[28] The ensuing events, however, undermined politics as a medium of struggle for black Bostonians.

THE BILL FAILS IN THE SENATE

If George Frisbie Hoar cannot be strictly classified as a Boston Brahmin it is only because he had moved from his native Concord to practice law and politics in Worcester. His paternal ancestry could be traced to early Puritan settlers. His father had been a friend of Ralph Waldo Emerson's, and was once violently expelled from South Carolina while on a mission on behalf of African-American seamen. His maternal grandfather was Roger Sherman, a signer of the Declaration of Independence. Hoar himself, born in 1826, studied at Harvard and worshiped as a Unitarian.[29]

His father and elder brother were early members of the Free Soil Party. George Frisbie Hoar was a member of the new party too, and later a leader of the Kansas Emigrant Aid Society and the Republican Party. His political idol was Charles Sumner, whose policies he followed throughout the 1850s and 1860s. He won election to the Massachusetts House in 1852 and the U.S. Congress in 1868, where he served four terms until the General Court chose him for the Senate. Hoar was a Radical Republican on sectional questions, but an opponent of spoils politics, a combination of views that placed him in the camp of Republican "Half Breeds," along with such men as future presidents Rutherford B. Hayes and Benjamin Harrison. Support for civil rights was alive in Hoar as it was in no other senator in 1890. Sixty-four years old in that year, he was the last man of the 1848 Free Soil movement serving in the Senate when he died in 1904. His tenure was marked by strong advocacy for a variety of social reforms, and conservative positions on economic issues such as the tariff and currency. He was the right senator to lead the fight on the elections bill.[30]

Despite the Republican Senate majority, Hoar was nervous about the fate of the bill even before the November election. As early as August, the majority of ten seemed fragile. "I am more anxious and disturbed about the political situation than I have ever been before in my life," Hoar confided to a friend. This was a strong statement from a political veteran of the Civil War and Reconstruction.[31] As Hoar feared, Republican Stalwart politicians under the leadership of Pennsylvania's Matthew S. Quay wanted to give precedence to the tariff and postpone the elections bill until the second session of Congress, commencing in December. Only after all but one Republican agreed to give the bill priority in December did Hoar consent. The four-month delay, however, gave the Democratic South and its allies a chance to regroup. During the break, the *Atlanta Constitution* threatened a southern boycott of northern products if the Lodge bill passed. Northern businessmen became alarmed, and began pressuring their senators to vote nay. Senators from New York, Nebraska, Minnesota, Pennsylvania, and Rhode Island voiced skepticism about the bill. Republican ranks began to crumble.[32]

Massachusetts businessmen showed little interest in the bill. The overwhelming concern of Hoar's business correspondents was with the tariff, and generally only as it affected their product. Alone, the Home Market Club linked the tariff and the election bill as complementary and equally deserving of the approbation of manufacturers. "Indeed, a protective tariff, or any other wholesome measure, can have but an uncertain tenure unless the freedom and purity of elections can be guaranteed," club secretary Albert Clark observed.[33]

Some southern Republicans, formerly northerners, wrote to Hoar of their fears. About 130 citizens of Anniston, Alabama, "recently removed from the Northern and Western states," sent a remonstrance against the bill, protesting that it would hurt the Republican Party, and their own business as Yankee merchants and artisans. A former Worcester Republican, now living in Florida, spelled out the underlying white fear: Negro "domination," which simply meant that black men might win office. The correspondent, however, thought it the better part of valor to accept the wishes of the native southern whites. Hoar also heard from courageous southerners, black and white, who backed him, but now that the stakes were higher it was obvious that pressure was mounting against the bill among southern Republicans of northern background, who might have been counted upon for support.[34]

When the Senate reconvened in December, the Democrats mounted a delaying filibuster. Hoar delivered an impassioned rebuttal on 29–30 December, but oratory swayed no senatorial votes. In early January two silver state senators joined the Democratic effort to set the elections bill aside. Hoar and his remaining allies could not muster enough votes to bring the bill back to the floor, and by 26 January, it was dead. A coalition of southern Democrats, northern businessmen and machine politicians, Mugwumps, and silver senators defeated the Federal Elections bill in the Senate.[35]

In Massachusetts, the effect on the Brahmins who had championed black voting rights was powerful. Lodge was bitter about the bill's defeat in the Senate. When a Missouri congressman attacked him on the issue in the aftermath, he delivered a stinging rebuke. He never addressed the suffrage question again, even during the years of Republican resurgence. W. E. Barrett, editor of the *Boston Journal* and now Speaker of the Massachusetts House, urged the state's Republicans to abandon the elections bill and turn to new issues. Massachusetts Republicans should campaign to develop the state's public schools, and compromise on the tariff. The Republican Party in the South was a dead letter. Implicit in Barrett's assessment was an abandonment of black rights.[36] Hoar's biographer concludes that "in Hoar's public career the conflict over the elections bill marked a definite turning point."[37] This was the last time that Hoar, Lodge, the Republicans, or Massachusetts would lead an idealistic crusade for the African-American in Congress. There was little now for the Brahmins to do but look on, either indifferently or aghast, at the new rise of codified racism in the South, and discourse favorably on the concomitant ascension of Booker T. Washington to the role of unofficial spokesman for the race.

BRAHMINS AGAINST A "FORCE BILL"

Within Massachusetts, Brahmin opposition to Lodge's bill was more vigorously expressed by the newspapers than by politicians. Democratic and Mugwump candidates understood that the issue did not interest their voters. For the Democrats in 1890, a downward revision of the tariff was the key question. Mugwumps, as usual, pushed for civil service reform. The Democrats won a sweeping victory in 1890 behind the brilliant campaign oratory of William Eustis Russell, who argued for sectional reconciliation and ignored civil rights. The *Boston Globe*, committed to the Democratic faction loyal to former president Grover Cleveland, took up the attack on Lodge's bill. Mug-wump politicians won several congressional seats, but as they generally concerned themselves with local issues, we shall briefly discuss Thomas Wentworth Higginson as the representative man of this group on race rela-tions. In print, the *Boston Evening Transcript* spoke for the divided conscience of the backsliding Brahmin racial liberals.

The national Democratic view of the race question was dramatically ex-pressed in Boston by *Atlanta Constitution* editor Henry W. Grady in a 12 December 1889 speech before the Boston Merchants' Association. An earnest exponent of southern industrialism and alliance with northern capital, Grady understood that a prerequisite for sectional harmony was the elimination of the race problem from politics. Speaking with former president Cleveland, Andrew Carnegie, and others, Grady acknowledged the difficulty of present-ing his case in the home of Wendell Phillips and Charles Sumner. He re-minded his listeners that although both sections had been stained by slavery, whose passing he was glad of, it had in fact been a civilizing mission that brought happiness to the savage. Now the line between North and South was "but a vanishing shadow." The (white) South faced the difficult problem of living side by side with a "kindly and dependent race," which it could do only with the North's help. The Negro was making determined economic prog-ress, owning $10 million of property in Georgia. While black citizens paid one-thirtieth the taxes of whites, they received half the educational services. Artisan trade was more open to the southern Negro than the northern, Grady asserted. Yet, it would mock democracy if "ignorant and purchasable votes," easily swayed by demagogues, were to rule by force of numbers over the whites. "The negro vote can never control in the South, and it would be well if partisans at the North would understand this." The editor was sure that his revered "old black mammy" was herself looking down from heaven to bless this course. He concluded with a moving peroration exalting American na-tionalism, a future without sectionalism, and the divine mission of the United States to advance democracy. Even the Republican *Boston Journal*, which editorially questioned the veracity of Grady's remarks, headlined its story "Editor Grady Brings Tears to the Eyes of His Auditors."[38]

Grady's untimely death at age thirty-nine a few days later, after his return to Atlanta, further softened the feelings of Bostonians for white southerners. The *Journal* praised him, suggesting that he would have been a congressman had he lived. The Democratic *Boston Post* noted that Grady's last speech was given at Plymouth Rock and compared his eloquence to that of Wendell Phillips. He had had a profound effect upon the industrial development of his section and the nation, the paper concluded. The *Journal*, however, also ran a reminiscence by its Washington correspondent, upon whom Grady had called while en route to Boston. This writer noted that Grady's mood had been full of foreboding regarding race relations. He had recently protested a white invasion of an African-American residential district near Atlanta, during which black men had been flogged. He feared that "vicious colored leaders" might instigate a race riot. The *Journal* thus implied that Grady knew all along that a storm of race hatred was gathering in the South.[39]

Among the honored guests at the Merchants' Association banquet was former Cambridge mayor William E. Russell, unsuccessful Democratic candidate for governor in the last two elections. The youthful Russell was a descendant of early Puritan settlers, and a graduate of Harvard and the Boston University Law School, where his father was on the faculty. His tenure as mayor in the mid-1880s had been marked by efficiency in government, budget balancing, and increased municipal services. He was one of the rare Brahmin politicians of either party who possessed a genuinely democratic temperament. Despite some friction with municipal unions, he crafted a working alliance with Irish leaders in Boston and Cambridge, and had only narrowly missed election in the recent gubernatorial race.[40]

In February 1890, he repaid Grady's visit to Boston by bringing a party of thirteen businessmen to Atlanta's first Chamber of Commerce meeting. Grady's last letter, written to a Georgia colleague, had praised Russell, who apparently agreed to the trip during the editor's Boston sojourn. Russell proceeded to deliver a northerner's version of Grady's speech to his southern audience, celebrating the industrial growth of the South and the possibilities for commercial exchange. The role of government was to facilitate this process. In his only oblique reference to the rights of African-Americans, Russell extolled the Supreme Court for undoing "much legislation founded upon sectional prejudice and enacted for sectional or partisan purposes." Youth was a key theme of the address: Russell and his generation, who had been children during the Civil War, would look not to the past but to the future. He concluded by calling for reform of the ballot (meaning the secret ballot, not Lodge's bill), civil service, and tariff. Upon his return to Boston, Russell assured the manufacturer Edward Atkinson that race relations in the South were in fact harmonious.[41]

A few months later, Russell, still in his early thirties, launched his third campaign for governor. The Massachusetts Democrats were experiencing a hopeful revival as the Lodge bill was launched. The party's rising fortunes were based on the confluence of inflation and Republican high tariff policies; Russell and Democratic congressional candidates addressed these pocketbook issues and said little about the Lodge bill. The *Boston Globe*, however, under the ownership of Charles H. Taylor and his sons, campaigned enthusiastically against the bill. Taylor and Russell were political allies in the Grover Cleveland wing of the party, and Taylor served on Russell's staff after the latter was elected governor.[42]

The *Globe* portrayed any federal attempt to regulate the elections as mere sectionalism and partisanship. While Lodge was planning his tactics in the House, New Hampshire Senator William E. Chandler was formulating a similar measure in the upper chamber. "No Revival of Sectionalism Wanted," the *Globe* warned in an early attempt to head off reform. The "insult" to the South would jeopardize southern votes for an American site for the World's Fair. Northern talk of ballot reform was simply a cover for a power grab that would give the captains of industry the high tariff rates they craved.[43]

When the bill emerged in the House, the *Globe* blasted it as part of the Republican campaign to stifle the Democratic House minority by tightening rules of procedure. The "Force Bill" was a conspiracy by House Speaker Thomas Reed and Lodge to enforce Republican rule. Waving aside the notion that most Negroes voted Republican, the *Globe* derided the federal inspectors that the bill would send southward as Republicans with police powers. "Never has legislation been carried on with such high-handed audacity," the *Globe* alleged, as it was in Congress under "dictator" Reed.[44]

Not only was the bill unfair; it would also cost the voters a fortune to enforce. To pay for the "Army of 300,000 Republicans" ready to descend upon the South would cost $16 million, a lead headline declared. In rebuttal, Lodge estimated that there were 140 election precincts per congressional district. His bill mandated three inspectors for each precinct when an election was challenged. He further estimated only twenty challenges. Rounding off the arithmetic to produce a lower figure, Lodge foresaw eight thousand supervisors per election. The *Globe* reporter countered that every district in the country would see a challenge. Furthermore, Lodge had neglected to count the cost of three deputy marshals who would accompany the three inspectors. With 330 congressional districts, at a cost of $50,000 per district, the country would indeed require 300,000 inspectors and marshals at a cost of sixteen million dollars.[45]

The accuracy of either side's self-serving predictions cannot be reckoned. What was more revealing was the *Globe*'s threat to pervert the intent of the bill by pressing spurious challenges. "The way to make a bad law odious is to enforce it," the editors declared. The Democratic Party itself would not stoop so low, the editors thought, but slyly surmised that "one hundred cranks" could be found in each district to challenge even the most lopsided of elections. The federal inspectors would work every district, Congressman Lodge's not excepted.[46]

When the bill passed the House, the *Globe* predicted that the voters would provide the ultimate chastisement in November. In the South, white voters fearing Negro domination, even if that fear was unjustified, would flock to the Democratic standard. Northerners too, would feel "disgust" if "the bill to promote fraud" became law. The *Globe* foresaw that "this will be a democratic tidal wave year, like 1882 and 1874."[47]

The Mugwump tendency was less cohesive than even that of the fractious Democratic Party. Politically heterogeneous and always in motion, its roots lay in the Liberal Republican revolt against President Grant. Independents cared mainly about civil service reform and the corrupting effect of the spoils system upon government. They gradually set aside Reconstruction issues. Mugwump disgust with the Blaine nomination in 1884 led to a hot fight in the Massachusetts Republican Party, whose bad feelings lingered past 1890. Lodge was on the receiving end of this antagonism. Independents with political ambitions of their own had reason to resent a man they perceived as a political opportunist.

However, the Mugwumps suffered from an elitism that was politically paralyzing. It was a much-remarked-upon phenomenon of the time that men of the upper class were withdrawing from politics, which was becoming increasingly ungentlemanly. According to Geoffrey Blodgett, the Mugwumps were "college-bred, Protestant, urban and middle class." They held a wide range of views on economic questions, agreeing only on civil service reform. While they did not possess great voting strength, they were sometimes financially powerful and always articulate. Among the wealthy in this circle were John Murray Forbes, Boston's most powerful capitalist; Robert Treat Paine, philanthropist; investment house heads Henry Lee and Henry Lee Higginson; and Charles Cabot Jackson, Martin Brimmer, and Charles Francis Adams. Academics supporting Independent policies included Charles Eliot Norton, William James, and Charles W. Eliot. Moorfield Storey, Thomas Wentworth Higginson, and John F. Andrew, son of the Civil War governor, were other prominent leaders.[48]

Independents also held a range of views on civil rights. No individual, however, exemplified the retreat of this milieu more dramatically than Thomas Wentworth Higginson. A descendant of Puritan divines, he himself became a Unitarian minister of radical proclivities. In the antebellum period he was the architect of daring plans to free fugitive slaves from federal hands. He joined the financial backers of John Brown and was the most steadfast of the "Secret Six," the only one who was convinced that Brown's plan might work, and the only man to stand his ground after Brown was caught and his incriminating papers found. During the Civil War, he commanded a regiment of South Carolina freedmen. *Army Life in a Black Regiment*, his postwar account of that experience, testified to the fighting capabilities and great courage of the African-American combatants, although its paternalist assumptions were all too common in 1870. During Reconstruction, which he at first ardently supported, he began to lead a literary and contemplative life. Along with this change in his personal routine came new doubts about how the freedpeople would advance themselves. Higginson participated in the Liberal Republican campaign that relegated African-American rights to second place behind civil service reform. In this spirit he unsuccessfully ran for Congress in 1888 as an independent Democrat. This ideological journey was typical for men of Mugwump stripe, but Higginson's case is the most pronounced because of his outstanding record as an abolitionist and his unique Civil War experience. If any Boston Brahmin could have been expected to speak out for civil rights until his dying breath, it was Higginson, but he reflected too much the mood of his social group and time by 1890.[49]

This mood was put in print daily by the *Boston Evening Transcript*. The newspaper was founded in 1830 by Henry Worthington Dutton, a poor boy from western Massachusetts, and Lynde Minshull Walter, a Harvard-educated Episcopalian. In the antebellum period, the paper followed the line of Boston's Cotton Whigs—generally antislavery but also anti-abolitionist. The paper supported conservative Whiggery until Daniel Webster's Seventh of March 1850 speech, and then gradually toughened its antislavery stance, supporting Abraham Lincoln in 1860.[50]

The original owners gave the editorial staff considerable leeway and the Dutton family continued this policy throughout the century. In 1881, Edward Henry Clement, the son of a mercantile family, assumed the editorship. Clement was raised with abolitionist ideas and served William Tecumseh Sherman during the Civil War as a journalist after the capture of Savannah. Like Henry Cabot Lodge, Clement was a Republican who voted for Tilden in 1876; unlike Lodge, however, he opposed Blaine in 1884. A low tariff man, he supported Cleveland several times against Republicans. Clement took an active interest in questions regarding African-Americans and sought to advance the race's interests, as he understood them, as editor.[51]

The *Transcript*'s opposition to the Lodge bill thus reflected and reinforced the retreat of the Brahmin elite from confronting the South on its increasingly restrictive racial policies. Nevertheless, a certain ambiguity pervaded Clement's argument and he sometimes seemed uncomfortable with his own conclusions. The newspaper's vacillation displayed the fading of the civil rights dream in the Brahmin mind, like a light flaring uncertainly before it flickered out.

The *Transcript* embraced President Benjamin Harrison's 2 December 1889 speech that signaled a new direction on southern policy, although it did not comment directly on that small section of the address. When Jefferson Davis died a few days later, Clement contrasted the South's progress to Davis's reactionary vision. Toward the end of the month, after Henry Grady died, Clement observed that most northerners disagreed with the editor, but respected him. "He saw Negroes as hewers of wood, but did not countenance outrages against them, and took risks to denounce them." Unlike Grady, Clement respectfully advocated the social equality of the Negro. At the same time, he downplayed the political struggle, vowing that in this "new social crusade," Bostonians "will again be found . . . in the forefront of radical and hopeful opinion."[52]

In concrete terms, the "new social crusade" meant that Clement was ready to abandon the old civil rights crusade. When Henry Cabot Lodge announced an intention to protect the ballot in the South, the *Transcript* demurred. Lodge, the editor protested, was misreading lessons he should have learned as an historian of federalism. Congressional elections were actually state elections. Just as the people of Massachusetts would resent federal supervision of their elections, so should the good people of the South. As for African-Americans, the *Transcript* rosily foresaw a gradual elevation of the Negro from his bondage to ignorance, and a concomitant lessening of racial tension in the South. The Blair education bill, therefore, did earn the newspaper's praise.[53]

Toward the Lodge bill, the *Transcript* observed a discreet silence at first. As the House vote drew nearer, Clement could comment only abstractly. "The public will draw its own conclusions as to the extent party politics or a real desire for fair and pure elections dominates" considerations regarding the bill, he mused. The Congress would be on "doubtful ground" to pass the bill, but it was constitutional. If the Negroes were in fact Democrats, as southern Democrats claimed, then the bill "will serve to dissipate a prevalent error at the North, and so promote harmony and friendship between the sections." At best, his position was agnostic.[54]

Then the bill passed the House, and Clement turned against it. Now he predicted that "the short-lived infant" would be strangled in the Senate. The bill was "a monument . . . of misplaced energy and maladroit strategy on the part of Speaker Reed, Congressman Lodge, and others." Then in August, when this prediction seemed accurate, Clement grew mournful about his impending victory. He regretted that the "New Republican Party, which has taken the tariff idol, that Lincoln and Sumner knew not, for its fetish. Pennsylvania leads now, the New England ideal is disestablished." Five months later, when the bill failed to come to a vote, the newspaper seemed more grim than gratified. In an editorial that did not mention African-Americans, Clement concluded that the bill had been nothing but "partisan legislation" that flew in the face of public opinion.[55]

The November Election

Between the House and Senate votes came the November election, and in the nation's economic difficulties, the hopes of challengers soared. Mugwump independents running for Congress as Democrats included John F. Andrew, son of the Civil War governor, George Fred Williams, and Sherman Hoar, nephew of the senator. The North Shore Democrats could find no one to run against Lodge, so they imported William Everett, son of the famed orator Edward Everett, from Quincy. Everett the younger was a Harvard faculty member who lived in genteel poverty and relative obscurity.[56]

The *Lynn City Item*, a Republican paper, took the Democrats' choice of Everett as a "confession of weakness." Everett was clearly "a sacrificial lamb" doing noble party duty, but destined for defeat. Lodge had handily drubbed his last opponent by five thousand votes. In addition, Lodge's friend and ally Reed had won a whopping victory in a special Maine election, speaking out on behalf of the voting rights bill during the campaign.[57]

Lodge nevertheless ran hard, and proudly proclaimed his role as shaper of the elections bill. At the Sixth District Republican convention, speaking before a large audience, he won the heartiest applause when he championed fair elections and political morality. In another speech the same day he blasted those who deserted the Republicans for "the party of hatred." The country "owe[s] to the Negro the protection which the Constitution has pledged to him," Lodge insisted, and charged that his opponents could only fear reform if they had something to hide. Massachusetts had led the way in the antislavery struggle and the Civil War; the state had the best and earliest fair elections bill itself. As Massachusetts had led in those crusades, so she led now. The issue was more important than the tariff or currency questions. Lodge ended with classic "bloody shirt" rhetoric, but the passion that he displayed on the question reflected genuine commitment and flowed out of the man's upbringing, education, and life experience.[58]

Lodge, of course, did not campaign as a single-issue candidate. He defended the whole range of Republican issues, including the recently passed McKinley tariff, the House Rules reform that strengthened the Speaker, a big Navy, immigration restriction, veterans' benefits, and his ability to bring home the federal bacon. Democratic opponent Everett attacked him on the tariff, House Rules changes, and the elections bill. Democratic gubernatorial candidate Russell claimed that Lodge had sacrificed New England's interests to the protectionist manufacturers of Pennsylvania. The *Globe* denounced Lodge's bill as "a sort of perpetual Hayes-Tilden, 8–7 counting out fraud." The voters should defeat Lodge, or at least reduce his majority, to send a message that the country did not want the bill.[59]

The voters did send a message, but on which issue? Lodge barely squeaked past Everett, winning 14,558 votes to Everett's 13,562 with 997 for the Prohibitionist. The Democrats added four new congressmen, including Mugwumps Andrew, Williams, and Hoar. Russell resoundingly defeated governor John Quincy Adams Brackett. Nationally the Republicans suffered their worst defeat since the Civil War, losing control of the House.[60]

Lodge and Hoar put the best possible face on the loss. The congressman bravely acknowledged the extent of the defeat, and blamed it on "one cause, the passage of the tariff bill . . . and the skilfully managed scare about high prices." He accepted his lower vote total as a warning for him on the tariff. "As to the election bill, if that had been the issue the result in Massachusetts would have been very different, for the people of this state will always sustain measures for honest elections." He vowed adherence to the principle of the bill and predicted that its promise would one day be fulfilled.[61]

Hoar claimed the result was but an exaggeration of the usual midterm check on the presidency, a process that had gone on for sixty-six years and signified little. Actually, the longer term trends showed that the Democrats had little to celebrate, Hoar thought. The South comprised sixteen of thirty-seven states in 1874, but today seven new states had no slave past. In addition, the northern Democrats, while refusing to support the elections bill, never defended actual southern elections, "those Isthmian games of murder and fraud." In his standard stump speech, Hoar argued that the South had stolen some thirty-nine to sixty congressional seats at the last election, and that the vote of one southerner counted as ten votes in Massachusetts. Ultimately, Democratic currency policies would work against the Democrats, for "the party of the clipped dollar and the party of clipped citizenship are the same."[62]

For black residents, even the Boston atmosphere seemed to change. Where once harmony apparently reigned, now threats of exclusion appeared on all sides. At the New England Conservatory, southern white students demanded that two African-American women be barred from dormitories. One of these, Maud Cuney, would not give in. The Colored National League threatened to sue, and the conservatory rebuffed the southerners. Next a black woman was kept out of a restaurant. A South Boston resident suddenly found evidence that Crispus Attucks had not been killed at the Boston Massacre after all. At Phillips Exeter Academy, southern students objected to the choice of a black student as class orator. These unrelated cases of white hostility, following so swiftly upon the heels of the Democratic victory, suggest either a new boldness on the part of racists, or a new awareness by the *Age's* Boston correspondent of the significance of episodes he might previously have dismissed.[63]

Failure is often the occasion for recrimination, and the defeat of the Lodge bill inspired that as well. When Massachusetts Republican leader William E. Barrett called upon his party to forget old issues like the race problem in the South, *Courant* editor Street urged black voters to turn against Barrett when he ran again. "What kind of martyr's crown are you bidding for, Editor Street?" an angry Timothy Fortune objected. A few months later Street apparently departed from the *Courant*, which now vowed to be a "dignified and sensible ally of the *Age*." Fortune was more forgiving toward a youthful Harvardian who felt that "the [white] South has some excuse for its present attitude" toward black voting rights. The Harvard man said that "a good many of our people south of Mason and Dixon's line are not fit for the responsibilities of republican government." Fortune dismissed this as "humbug" but predicted, correctly, that the youthful W. E. B. Du Bois would change his opinions with experience.[64]

Despite this brave rhetoric, the national and state Democratic victories surely encouraged the bill's defeat in the Senate. The *Globe* observed that "Mr. Lodge and Senator Hoar are informed that their state is not with them in their effort to revive sectionalism," and even the *Lynn City Item* attributed Lodge's low vote to "northern doughfaces," a tacit admission that the tally hinged in part on his bill. It is more likely, however, that the bill played little part in the state election and only a secondary role in Lodge's district; the tariff and state issues were probably more important.[65]

Henry Cabot Lodge never again expressed interest in African-American rights. Elected to the Senate in 1893, he turned his attention to immigration restriction and foreign policy. Both these issues inclined Lodge to racialist thinking. His friendship with Theodore Roosevelt deepened this tendency. When President Roosevelt discharged African-American soldiers from the Army after the Brownsville, Texas, incident of August 1906, Boston's black community excoriated the president's ally in the Senate. Nothing more dramatically symbolized the Brahmin retreat than the evolution of Lodge's position from 1890 to 1906.

All along, Lodge had been a racialist on the immigration question. Like Henry Adams and others, he advanced the theory that democracy was a special attribute of the Anglo-Saxon "race," and that other "races" did not possess its peculiar virtues. In the late 1890s, he advocated a literacy test as a means to keep out immigrants from southern and eastern Europe.[66]

Lodge was also a staunch interventionist in the buildup to the Spanish-American War, an advocate of annexation of the islands won from Spain, and the architect of a coverup of American atrocities in the Philippines during the war to secure American control there. In Boston, Mugwumps formed the core of the antiwar campaign, with Senator Hoar allied to their position. As Senate chairman of an investigating committee, Lodge presided over partisan hearings designed to paper over the brutality of the war in the Philippines. The Mugwump *Boston Herald* charged that "our troops in the Philippines . . . look upon all Filipinos as of one race and condition, and being dark men, they are often therefore 'niggers,' and entitled to all the contempt and harsh treatment administered by white overlords to the most inferior races." The roles of Lodge and the Mugwump critics of 1890 were now reversed.[67]

This confluence of attitudes matched that of Lodge's friend, Theodore Roosevelt, who greatly disillusioned his African-American supporters. A few days after the November 1906 elections, Roosevelt dismissed without trial three regiments of African-American troops who had refused to cooperate with an investigation into an alleged shooting incident at Brownsville, Texas, during August. Nationally, the African-American community protested Roosevelt's decision. In Massachusetts, a delegation of African-American veterans, including Civil War hero Sergeant William Carney of New Bedford, visited Governor Curtis Guild Jr. They urged him to intercede with Roosevelt, but the president stood by his decision. When other senators began their own investigation, Lodge suggested that Secret Service men block their inquiries, and gratuitously attacked the record of the black soldiers prior to the Brownsville affair.[68]

George Frisbie Hoar never abandoned his long-range civil rights goals, but these were relegated to a far-off future as he turned his attention to other issues. He no longer thought that much could be accomplished by legislation on behalf of African-Americans. Early in 1895, a despairing African-American editor in Cincinnati wrote to him, wondering if it were not perhaps best that the colored people allow themselves to be deported to Africa, as an Alabama senator was demanding. Hoar suggested that his correspondent look on the bright side. Southern whites would not seek the deportation of the people upon whose labor the region depended. Beyond that, colored Americans were better off than most non-Americans, and by practicing the

Puritan virtues their condition would improve still more. "The Negro question is to be settled in this country by the personal worth of the Negro," he concluded.[69]

Governor Russell, like most Massachusetts Democrats, said and did little about national race relations after 1890. His concern was to unite a Democratic Party that was splintering over the currency question. After serving three one-year terms as governor, he returned to his private practice. In 1896, he sought the presidency as the true heir of Grover Cleveland, only to be overwhelmed by William Jennings Bryan, whose "cross of gold" speech at the convention followed Russell's. Russell died a few weeks later, like Henry Grady, just short of celebrating his fortieth birthday.[70]

If Russell did not disappoint African-Americans because he never cared about them anyway, Thomas Wentworth Higginson's career symbolized the retreat of Brahmin radicals who dedicated their early lives to abolition. He wrote and lectured on literature, becoming a highly regarded member of respectable society, but the rights of African-Americans ceased to be a preoccupation. Still, just before his death in 1911 at the venerable age of eighty-eight, he sought out membership in the National Association for the Advancement of Colored People.[71]

The failure of the Lodge bill led to strained relations between African-American and white Republicans. Both the Equal Rights Association and the Colored National League demanded that the Republicans nominate a black man on their state ticket in 1891. They proposed William H. Dupree, chairman of the former group, as candidate for state auditor, and vowed to run him as an Independent if the Republicans refused. Dupree later changed his mind, and the black politicians then switched to William O. Armstrong. With or without African-American prompting, the Prohibition Party decided to nominate Armstrong as *its* candidate. Then Dupree appeared at the Republican convention, seeking its nomination, which suggests that he wanted the office but not a confrontation with the party. The Republicans brushed him off, and convention chairman Henry Cabot Lodge "delivered an address that the democratic dailies were unable to pick a flaw in," the *New York Age* observed. Not even Timothy Thomas Fortune knew what to do about this dilemma. "The Massachusetts Afro-Americans are an unusually intelligent, independent, and courageous people," he averred, but could offer no advice from afar. The Bostonians went ahead and built a meeting for Armstrong. Some speakers assailed the Republicans, one praised the state Democrats, and Armstrong of course lauded the Prohibitionists. In November he ran ahead of his ticket, but all received few votes in the Democratic victory. The unity behind the Republicans was temporarily shattered, and the argument in favor of political independence gained ground.[72]

In the years after 1890, the *Boston Evening Transcript* continued as the voice of respectably upper-class Boston. The paper remained under the editorship of Edward Henry Clement until 1905, when he was removed in favor of a man more responsive to the ownership's conservative views. From 1901 to 1920 he authored "The Listener" column, advancing his mildly reformist views on women's suffrage, temperance, and pacifism. On racial questions he remained unchanged: a believer in and advocate of Negro progress, a defender of African-Americans against racial violence, a gradualist on civil rights.[73]

The *Boston Globe* paid much less attention to racial matters. The African-American appeared in the *Globe* from 1890 to 1920 mostly as a troublemaker and participant in violent affrays. While the *Globe* opposed lynching, as did virtually all northern newspapers, it showed little interest in civil rights. After the turn of the century, the paper ran a cartoon, "Mr. Asa Spades," that mirrored the white culture's image of the African-American as a harmless buffoon. Neither the *Globe*'s news coverage nor its rare editorial comment did much to counter this image.[74]

The years after the defeat of the Federal Elections bill were marked by a prolonged retreat by Boston's white Brahmins on the question of black political and civil rights. African-American Bostonians never abandoned the fight, but political action seemed less efficacious after 1890. In the aftermath of the failure of politics, a strategy of self-help and economic advancement became more compelling as a strategy of race advancement. What this meant in a city that already granted political and civil rights will be explored in the following chapter.

HAVE YOUR MEALS AT
.... THE SOUTHERN DINING ROOM............
THOMAS E. LUCAS, Proprietor
Good Food and Prompt, Attentive Service have made this a most
desirable dining place for discriminating people. Cool, Clean, Commodious
894 Tremont Street — — Boston, Mass.

Southern Dining Room. Courtesy of the Boston Public Library.

TWO

❧❧❧❧❧❧❧

Booker T. Washington
and Boston's Black Upper Class

BOOKER T. WASHINGTON was the most powerful African-American leader of his time; he may have exercised more influence over the ideas of black Americans at the height of his power, between 1895 and 1906, than any other leader in history, with the exceptions of Frederick Douglass or Martin Luther King Jr. One of the many paradoxes of his life was that he denied any interest in politics and disdained ideology, yet acted upon the political and intellectual world of both races with great force. In part, his stated lack of concern with power and ideas was disingenuous; in part he simply absorbed the pragmatic, commercial spirit of his age, and translated it into a bargain between the races with an unconsciousness that gave his program all the more appeal.

In Washington's mind, that program was fashioned to meet the needs of the mass of African-Americans, from whom he himself had come. These rural black southerners, freedpeople or their descendants, working as sharecroppers, laborers, farmers, or artisans, were overwhelmed in the period 1890–1920 by white reaction. The relation of forces between African-Americans, increasingly abandoned by northern supporters, and the leaders of the white South, allowed the whites to dictate the terms of the 1895 Atlanta Compromise. Washington's famous 1895 speech registered his appraisal of current political reality, not his long-term vision. However, what might seem a realistic, if minimal, program in the South looked like capitulation to some northern African-Americans. Since the opposition to accommodation came primarily from Massachusetts men such as William Monroe Trotter or William Edward Burghardt Du Bois (then teaching at Atlanta University), the question arises, How did black Bostonians who defended Washington do so?

That question may best be approached through the interpretation of Washington's life offered by his biographer, Louis R. Harlan; the work of

Harlan and Raymond L. Smock in the published Booker T. Washington papers; and the perspective of August Meier in *Negro Thought in America, 1880–1915*.[1] These historians argue that Washington was not simply an accommodationist, although he fought a secret and dirty war against his northern opponents who denounced him as such. His "secret life" held a second dimension: behind the scenes he organized legal battles against Jim Crow laws and disfranchisement.[2] Even his public rhetoric was fraught with ambiguity. As Harlan reminds us, he never defined the phrase in the Atlanta Compromise speech: "those things of a social nature in which the races might remain separate."[3] Further, it must be remembered that Washington never took the terms of the Atlanta Compromise as permanent. His many northern supporters, African-American and white, could focus on the image of Washington the builder. At the heart of their vision was not the enduring subordination of African-Americans, but the gradual rise of a people toward full equality through industry, education, and patriotism. By trying to silence all opposition within the African-American community, however, he guaranteed a polarization into two broad camps, each of which shared some of the other's values. The heated atmosphere discouraged thoughtful dialogue and encouraged a war of rhetoric.

This chapter explores Washington's relation with Boston's black community, and more especially with its upper class. Booker Washington tried to control the national African-American community, and he did that by acting upon the leadership layer: arranging patronage and power for friends, pushing enemies to the margin. Boston was a hotbed of opposition toward him, but it is also true that for a while it was an important base of support for him. In the beginning of his career as a school principal, especially before the 1895 speech that made him famous, white Bostonians were among his most important financial backers. But the 1903 confrontation with Monroe Trotter in Boston showed that he was still the authoritative figure in the black community as well. Only the subsequent deterioration of national race relations during the second Theodore Roosevelt administration lent sufficient force to the militant perspective to establish Trotter's leadership in Boston's African-American community.

If Washington's support was broader than Trotter's in 1903, it was also thinner. Black Bostonians who liked Washington's message generally did not agree with his public posture of downplaying civil and political rights. They endorsed the work of the Tuskegee Institute, but they did not necessarily agree that African-Americans should shun higher education. Upper-class black Bostonians approved of Washington's respectful attitude toward cultured whites, and his adoption of their values. Like him, they sent their

children to predominantly white schools, summered on the shore, and preferred the symphony to ragtime. However, because they lived in abolitionist
Boston, they could not simply present national race relations in accommodationist terms. As they observed a worsening of race relations in Boston and
the country as a whole, their support for Booker Washington became more
defensive. More than other Americans, the spirit of their city compelled them
to consider what William Lloyd Garrison, Frederick Douglass, or Wendell
Phillips might say if they were still alive.

Booker Washington himself had important roots in Boston. His intellectual heritage was of New England: Puritan, Yankee capitalist, and even abolitionist molded Washington's thought. His first teachers were Viola Knapp
Ruffner of Vermont and General Samuel Chapman Armstrong, the founder
of Hampton Institute and son of Massachusetts missionaries. As a builder of
Tuskegee Institute, he looked first to Boston and New England for financial
support, which came in large part from such neo-abolitionist families as those
of George Stearns and Brahmin businessman Henry Lee Higginson. His
wife, Olivia A. Davidson, attended the Massachusetts State Normal School
at Framingham through the efforts of Boston's Mary Hemenway, and he
established a summer residence at South Weymouth, on the state's South
Shore.[4] His ghostwriters, Max B. Thrasher and later Robert Park, were Bostonians. He probably chose Boston for the first convention of the National
Negro Business League because he knew Boston best of the northern cities.
He included an elegy to the city in *Up From Slavery*, and he was a stranger
neither to Beacon Street nor to Harvard Yard. If he was a product of the
South, he was also a product of the New England philanthropic intervention
into the South, just as the leaders of Boston's black community were. In that
sense, Booker Washington was one of them.[5]

Four interrelated factors prevented conservatives among Boston's black
upper class from leading the community as a whole during the Age of Washington. These problems were in part replicated nationally and were in part
more specific to Boston. They help explain why militants gained the upper
hand more forcefully in Boston than in other cities. First was a general dilemma that Bookerites everywhere faced: ostensibly, their leader's philosophy
was nonpolitical, and in the face of a political challenge they were disarmed.
Second, Boston's black upper class stood particularly aloof from the rank
and file. Third, Boston's African-American businessmen were economically
weaker than their counterparts in other cities. Finally, the white support for
Washington was morally authoritative in Boston; thus when it began to frac-
ture, black Bostonians who supported Washington were cut adrift. Lacking a

deeply rooted base in the community, not entirely agreeing with Washington anyway, the conservative upper class was transformed.

The first problem Boston's Bookerites faced was common to his backers everywhere. Washington counterposed his philosophy of self-help, deference, and economic uplift to the open struggle for civil rights. Throughout the 1890s the two sides met in annual struggle at meetings of Timothy Thomas Fortune's Afro-American Council, which Washington dominated. However, this was not a mass organization that Washington strove to build, for he did not believe in such things. He professed not to lead. Similarly, the National Negro Business League was open only to the small number of businessmen and professionals, and it refused to act on political developments. William Monroe Trotter's various groups, later W. E. B. Du Bois's activist Niagara movement, and finally the National Association for the Advancement of Colored People, were all projects open to the rank and file that solicited members. Ultimately, the Bookerites had nothing to counterpose to them.

As sociologist Adelaide Cromwell Hill observed, Boston's black upper class was "an exclusive society into which one definitely did or did not belong." Historian Willard B. Gatewood agreed that "Boston's aristocrats of color tended to be socially exclusive while also cultivating connections with whites." They valued lighter skin color, attended white churches, and joined interracial boards of municipal institutions. While families with long residence in Boston formed the core of this society, it was possible to learn or earn one's way to acceptance. Southern migrants who were well educated or wealthy also belonged to this class of proprietors and professionals. Prominent families of both sorts included the Ruffins, Ridleys, John Lewises, Grants, Benjamins, Lews, Wilsons, Duprees, William Henry Lewises, Sampsons, Trotters, and others.[6]

Novelist Dorothy West in *The Living Is Easy* and memoirist Walter J. Stevens in *Chip On My Shoulder* drew portraits of this society. Both books depict the aloofness of the upper class and its economic weakness. The very titles of their books suggest a world of comfort, pride, and self-confidence, but it was also a world not far removed from vulnerability. Bart Judson, the "black banana king" of West's novel, is based on the author's own prosperous father, whose parsimoniousness was rooted in his impoverished past. Stevens's father owned a small restaurant, and the author moved in the black upper class as a clerk in the mayor's office and afterward as a steward in a Harvard club. Both stories show that people in the upper class knew that their economic situation was insecure. The discussion of the National Negro Business League in this chapter will develop this point.[7]

A final conundrum for Boston's black upper class involved its own relation to the white world. During the Gilded Age and Progressive Era, upper-class African-Americans modeled their culture in part on white society. In Boston, because of the city's unique antislavery tradition, this pattern was probably more pronounced than in other cities. Booker Washington's support among such neo-abolitionists as William Lloyd Garrison Jr. and Francis Jackson Garrison, sons of the abolitionist editor; or Thomas Wentworth Higginson and Mary Stearns, who had conspired with John Brown, gave him a credibility he would not have in cities where such people were not already written into legend. Prominent Harvard academics such as Charles W. Eliot, president of the institution, the philosopher William James, geologist Nathaniel Southgate Shaler, and literature professor Barrett Wendell were all Washington supporters. But as white moderates lost interest in black progress, and when the radicals founded the National Association for the Advancement of Colored People, Booker Washington's white Boston base became significantly attenuated. Some of the ground was cut out from under upper-class moderates.

The extent to which African-American Bostonians felt hesitant about Washington's perspective within and among themselves can be seen in a series of public meetings held around the turn of the century, before the launching of William Monroe Trotter's *Guardian* hardened the groupings into factions. A large interracial audience of prominent people came to hear Washington speak on 21 March 1899 at the Hollis Street Theater. On the platform also were Atlanta University professor W. E. B. Du Bois, and the poet Paul Lawrence Dunbar.[8] The following year he launched the National Negro Business League in Boston. In 1901, he addressed the Wendell Phillips Club, Boston's most exclusive African-American men's club. All three meetings showed that Washington had great authority among black and white elites.[9]

But the hard ugliness of southern reality intruded into the picture of gradual economic uplift that Washington unfailingly painted. A few weeks after Washington's 1899 Boston speech, a huge mob brutally tortured Sam Hose to death near Atlanta. Boston's militants had already planned a meeting to commemorate the anniversary of Charles Sumner's election to the U.S. Senate. Gathered at Young's Hotel, they hissed President William McKinley for failing to denounce southern outrages against black people, and they hissed again at the mention of Tuskegee Institute. Booker Washington did not comment publicly on the Sam Hose lynching, but his Boston supporters joined with his opponents to do just that a few weeks after the Young's Hotel meeting. Black and white speakers including attorney William Henry Lewis, Reverend Samuel M. Crothers, Archibald Grimké, Thomas Wentworth

Higginson, former state attorney general Albert E. Pillsbury, and former governor John Quincy Adams Brackett addressed a spirited audience at the People's Temple in early May. This public meeting indicated that to be a Booker Washington supporter in Boston did not preclude speaking out for civil rights.[10]

A study of four representative groupings shows the breadth of Washington's following among Boston's "aristocrats of color." While some remained earnest Bookerites for many years, others changed their views with the times when accommodation seemed not to work. The founders of the *Colored American Magazine* endorsed Washington's constructive efforts and questioned militant tactics, but they also insisted upon full equality. In 1905, Washington engineered the appearance of *Alexander's Magazine*, which oscillated between accommodation and militance. The National Negro Business League, launched in Boston in 1900, tried to build up a black commercial class. Finally, white Bostonians, liberal and radical, contributed to Tuskegee and at least for a while, to gradualism.

THE *COLORED AMERICAN MAGAZINE*

The *Colored American Magazine*, published by the Colored Co-operative Publishing Company, first appeared in May 1900, vowing its devotion "to the higher culture of Religion, Literature, Science, Music and Art of the Negro, Universally." The professional quality of its prose, photography, layout, and printing suggested that it had gathered sound financial backing and had hope of securing more. Headquartered at 232 West Canton Street in the South End, the magazine proudly declared, after a year of publication, that its production values showed it to be the first fully up-to-date magazine in the history of the race. It lasted four years in Boston until financial difficulty forced its transfer to New York and indirect control by Booker Washington.[11]

The *Colored American* was the project of four Virginia migrants and one Bostonian whose stories typified the values of hard work, perseverance, and thrift. The Virginians were all young men in their late twenties who arrived in Boston a few years before launching the magazine. Walter W. Wallace, the managing editor, was the descendant of Hampton graduates; he worked in Boston as a prescription clerk in a drugstore. Jesse W. Watkins had been a miner and electrician but by 1901 he owned real estate in Virginia and was a prominent Boston lodge member. The treasurer, Harper S. Fortune, was a musician and legal clerk, and the advertising manager, Walter Alexander Johnson, worked by day for a publishing company. These unknown and largely uneducated young men turned out a remarkably sophisticated publication with a national circulation.[12]

The real workhorse of the magazine, who become the editor in 1903, was Pauline Elizabeth Hopkins. She was the oldest of the group, born in 1859, the only Bostonian, and the only woman (the magazine did have other female contributors, but none so prolific as Hopkins). Born in Portland, Maine, to a Virginia-born father and a mother descended from Boston church leaders Nathaniel and Thomas Paul, Hopkins's parents moved to Boston where she graduated from high school. As a student she read books by African-American novelist William Wells Brown and wrote a prize-winning essay on temperance. After graduation she worked as a stenographer and performed with her family in theatrical productions. In the late 1890s she worked on a novel, *Contending Forces: A Romance Illustrative of Negro Life North and South*. The *Colored American* printed it separately, and serialized three subsequent novels. She published seven short stories and numerous biographical articles in a series on famous African-Americans. After the magazine moved to New York she virtually ceased writing, returned to stenography, and died in 1930 in a fire. There were no obituaries. She had been the central contributor to one of the country's leading African-American literary magazines, and she died in obscurity, not to be noticed again until the 1970s, when feminist literary critics rediscovered her work.[13]

Hopkins toiled in the unsubtle genre of magazine fiction and hewed close to the conventions of literary melodrama. As her plots twisted and turned, heroines clung to their virtue, heroes displayed their courage, and villains seduced and abandoned their prey. At the end of many exciting adventures, virtue was inevitably rewarded and vice exposed and condemned. Her work was unabashedly sentimental and her moral values steadfastly Victorian; she offered a simple presentation of good and evil, unalloyed. Hopkins was, however, a race-proud feminist, and as such she was twenty years ahead of the better known writers of the Harlem Renaissance.[14]

Despite Hopkins's literary flair, the financial weakness of the community and the reluctance of white creditors to lend money made the project a risky business. Editor Wallace after little more than a year was forced to appeal to Booker T. Washington for financial support. Washington bought some stock and later Boston's William H. Dupree came to the rescue as financial angel and publisher, but he could not keep the magazine afloat. When the money ran out, Washington moved the magazine to New York and the close editorial supervision of his ally Fred R. Moore. During its Boston incarnation, the editors looked toward Washington as the leading black American and always wrote favorably of him, but he never tried to dictate its policy.[15]

The general tenor of the magazine was one of high-minded self-improvement, and the editors displayed their erudition as proof that African-Americans could assimilate into respectable white society. They focused on achievement in the arts and sciences, intending to reach the upper-class audience. The January 1901 edition, for example, featured articles on Virginia University; Elijah Lovejoy, the abolitionist martyr; "Boston's Smart Set," which spotlighted African-American society women; and a regular feature, "Fascinating Bible Stories." Another regular series described the bravery of colored troops in the Philippines. Washington himself was lionized on occasion, but sparingly. Augustus M. Hodges wrote one such piece, finding "The Solution to the Negro Problem" in Washington's formulas.[16]

The first editorial marked the political course the magazine vowed to follow. Wallace denounced the white South for its racist policies, the Supreme Court for its retreat on the Fourteenth and Fifteenth Amendments, and the New England pulpit for its silence. While determined to speak out for justice, Wallace defended Booker Washington against complaints "that he caters too much to the opposite race at the expense of his own." This was an unwarranted charge against a "benefactor" who "does not deserve censure, criticism and calumny."[17] The Colored American thus shielded Washington from his critics, but also condemned lynching, segregation, and disfranchisement.

Washington's politics were at their weakest in his handling of racist violence. He tended to discuss lynching in general terms, stressing its debasing effect upon the perpetrators and the white population. He sometimes said nothing about particular outrages, or complained privately to the appropriate official. Typical of his behavior in this period was his tepid response to the Sam Hose lynching, upon which he refused to comment. Instead he wrote a letter of protest to the governor of Georgia, which his friend Timothy Thomas Fortune convinced him to suppress. Washington then left the country on vacation, and from London addressed a weak letter of concern to the southern newspapers, in which he appealed evenhandedly to whites to cease the practice and to blacks to behave in a more law-abiding spirit.[18]

By contrast, the Colored American regarded lynching as a crime against colored people whose responsibility rested with the perpetrators, not the victims. It appealed to the sentiment in favor of due process of law. On rare occasions, it published contributions supporting the right of African-Americans to defend themselves against such mobs. While it did not publicize the campaign of Ida B. Wells to make lynching a federal crime, probably for fear of going beyond Republican policy, the editors typically expressed outrage and called for urgent measures.

While Booker Washington stressed the relationship between criminality and lynching, the Boston editors blamed race hatred. One such article, by Reverend Quincy Ewing of Greenville, Mississippi, compared mob action to anti-Semitic pogroms of the Dark Ages. He called on Mississippians to stamp out lynching by denying state funds to counties that failed to suppress the practice, and to remove sheriffs who would not prosecute lynchers. When President William McKinley was assassinated in Buffalo, New York, an African-American fairgoer wrestled the gunman to the ground. The editors printed his story, and equated lynching with anarchism. After a 1903 lynching at Wilmington, Delaware, the *Colored American* editorialized against a "community corrupted in civic ideals and void of civic and moral virility." The editors contrasted the official repression of pogromists in czarist Russia with the official tolerance of lynchers in the United States by reprinting an anti-lynching *Boston Herald* article. Booker Washington's supporters in Boston reflected the disgust for the summary executions shown in the North.[19]

Washington's approach to the suffrage problem was more complex than his general silence regarding lynching. His public posture was to accept the new disfranchisement legislation passed by state legislatures or special conventions, but to insist that property or education requirements be applied fairly to both races. Privately, however, Washington arranged legal challenges to disfranchisement in Louisiana, Alabama, and Georgia. Some Bostonians, such as the attorney Richard P. Hallowell, who worked on these appeals, knew his role.[20]

The *Colored American* editors did not accept Washington's public views on disfranchisement. They published articles by Hallowell and Moorfield Storey that took up the wider intellectual assault on the Fifteenth Amendment. The *Boston Herald*, Secretary of State Elihu Root, *Outlook* editor Lyman Abbott, the *Charleston* (South Carolina) *Evening Post* and the *New York Sun*, all declared Negro suffrage a failure. Hallowell defended radical Reconstruction policies, arguing that "in the South, white suffrage is comparatively a failure" since it was used "as a potent weapon in their effort to degrade the Negro to the social condition of social servitude." He defended the Reconstruction regimes from the charge of corruption and contrasted them to the record of the Redeemers with scholarly thoroughness and an impassioned tone. In South Carolina, "no white man today, as I know from personal experience, can . . . treat the colored man as an ordinary citizen of the United States without making himself liable to insult and cowardly assault." Moorfield Storey insisted upon the duty of the emancipators to follow through on the work they had begun. "The same reason that led us to abolish slavery forbade us to establish any legal inequality between man and man."[21]

The magazine was also a step ahead of Washington in its evaluation of the

May 1900 Montgomery Race Conference, organized by the Reverend Edgar Gardner Murphy, a Montgomery Progressive. Washington hoped that the conference might facilitate interracial dialogue, and he worked for its success even after blacks were relegated to a Jim Crow section as voiceless observers. The Tuskegee campus newpaper described the conference in neutral tones, although the meeting's effect was to encourage disfranchisement.

The Boston editors published a less sanguine appraisal. M. F. Hunter found that "the Negro has come out of the crucible of analysis and decision with less than justice done to him." He concluded that "the conference showed the bitterness of the white man of the South," and he placed the blame for the breakdown in race relations on the whites. A subsequent issue rebutted a speech that Washington had endorsed.[22]

In the wake of the July 1903 Boston "Riot," in which William Monroe Trotter disrupted a Washington speech, the *Colored American* maintained a discreet and lengthy silence. It did not respond until November, when it reprinted a pseudonymous piece by Kelly Miller, of Howard University, who occupied a middle ground between the contending camps. Dismissing the confrontation as "regrettable," Miller coolly compared and contrasted the relative strengths and weaknesses of Washington with those of Trotter and W. E. B. Du Bois, whose *Souls of Black Folk* appeared just before the affray. In the October issue, the editors had warmly greeted Du Bois's book as a "powerful blow at lynching advocates, Jim Crow cars, and peonage" but prudently kept silent on its critical evaluation of Washington. A two-part series in December 1903 and January 1904 rebuked the disruptors. A. Kirland Soga, a South African correspondent, argued that Harvard-educated Boston Negroes, who enjoyed the liberties of their city, a "beacon light of civilization," should not turn their fire on a beleaguered representative of southern Negro education. Trotter's questions to Washington seemed merely cheap polemical tricks. Soga argued that "the honor of the race leaders, and of the race itself makes it imperative that they should be protected against the brutality of black mobocrats, and the prestige of the race is degraded not enhanced by such sights as Booker Washington being escorted under police protection to his carriage to escape from violence." Every out-group fears making a spectacle of itself, and the *Colored American*, seeking to present a positive image of the race, was embarrassed by Trotter's creating such an ugly scene.[23]

The editors were caught in the dilemma of being genteel Bostonians. On the one hand, they valued Washington's good work, financial backing, and powerful influence. On the other hand, they wanted an end to Jim Crow, lynching, and disfranchisement and said so openly. Yet Trotter's rude solution to this dilemma—rallying the plebeian elements against the respectable—also seemed wrong, but the editors could not forthrightly declare this. Kelly Miller in distant Washington, D.C., and A. Kirland Soga in faraway South Africa had to speak for them. Their muteness symbolized the contradictions of an upper class beginning to lose its influence.

ALEXANDER'S MAGAZINE

The *Colored American Magazine* was an independent journal that looked to Booker Washington for guidance and some financial aid. During its brief Boston incarnation it stayed within the Tuskegee orbit while retaining its critical independence. *Alexander's Magazine*, by contrast, was a Washington operation from the beginning. One Washington tactic was to put Trotter out of business by organizing a rival Boston newspaper. After two such short-lived attempts—the *Advocate* and the *Enterprise*—failed, he tried a third, the *Boston Colored Citizen*, under the direction of Peter J. Smith and J. Will Cole. Smith consistently pestered Washington for money, and the disgruntled educator imported Tuskegee graduate and former Boston resident Charles Alexander to take over the reins. When this paper failed within a year, Alexander launched a monthly in 1905, *Alexander's Magazine*. What began as a conscious effort to build a pro-Washington literary mouthpiece in Boston ended in Alexander's offering the magazine to the NAACP in 1909. A combination of the Boston political-intellectual environment and national developments, especially the Brownsville incident and the Atlanta Riot of 1906, curtailed the possibility of establishing an accommodationist journal in the city.[24]

The *Colored American Magazine* was published during the height of Washington's power, which was linked in great measure to President Theodore Roosevelt's patronage. The life of *Alexander's Magazine* was roughly contemporaneous with the president's retreat on African-American rights during his second term, which made its task more difficult. Alexander's earlier career suggested he was himself stamped out of the Tuskegee Machine. He was teaching printing at Wilberforce when Washington brought him to Boston. Despite Alexander's personal limitations, he produced a lively if uneven journal that reflected the tension between Tuskegee financing and a sober view of worsening race relations from liberal Boston. Alexander grew as a writer and polemicist. His contributors included Reverdy C. Ransom, a lifelong Washington opponent; Archibald Grimké, the distinguished writer and former diplomat, who edited the magazine in the fall of 1907; and Walter F. Walker, corresponding from Liberia. White writers appeared more regularly in *Alexander's* than in the *Colored American Magazine*. These included the old abolitionist Frank Sanborn; settlement-house worker John Daniels, who wrote the book reviews; and occasional reprints from Edward H. Clement, a moderate editor of the *Boston Evening Transcript*. This would be an impressive roster for any magazine.[25]

At its most dull, *Alexander's* ran tedious celebrations of Tuskegee and other African-American institutions, laden with Washingtonian clichés. The first issue, for example, contained a reprint from the *Baptist Missionary Magazine*, relating the work of the Hampton Institute in Africa. Subsequent issues usually included similar features on black colleges in a public relations vein. Alexander devoted a considerable amount of space to the pomp surrounding Washington's installation as a Mason in Boston. If such articles were predictable, they were nevertheless assertions of determination to build enduring institutions rooted in the community: church, school, and lodge.[26]

Alexander's Magazine regarded Trotter and Du Bois as opponents, but never fairly engaged them or their ideas in open intellectual combat. Trotter was an offstage nuisance, a sectarian to be occasionally denounced but never named. In an otherwise innocuous piece on "Negro Journalism" the editor disparaged those who "engaged in this sacred calling who openly pervert its functions. They form the growling, grumbling, gossipping . . . pessimistic element." Another article called Trotter and his friends a "selfish, bigoted, non-race loving class—men who know little about the Negro in or outside of Boston . . . the solid [Negro] businessmen in Boston are with Booker T. Washington, quietly doing constructive work." Du Bois commanded more respect. Alexander treated him as a fallen angel who had separated himself from the radiance of Tuskegee. Reviewing *The Souls of Black Folk*, which had been out for two and a half years, John Daniels urged prospective readers to take it "not as an argument, as an anti-Washington protest, but as a poem, a spiritual, not intellectual offering, an appeal not to the head but to the heart." When the Niagara movement's journal *The Moon* appeared, Alexander called it "abominable," despite Du Bois's literary skill. In a tone of snide condescension *Alexander's* condemned the second meeting of the Niagara movement as a gathering of speechifiers intent on destroying Booker T. Washington. Ironically, the magazine singled out as the worst offender the same Reverdy C. Ransom who contributed to *Alexander's* both before and after the meeting. It then reprinted, without comment, part of the Niagara movement's platform. Throughout, Alexander treated Du Bois with ambivalent disdain and respect, but never fairly appraised his ideas.[27]

Alexander's covered the local political scene with a mixture of pragmatic opportunism and scarcely concealed disgust. By 1905, African-Americans had been driven out of the state's elective offices and the only practical political activity left was to determine which candidates promised to appoint more black office-seekers. *Alexander's* hewed to the Republican candidate of the moment, tending toward bland approval of both sides in contested primaries. It hailed governors Eugene Foss, Curtis Guild, and Eben S. Draper as patriots. Trying to hold the victors to account, *Alexander's* called upon Senators Henry Cabot Lodge and Winthrop Murray Crane to break personal relations with South Carolina's Ben Tillman.[28]

All of this easily fit into the framework of any northern pro-Washington journal. The Atlanta race riot, Theodore Roosevelt's wholesale dismissal of African-American troops at Brownsville, and the rhetorical retreat of Presidents Roosevelt and William Howard Taft on civil rights led to a furious storm of condemnation by *Alexander's* that went completely beyond the bounds of Washington's terms. In the end, however, Alexander was bribed, and wound up lamely supporting Taft. In a fit of frustration with the president it had just endorsed, the magazine folded a few months after his inauguration, and as the NAACP was born.[29]

The journal vented its ire at the entire government in 1906. "We have heard nothing from President Roosevelt recently concerning the 'square deal' for the Negro citizen of the U.S.," the editor complained. "When we realize that there is not a single man in the House of Representatives at Washington or in the Senate who has the courage to say a single word in defense of the Negro at the present time, and there is not a Negro there to speak for himself . . . the situation is pathetic to say the least."[30] An all-white Congress was not yet something to be grimly taken for granted.

The Atlanta race riot broke out a few months later, beginning 22 September. After five days of violence against African-Americans, ten were killed, many injured, and much property destroyed. In the aftermath, city leaders formed an interracial committee to promote peaceful cooperation between the races. However, they made no attempt to prosecute the perpetrators of the violence. Jim Crow remained the law, and black Georgians lost their vote after the 1906 gubernatorial election.[31]

Alexander grew steadily more distraught. In October, the journal noted the gains Atlanta Negroes had made since emancipation, condemned the violence, and found a hopeful note in the formation of the interracial committee. But the next month, the judicial aftermath had begun, and Alexander wrote, "the grand jury indicts sixty Negroes for murder, and sixteen white men for riot! If that is white Atlanta's official expression on the subject, then it is useless for anyone to pretend that Atlanta has any sense of justice." However, the magazine's patron was doing exactly that. Taking care in the next issue to applaud Washington's speech at the Afro-American Council in which the Tuskegean urged black people not to hate all whites, Alexander unstintingly praised Du Bois and his Atlanta postmortem, which called for prosecution of the perpetrators; condemnation of the politicians who created the environment that facilitated the riot; restoration of the vote; and reduced representation for Georgia in Congress if the vote were not granted.[32]

Next came the ugly climax to an earlier incident. On the night of 13 August, unknown persons shot up a section of Brownsville, Texas, killing one man and wounding another. For months previous, the city had treated African-American troops in the garrison there with hostility. The authorities accused the soldiers, but some journalists of that time and recent scholars argue that the men were framed. After the men refused to incriminate each other, President Roosevelt consulted Booker Washington at a 30 October White House meeting. Washington advised against harsh action and tried to influence an upcoming presidential speech on lynching prompted by Atlanta. Roosevelt waited until after the November elections, and then discharged all the soldiers without honor. Then came Roosevelt's December speech on lynching. "The greatest cause of lynching is the perpetration, especially by black men, of the hideous crime of rape," the president declared. The best prevention of this crime was a Tuskegee-type education. The principal of Tuskegee did not demur on any of this. For some of Washington's supporters, including Timothy Thomas Fortune, editor of the *New York Age*, this was too much.[33]

A similar split developed more slowly in Boston, although Alexander was not so important to the Tuskegee Machine as Fortune. In January 1907, Alexander ran "The True Story of the Brownsville Affair," a reprint of a *Boston Herald* article whose investigative journalist found that "the integral error . . . of the whole unhappy incident lies in the military assumption that the unsworn testimony, the gossip and hearsay of Brownsville is to be accepted as conclusive evidence of the guilt of the Negroes." In May, Archibald Grimké, writing in *Alexander's*, denounced Roosevelt's action as "Draconian," and "a blow dealt to the whole race," in an article praising the congressional investigation begun by Ohio Senator Joseph B. Foraker.[34]

The Atlanta riot and the Brownsville incident caused Alexander to call for an end to the factional struggle on both sides. In a perceptive editorial, he summarized the various strengths of the National Negro Business League, the Afro-American Council, and the Niagara movement, concluding, "there is evident good in all these modus operandi, but neither one unaided will reach the desired goal. What is needed is a combination of the three, a pool or a trust." This call for unity was far from the mind of Washington, Trotter, or Du Bois, and it went unheeded.[35]

Washington did not want to lose Fortune or Alexander, but he labored especially hard to keep Archibald Grimké within the fold. By the autumn of 1907, when Grimké took over the editor's job at *Alexander's* for three issues, the two men had been in uneasy alliance for almost a decade. Grimké (1849–1930) was the son of a master and his slave; during the Civil War he escaped from Charleston to freedom, education, and his famous Boston aunts. Sarah Grimké and Angelina Grimké Weld introduced Archibald into abolitionist Boston society. Their nephew graduated from Harvard Law School, strolled with Wendell Phillips, and edited the community newspaper, the *Hub*, during the mid-1880s. When white Republicans failed to support the newspaper financially, Grimké gravitated toward the independent group, among whom he had friends. His Democratic leanings earned him an appointment as consul to Santo Domingo in the second Grover Cleveland administration. In 1898 he returned to the United States, dividing his time between Boston and Washington, D.C., where his influential brother Francis was a prominent minister and Booker Washington supporter.[36]

During the next decade Grimké established himself as a significant national African-American leader through his writing and lecturing. Grimké's biographer, Dickson D. Bruce Jr., persuasively suggests that Grimké viewed Washington as a cunning dissimulator who showed whites a deferential mask while laboring for full equality. In this framework, Grimké may have reasoned, it made sense for Bostonians like himself to speak out, but for recipients of philanthropy in the South—like Washington—to hide their full agenda. Grimké was then writing a paper on the antebellum free black insurrectionist Denmark Vesey, Bruce argues, and Grimké may have seen Washington as a careful dissembler, as Vesey was.[37]

Trotter's 1903 attack on the educator disturbed this alliance. Grimké attended the Boston "riot" meeting but did not disrupt it. Nontheless, Washington suspected that Grimké and others stood behind Trotter, and he attacked Grimké publicly. Grimké in turn testified on Trotter's behalf at the latter's trial, but he never felt comfortable with the prickly Trotter. Washington and Grimké reconciled at a leadership meeting in New York's Carnegie Hall in January 1904. He then became a writer for the *New York Age*, which was firmly in Washington's camp.[38]

This alliance lasted for two and a half years, and was ultimately terminated by the Brownsville incident. Grimké's heated columns on the subject distanced him from Washington. He joined the Niagara movement, causing a split between Trotter, who felt betrayed by Grimké, and Clement Morgan, who valued his participation. As the Boston branch of the Niagara movement wallowed in internal disarray, Grimké took over the editorship of *Alexander's Magazine* in the fall of 1907. He had never definitively broken with Washington, and he still approved of the Tuskegee mission. Alexander, too, was disgusted by Brownsville and the views of the two men were near enough to permit collaboration.[39]

In his first turn as editor Grimké complained that Secretary of War Taft and the "autocratic occupant of the White House" had mishandled the Brownsville incident and subsequent investigation by Senator Joseph B. Foraker. He challenged Taft's "astounding assertion about the Southern white man's being the 'Negro's best friend' " and reminded the Republicans that these same "friends" were taking away the Negro's vote. Citing administration failure to challenge discriminatory rulings in railroad cases, he concluded angrily that the president "has quietly acquiesced in the nullification of the Fourteenth and Fifteenth amendments to the Constitution." In the same issue he reported positively on the Niagara movement, which called for a Democratic vote in the North. As a case in point he offered Republican Senator Henry Cabot Lodge, who, Grimké alleged, no longer cared about the wrongs done to colored citizens. In November 1907, Grimké endorsed Democratic mayoral candidate John F. Fitzgerald. That same month he left *Alexander's*, which soon reverted to Republican regularity. This marked Grimké's last dalliance in the Tuskegee camp.[40]

Atlanta and Brownsville cast long shadows over African-American politics as the 1908 election approached and Roosevelt's appointed successor, Secretary of War William Howard Taft, who executed the Brownsville dismissal, loomed as Roosevelt's heir apparent. Washington predictably backed Taft, hoping to turn support for the Republican mainstream into patronage. Alexander sided with Senator Foraker through the convention, and then had to be bought off before supporting Taft. Comically, the Republican Negro Bureau, now run by a white functionary, almost paid the wrong people at the convention. The Taft machine did not even know which black Bostonians it thought it owned. During the general election, Alexander could muster only a lukewarm pro-Taft editorial.

After the election, the president-elect made a speech before the North Carolina Society of New York in which he pledged to leave the South alone, and rejected the Negro plank passed at the 1908 convention. *Alexander's* flirted with independence again, protesting that "if this repudiation . . . does not open the Negro's eyes to the fact that he can no longer depend on the sympathy and traditions of any party" he was blind indeed.[41] Within a few months of the election, Alexander stopped publishing. Like the *Colored American*, *Alexander's Magazine* reflected the ambivalence of Boston's black upper class, but because it appeared later, its contradictions were more pronounced. After Atlanta and Brownsville it was more difficult to continue repeating that thrift and honesty would bring their own rewards. Neither Alexander nor Grimké could maintain that perspective and both headed, separately, toward the NAACP.

THE NATIONAL NEGRO BUSINESS LEAGUE

If there was a quintessential Booker T. Washington organization, it was the National Negro Business League (NNBL). Washington led its founding at the 1900 Boston convention and remained its president until his death in 1915. Yet, as Louis R. Harlan and August Meier have pointed out, Washington took the idea for the league from W. E. B. Du Bois, whose 1899 Atlanta University conference, "The Negro in Business," proposed to develop such a group; the Afro-American Council later that year assigned Du Bois the task of organizing it. Acting outside the framework of the Afro-American Council, Washington issued a convention call in June 1900, to the consternation of his political opponents. Despite the squabble for organizational control, Meier and Harlan suggest, lay a temporary ideological agreement. Both men shared the idea that the race would rise in accordance with the entrepreneurial spirit of the age.[42]

Having stolen a march on the competition, Washington was in a position to put his own stamp on the new organization. Pressed by his rivals to explain its purpose, Washington responded through a white journalist that there would be a division of labor between the political Afro-American Council and the commercial NNBL. A business league led by Du Bois or Ida B. Wells, another critic of this venture, might be more emphatic about the need for political struggle. While Du Bois agreed with the notion of a business league in general, William Monroe Trotter did not. At a 16 August meeting in a Boston church shortly before the NNBL founding convention, an evenly divided audience discussed how to approach the new organization. Former city councilman Isaac B. Allen supported the new group, and William C. Lane of Cambridge urged participation in the NNBL, but with the goal of politicizing it. Trotter, who had not yet launched his weekly newspaper, condemned the upcoming convention and called instead for a new political organization. Trotter at once saw the NNBL as a diversion, and a tool of Washington in the intraracial struggle.[43]

Herein lay the first of the NNBL's contradictions. It was born as an economic organization, and clearly could have a useful role to play as such. On the other hand, it developed in struggle against the radicals, and naturally adopted a conservative agenda. Despite its supposedly apolitical nature, it acted as a counterpole of attraction to radical efforts.

There was a second contradiction as well. Again and again Washington would explain that economic productivity knew no color line. His speeches at NNBL conventions were generally a string of clichés in the Horatio Alger vein. At the same time, Washington understood that race prejudice would keep the Negro businessman marginalized. NNBL conventions were characterized by a cheerful atmosphere of small-town boosterism and innocent hope, the same kind of business optimism that supplanted the Jeffersonian myth around the turn of the century for white Americans. In the age of Jim Crow and lynching, an air of unconscious irony pervades the same rhetoric in the mouths of African-American conventioneers. As a student of the NNBL concludes, "the portrayal of Negro business as worthy of imagined respect and social prominence equal to that of their white counterparts was mythological and a venture into the rhetoric of unreality."[44] There was a need for a National Negro Business League. However, African-American business success also depended upon the winning of political and civil equality. A symbolic rendering of the mutual interdependence of political freedom and economic progress was the notorious 1892 lynching of black proprietors in Memphis. White competitors wanted their market, and this hostile takeover launched local journalist Ida B. Wells on a lifelong antilynching campaign.

The leaders of Boston's African-American business elite personified both of these conjoined dilemmas. Lacking a political organization, they could not or would not lead politically. Frozen out of easy access to credit, capital, and white customers, they were in general respectable but marginal businessmen providing services to a poor community. That is, they could not even lead economically. The notable success stories to be briefly discussed here are the exceptions that prove the rule, as the following statistics suggest.

In 1914, sociologist John Daniels found 353 men, or 7.8 percent of black men at work, and 136, or 5.9 percent of working black women, in the professional and proprietor category of the 1900 census, the last figures available to him. Of those 353 men, in descending numerical order, were 60 musicians or actors, 50 retail merchants, and 47 livery-stable keepers. Of "manufacturers and officials" there were seven, and "bankers," one. Of the 136 women, 55 were boarding- and lodging-house keepers and 33 were actresses or musicians. The remainder of both sexes were scattered among artisan, professional, and small business categories. By his own impression, Daniels saw little change over the fourteen-year period. Thus Boston's African-American "middle class" was small in percentage of total population, and employed at humble pursuits, both in status and economic remuneration.[45]

There were exceptions to this picture. John H. Lewis led the first convention's workshop on "merchant tailoring." Born in Heathsville, North Carolina, he began with a $100 operation in Concord, Massachusetts, and by 1896 had a $150,000 per year Boston business with a largely white clientele. He was one of the richest African-Americans in the country and was the prototype of the man Washington hoped would lead the race. Joseph Lee, a baker, invented a bread-crumber and bread-kneading machine that mechanized the industry. Money earned from these devices enabled him to open restaurants in Boston, Auburndale, and Squantum. The largest wig manufacturing shop in New England, supplying theatrical companies and individuals, was owned by Gilbert C. Harris, originally a Virginian. These three businessmen, along with others such as Basil F. Hutchins, undertaker, or the owners of the Astor Hotel, which catered largely to Pullman porters, are prominent examples of financially successful black Bostonians of the period. Taken as a group, their marginality in relation to Boston's white capitalists need hardly be argued. Actual leadership of the league fell to Dr. Samuel F. Courtney, chairman and longtime friend of Washington's; Peter J. Smith, editor of a pro-Washington newspaper; and Louis F. Baldwin, a Cambridge city councillor and brother of the more famous Cambridge school principal Maria Baldwin. These less wealthy members represented the rank and file of the organization better.[46]

The average member was typified by people like R. L. Ames, a grocer who complained at the founding convention that "we are extremely handicapped in Boston," because of white competition in mixed neighborhoods like the South End, where whites avoided black-owned stores. The small size of Boston's black population retarded the growth of a business class that could grow in other cities whose new industrial jobs attracted black migrants. Boston's African-American merchants or artisans now had to compete with a burgeoning immigrant population that displaced black workers from certain established businesses, such as barbering or catering. Modernization would soon replace the livery stables owned by black proprietors as automobiles and elevated trains drove the horse from urban streets. By 1915, the more successful Lewises and Lees had not visibly multiplied, in part because start-up capital had to be bigger as cities and business enterprises grew. The more representative officers and board members of the NNBL remained obscure figures.[47]

On a national level, the NNBL did expand organizationally from 1900 to 1915. Three hundred people attended the 1900 convention, and three thousand attended fifteen years later when the convention returned to Boston. Several Boston newspapers noted the large number of automobiles owned by the 1915 conventioneers. Boston Mayor Thomas N. Hart attended in 1900, and Governor David I. Walsh did in 1915. There was even a dispute at the latter convention about rebuking Mayor James Michael Curley for failing to ban the movie *The Birth of a Nation*. However, Booker T. Washington died a few months later, and the national organization faded.[48]

The Boston chapter illustrated the weakness of the NNBL, whose national contributions should not be dismissed. The business leaders who achieved success did not wish to lead the community politically. Economically, shopkeepers or providers of marginal services could not compete with new immigrants who were flocking to Boston. The NNBL could not call a middle class into being in a period of increasing race discrimination. In Boston, the rising commercial class did not rise far.

This social fact should inform a question raised by historian Louis Harlan. He recalls the work of Richard Hofstadter, who argued that the Progressive movement was fueled by a "status anxiety" on the part of the old white elite, which was surpassed by the newly wealthy captains of industry. Is it possible that the older black elite felt the same anxiety in relation to a new rising middle class, and that similar anxiety fueled the feelings of people like Trotter or Du Bois?[49] Probably not: the new black upper class was just too small, and its position in relation to white capital too tenuous to seem genuinely disconcerting to people like Trotter, or Butler Wilson, an NAACP founder. While there may have been some validity to the "status anxiety" concept for Boston African-American militants, it is more likely that their hostility to Booker Washington and his followers was rooted in their disagreement with his political strategy in an age of reaction.

WHITE WASHINGTONIANS

Influential white Bostonians were unanimous in their support for Washington's educational project. Some, like Harvard president Charles W. Eliot, also subscribed to his accommodationist views. Others, like the neo-abolitionist sons of William Lloyd Garrison, enthusiastically backed Tuskegee Institute while calling for full civil rights themselves. As James McPherson shows in *The Abolitionist Legacy: From Reconstruction to the NAACP*, the major contribution of second-generation white activists to African-America was the promotion of education. Faced with the reality of reaction, the next generation had to emphasize the positive to keep up their own spirits. While they urged Washington to be more bold in their private correspondence, they were not blind to the evolving relation of forces on the race question. Like Washington, they were builders. However, between the Brownsville, Texas, incident of 1906 and the Springfield, Illinois, race riot of 1908, they grew increasingly impatient, and finally launched what became the NAACP in 1909.[50]

Boston's mainstream elite, however, applauded Washington without ambivalence. They believed in a limited ballot in general, sanctioned southern segregation, and deplored lynching. The year after the Atlanta address, Harvard awarded Washington an honorary degree. The following year he spoke at the dedication of the Augustus Saint-Gaudens monument to the African-American troops of the 54th and 55th Regiments. Before a huge gathering of luminaries, Washington upstaged Governor Roger Wolcott, Mayor Josiah Quincy, and other city fathers. From the podium he spoke directly to Sergeant William Carney of New Bedford, who had carried the flag at the battle of Fort Wagner. The crowd sprang to its feet with cheers, and the orator won the heart of the city.[51]

The personification of the Brahmin elite academic was Harvard president Charles W. Eliot. During his long tenure at the helm of the university (1869–1906) he modernized the curriculum, and opened the gates to a select few African-Americans. This handful of students lived a marginal existence at the school, but were treated fairly by the liberal faculty. Eliot saw African-American progress in much the same terms as Washington did. When moderate black leaders honored Washington at a Cambridge banquet, Eliot declared that his fellow college president "has done more than any other in the world to open the way of equal education to his race." Harvard faculty members such as philosopher William James, historian Albert Bushnell Hart, and geologist Nathaniel Southgate Shaler welcomed Washington to Boston on several occasions.[52]

If the enthusiasm of moderates like Eliot might be expected, that of the neo-abolitionist Garrison family might at first seem surprising. However, virtually the entire neo-abolitionist Boston milieu concurred with this feeling. Some historians have taken this as proof of the weakness of the abolitionist legacy. By 1901, William Monroe Trotter was attacking Washington, and in 1903, W. E. B. Du Bois joined in a softer tone. Yet, the Garrisons or other families like the Hallowells continued to work with him for a few more years. As McPherson argues, there is not much point in reading too much into this. Support for Tuskegee did not equal endorsement of segregation by Boston's neo-abolitionists.[53]

Like his father, William Lloyd Garrison Jr. (1838–1909) was a universal reformer. He was interested in the rights of Chinese immigrants, economic equality, and votes for women. As if to dramatize the difference between the Gilded Age and the antebellum period, the eldest son was also a wool merchant and investment banker. These commercial values Garrison extolled at the first convention of the National Negro Business League, at which he likened Booker Washington to Benjamin Franklin. In 1908, Garrison gave a civil rights speech that Monroe Trotter in his newspaper contrasted to Washington's rhetoric. Garrison wrote in reply that Washington was "the most remarkable living American, black or white. . . . How easy for colored men with academic advantages, secure in the stronghold of anti-slavery sentiment, to affect disdain and engage in bitter speech."⁵⁴

Francis Jackson Garrison (1848–1916) was a respectable editor at Houghton Mifflin, comfortable owner of his home The Cedars, at Lexington, and éminence grise to his beloved nephew and protégé, Oswald Garrison Villard of New York, an editor at the *New York Evening Post* and the *Nation*. Garrison arranged Washington's trip to Europe in 1899 and corresponded occasionally with him until 1908, but more so than any other white Bostonian, perhaps more than any other white man. "I regard yours as the most valuable life in America today," Garrison wrote Washington in 1903, after the latter had trounced Trotter at the Louisville Afro-American Council meeting.⁵⁵

Underlying the respect between the two men was a common belief in both Puritan and Yankee values, and the meshing of Garrison's pacifism and civility with Washington's public posture of humility. Added to this was Garrison's antipathy toward Trotter, which drove him closer to Washington. Nevertheless, their correspondence reveals an underlying tension between Garrison's latent militancy and Washington's accommodationism. Typically, Garrison would warn Washington away from unprincipled Republicans such as Theodore Roosevelt or paternalistic southern reformers like Edgar Gardner Murphy, and Washington would put the best construction upon some compromise to which he felt constrained to agree.

Garrison freely offered Washington his thoughts on the maze of southern politics. In the wake of the 1899 Sam Hose lynching, for example, Garrison suspected that southern governors who opposed lynching but nontheless countenanced disfranchisement would seek to use Washington to cover their retreat on the latter issue. Garrison cautioned against appearing on the same platform with such men as West Virginia Governor George W. Atkinson or Georgia's Allen D. Candler. He was soon impressed by Washington's energy and diplomacy in securing the defeat of Georgia's disfranchising Hardwick Amendment, which Washington optimistically trumpeted as a turning point for the South.⁵⁶

Garrison next warned Washington away from the 1900 Montgomery Conference, the project of southern progressive and Episcopal clergyman Edgar Gardner Murphy. Murphy hoped that this national conference would assert the leadership of southern white moderates like himself. Garrison saw that such "moderates" favored the repeal of the Fifteenth Amendment as a means to that end. In fact the conference degenerated into paternalistic race-baiting that, Harlan concludes, "set the stage for disfranchisement in Alabama." Remembering his father's words, Garrison advised Washington that clergymen were often beholden to wealthy congregations, and thus were incapable of leading true reform movements. Placing the conference in its wider perspective, Garrison saw that "the advocates of a 'white man's government' are evidently going to pour in and capture the conference. Our war with the Filipinos has distinctly lowered the tone, and weakened the power and disposition, of the Republicans to make a proper stand against such a movement." He warned too against President William McKinley's willingness to repeal the Fifteenth Amendment if he thought it would help his reelection campaign. Washington disregarded Garrison's advice and sought to put the best face upon an anti–civil rights gathering at which he was fulsomely praised.[57]

Garrison willingly complied with Washington's simultaneous secret challenge to a Louisiana disfranchisement measure. Washington desired time and money from Boston's legal community, but he also wanted to keep his own role out of the press. Although Garrison loyally provided names and enthusiasm, attorneys Albert E. Pillsbury and Richard Price Hallowell participated skeptically in an enterprise they suspected would fail without Washington's public imprimatur. For related reasons the suit failed to get off the ground.[58]

A few years later, Garrison proved a faithful friend to Washington when Du Bois and Trotter, then in alliance during the early days of the Niagara movement, attempted to break Washington's hold over the African-American press through his secret support of special favorites. Though suspicious of Washington's maneuvers, Garrison stood by his trusted ally. In fact, the crafty Washington deceived his sophisticated northern backers in this case. Before launching the Niagara movement, Du Bois sent Oswald Garrison Villard the sketchy evidence he could piece together of Washington's financial control of the press. Villard cautiously sent it on to his uncle for consideration. "I think the evidence is pretty clear that W[ashington] is subsidizing the papers referred to," Garrison concluded. "Where the money comes from, I know not, but I should hope he would not regard it as a legitimate thing to subtract any of the contributions to the Institute for that purpose." After speculating on Washington's self-justification for such a course, Garrison suggested that "it may be that the time has come when W's best friends should utter a word of caution."[59]

Yet a few days later, Garrison wrote to Villard, "It will take a great deal more than what Du Bois has written or presented to shake my faith in Washington's purity of purpose and absolute freedom from selfishness and personal ambition. . . . Nor have I seen the slightest trace of personal jealousy, bitterness or resentment in him towards those who have been so [unclear] toward him. . . . I have never liked the bitterness betrayed by my friends the [Butler] Wilsons . . . when BTW was mentioned."[60]

Writing to Washington, Garrison was more circumspect than he first promised his nephew he would be. After complaining about the low quality of Charles Alexander's *Colored Citizen*, and Trotter's "covert efforts to discredit you," he asked for reassurance against the charge "that you have subsidized and bolstered up several papers, including the Citizen, have supplied them, (through Mr. [Washington's personal secretary Emmet J.] Scott) with syndicate matter in laudation of yourself and Tuskegee, and that you are constantly endeavoring by fair means or foul to stifle and crush out all opposition to you and your policy." Expressing his disdain for such notions, he nevertheless urged Washington to "write me freely about this whole matter. If I blow a blast I want to feel fortified at all points."[61]

Washington responded with obfuscation. He defended Alexander but damned Trotter as "utterly wanting in truth or honor" for alleging that he owned the *Colored American Magazine*, now removed to New York. "The fact is, I do not own a dollar's worth of interest in a single Negro publication in this country." If this was technically accurate, the next claim that he did not subsidize the Negro press was certainly false. Garrison did not wish to know the worst about Washington, and he did not learn what he did not want to know. Du Bois, a victim of the Tuskegee Machine, had a far less sentimental view of Washington than did Garrison.[62]

By early 1909, Villard expressed reservations about Washington's course in print, and his uncle, as usual, concurred. On the eve of the first NAACP conference Garrison wrote: "I am glad you have written so plainly and frankly to Booker Washington. I imagine he will stay away from the conference, and yet it seems strange to have a Negro conference without BTW; but I fear he would be much too politic in his utterances." In the aftermath of the meeting, Garrison was pleased with Washington's diplomacy in staying away, for, as the Tuskegean himself had advised Villard, Garrison observed, "his presence might have hampered discussion and . . . would surely have invited the embittered attacks of the Trotter gang and so done infinite harm." Just a few days later, however, Washington had been much less diplomatic on his home territory. "I do not at all like the tenor of Booker Washington's speech at the Business Men's Conference [probably the NNBL] as reported in yesterday's paper," Garrison wrote, "and it seems to me as if he had gratuitously slurred and reflected on the work and purpose of the [civil rights] Conference by minimizing the importance of the vote and magnifying the value of money." The alliance between the descendants of the abolitionists and Washington was over, as was the peak of the latter's power.[63]

In its place was a mixture of respect, hostility, and forced cooperation. Throughout his career, Washington had made a series of speaking tours through the South, addressing interracial audiences with his message of goodwill toward whites and the self-improvement of black people. "You are right in saying BTW's true line of work is in such missionary expeditions," Garrison wrote his nephew in December 1909. "Your uncle William [Lloyd Garrison Jr.] long ago said that his Tuskegee work was the least part of his mission, and that his journeys and speeches up and down the land were the most important and far reaching."[64]

The NAACP was too much of a threat to Washington's position and the personal enmity between Du Bois and Washington was too great for the latter to refrain from attacking it and attempting to foment discord. Washington tried to drive a wedge between its black and white members when Du Bois unwisely used association letterhead in an anti-Washington circular letter; later Washington arranged scandalous press coverage of an interracial dinner attended by some members under the auspices of the Cosmopolitan Club. Villard and Garrison attempted to negotiate a middle ground: for civil rights, but not anti-Washington. They feared the danger he might do among their white supporters who also contributed to Tuskegee. While organizing for the 1911 Boston NAACP convention, Garrison noted the presence of "so many Tuskegee and Hampton constituents on our Honorary Committtee that [Atlanta University President] Dr. [Horace] Bumstead hopes nothing will be said by [Constitution League President John] Milholland or Du Bois to alienate them." He recognized that Washington might have dissuaded his Boston-area white supporters from joining the association, but did not, for fear that the effort might backfire.[65]

Washington died in 1915, Garrison the following year. Toward the end of their lives, there was little communication between the two; they had taken different paths. That the proud descendant of the most notorious abolitionist should have worked in harmony with the apostle of accommodation between 1899 and 1909 shows much of the complexity of racial politics in Boston.

Maria Baldwin. Courtesy of the Boston Public Library.

THREE

❦❦❦❦❦

Race, Gender, and Class
The Legacy of Lucy Stone

RACISM AFFECTED ALL AREAS of American life, including the campaign for women's suffrage. This movement, rooted in the abolitionist crusade, turned increasingly to white supremacist arguments between 1890 and 1920 to motivate votes for women. Middle-class northern suffragists, fearful of the voting power of new immigrants, argued that the admission of literate and/or propertied women to the ballot would offset the votes of immigrants in the North or blacks in the South, who would fail the literacy or property tests. African-American women, by contrast, adhered to the notion that all people had natural political rights that must be respected.

Lucy Stone, the central leader of the New England suffragists from 1870 until her death in 1893, had impeccable credentials as an abolitionist of the William Lloyd Garrison stripe. She defended the Fourteenth and Fifteenth Amendements against the opposition of Susan B. Anthony and Elizabeth Cady Stanton. So too did her husband, Henry Brown Blackwell, who was editor of the *Woman's Journal*, the weekly newspaper of the New England suffragists from 1870, and after 1890 of the national movement. Their daughter Alice Stone Blackwell edited the newspaper from 1909 until its demise in 1917. She grew up in the circle of abolitionists, suffragists, and reformers inhabited by her parents. All three members of this remarkable family on the leading edge of American reform argued that women's suffrage would ensure white supremacy in the South. Henry Blackwell in particular tried to convince the white South that female suffrage would bolster white supremacy; all three wanted to encourage the growing southern suffrage movement. After the death of her father in 1909, and especially after the victory of women's suffrage in 1920, Alice Stone Blackwell became increasingly radical. No longer constrained by the tactical necessity of compromising with southern white feminists, she embraced a range of causes that included civil rights, defense of accused anarchists Nicola Sacco and Bartolomeo Vanzetti, and socialism.

Two leading African-American women of Boston, Josephine St. Pierre Ruffin and Maria L. Baldwin, stood for civil rights and women's suffrage in this period. Each in her unique way contributed to building viable institutions in the black community. African-American women had a different set of political priorities than white women. While Ruffin and Baldwin admired the white suffragists for their abolitionist backgrounds and current work, female suffrage was necessarily a lower item on their agendas. They organized as black women, but the emphasis of their work was on race, which in their eyes marked the great divide in American life.

Despite this difference in perspective, black and white feminists cooperated with one another to a limited extent. Both shared the same ultimate goal: the removal of race and gender bars to political equality. Their ideas were rooted in Emersonian notions of equal opportunity and individual transcendence. Both white and black suffragists in Boston also shared an elite class perspective. Despite their differing priorities, both African-American and white campaigners for women's rights were heirs to a New England reform tradition that united them in spirit and sometimes in action.

THE LEGACY OF LUCY STONE

Lucy Stone (1818–1893) lived a full life in the vanguard of nineteenth-century American reform. Born a simple farm girl in western Massachusetts, she decided as a child to attend college in order to learn to read the Bible in what she thought was its original language, to see if God had really created the genders unequal. Against her father's wishes, she worked her way through Oberlin College as a teacher, becoming the first New England woman to earn a college degree. After Oberlin she traveled as a professional lecturer for the abolitionist movement, and through participation in that crusade developed her early feminist inclinations. She soon confronted a central dilemma in American reform: How should the movements against racism and sexism relate to each other? In consultation with her abolitionist colleague Samuel May, she decided to lecture part-time, separately, for each goal so as not to champion both unpopular causes from the same platform. With the aid of William Lloyd Garrison and Wendell Phillips she organized the first national women's rights convention in Worcester in 1850, and the conventions were held annually thereafter except for 1857. Throughout the antebellum period

Stone led the life of a poor and itinerant organizer for abolition and women's rights.[1]

Like Susan B. Anthony, Stone was determined to stay single and independent of a man's will. Henry Blackwell (1825–1909) of Cincinnati wore down her resistance in 1855, and they were married by abolitionist minister Thomas Wentworth Higginson, with Stone keeping her own name, an unprecedented decision. Blackwell had a hardware business, but he also participated in bold antislavery actions that earned him the threats of Kentuckians from across the Ohio River. Two of Blackwell's sisters were the pioneering female doctors Elizabeth and Emily Blackwell. Stone and Blackwell moved to Dorchester in 1870 (the year after its annexation to Boston) and participated in a variety of reform causes. Blackwell edited the *Woman's Journal* from its birth in 1870 to his death in 1909.[2]

During the Civil War they supported the troops on the home front and raised their only child. The women's suffrage movement revived again after the war and divided into two camps, primarily over the question of the Fourteenth and Fifteenth Amendments. The New York–based National Woman's Suffrage Association, led by Susan B. Anthony and Elizabeth Cady Stanton, actively opposed the amendments because they introduced the word "male" into the Constitution. The National favored a women-only organization, a federal amendment to secure women's suffrage, and a wider feminist agenda, including easier divorce laws. They reinforced this program with a wide-ranging critique of church, big business, and state. Lucy Stone and Julia Ward Howe led the American Woman's Suffrage Association, which reversed these positions in favor of a single-issue coalition on the suffrage question, open to men, motivated by an appeal to male chivalry. The two tendencies formed separate groups in 1870, with the *Woman's Journal* as the organ of the American and two short-lived and erratic journals representing the National.

If the National was more radical in its feminism, it was also more conservative in its view of the race question. Both Stanton and Anthony had participated in the antislavery crusade, but they believed that after women got the vote, and only then, would other reforms be possible. Any means to the end of women's suffrage therefore seemed plausible to them, and they relied upon a notorious race-baiter, George Francis Train, for advice and funds. Stanton derided the enfranchisement of "Africans, Chinese, and all the ignorant foreigners the moment they touch our shores," and she referred to African-Americans as "Sambo." They actively campaigned against the postwar amendments. Anthony even asked her friend Frederick Douglass to stay away from the reunited National American Woman's Suffrage Association's Atlanta convention.[3]

Whatever their limitations, the New Englanders never used racist language and they supported the civil rights and enfranchisement of African-Americans. The New England suffrage campaign was carried out in an abolitionist milieu. Stone and Blackwell counted among their friends various members of the Garrison and Grimké families. American leaders Julia Ward Howe, Ednah D. Cheney, and Mary A. Livermore had all contributed to the anti-slavery movement. Stone was especially close to Wendell Phillips. If these reformers had gained in respectability, still they all had been radical reformers. As a group, they stood in contrast to the National leadership on the race question.[4]

By 1890, however, most of their differences had narrowed. During the twenty years of separation, women's suffrage won wider support as women increasingly entered the workforce and gained the confidence to press for their rights. Technological improvements freed housewives from domestic chores. University education gained ground in the middle class. As the South modernized and became more urban, the women's suffrage movement advanced. Massachusetts women won the right to vote on education questions in 1879, and Wyoming joined the Union with full female suffrage in 1890. Alice Stone Blackwell, representing a younger generation that took for granted the evolved consciousness of the late nineteenth century, helped engineer the reunification. In general, the principles of the American group prevailed. However, with the substance of the Reconstruction amendments under increased attack, neither side wished to link what seemed to be an extraneous issue to the suffragist campaign. The National retained the presidency of the new National American Woman Suffrage Association (NAWSA), but the *Woman's Journal* became the official organ of the association.[5]

In *The Ideas of the Woman Suffrage Movement, 1890–1920*, Aileen S. Kraditor accurately described the changes that took place in suffragist thinking during this period. Kraditor argued that "the suffrage movement was essentially from beginning to end a struggle of white, native-born, middle class women for the right to participate more fully in the public affairs of a society the basic structure of which they accepted." She noted as well that as the older, abolitionist-trained leaders passed from the scene, the new leaders who took their places were more conservative in their racial views. "In this period, too, the first suffrage organizations appeared in the South," she observed. "The Southern suffrage movement was a white woman's movement, and the participation of Southern individuals and organizations in the NAWSA signified a permanent break with the abolitionist tradition from which the women's rights organizations had sprung."[6]

Contemporaneous with this process was a broader evolution of the suffrage movement's argumentation from a demand for justice to an appeal to "expediency." This meant that suffrage leaders dropped the line that women should be granted the vote because it was their natural right, and replaced it with the idea that women's suffrage would guarantee the hegemony of the elites that were besieged by foreign immigrants or African-Americans. These groups also were demanding "rights," and the suffragists gradually distanced themselves from them and their line of argument. By granting the vote to educated or propertied women only, the proportionate weight of the respectable classes would be increased. Only by the end of the period did the separate working-class women's groups unite in action with the suffragists. When African-American women even tried to join, they were rebuffed.[7]

Kraditor's conceptual framework best explains what happened to the bearers of Boston's antislavery tradition as they went about the fight for women's rights. Limited by its Protestant middle-class orientation, operating in a city where an immigrant and Irish-Catholic working class was taking control, disillusioned by the results of Reconstruction, the Bostonians appealed to class hegemony to justify women's suffrage. As early as 1867, Henry Blackwell advanced the idea that women's suffrage could be limited to the literate and propertied. The presentation of this argument became more pronounced later, as wider layers of white middle-class reformers retreated on the race question.[8]

Between 1890 and 1920 the *Woman's Journal* argued that the best way to ensure white supremacy in the South was to enfranchise literate or propertied women voters. Sometimes this line was coupled with an appeal for adequate schooling, which would encourage racial equality in a distant future, but often it was not. The weekly took no notice of the violence that accompanied the disfranchisement of even literate and propertied African-American men during the same period. Although both civil rights activists and feminists were addressing the same question in American life—Who shall vote?—the white women suffragists divorced the questions of African-American and female suffrage completely. Gradually southern women introduced their views of the question, some of which were extremely racist, until at the 1903 New Orleans NAWSA convention, their vigorously expressed views on race went unanswered by the northerners.

Henry Blackwell's argument was blunt. In 1890, using statistics from the 1880 census for the southern states, he showed that literate white women outnumbered literate African-American women by 11 to 1. Advocates of women's suffrage, he argued, were calling only for the enfranchisement of literate and/or propertied women. Massachusetts, he proudly asserted, had a literacy and property requirement for male voters. Even in a state like South Carolina, where illiterates could vote, and the black population at least equaled the white population and exceeded it in some areas, the enfranchisement of literate women would guarantee white supremacy. "How can the negro vote be freely cast and fairly counted without endangering social order and political stability?" he asked. "The illiterate, irresponsible voters, who now too often constitute a legal majority, must be controlled by the honest ballots of the civilized, responsible members of the community."[9]

The question came up again in 1894, when the NAWSA scheduled its first convention in the South, at Atlanta the following winter. Elizabeth Cady Stanton extended Blackwell's argument, writing that all new voters, male and female, North and South, should be literate in English. This would help protect native-born American workers from the ignorant votes of foreigners. When reader Anna Gardner of Massachusetts protested that Stanton's proposal was really an antilabor measure that would weaken the poorest men and women, Blackwell sprang to Stanton's defense, crafting a more nuanced version of his earlier proposals. "Circumstances alter cases," he argued. In cities like New York or Chicago, with their large immigrant populations, an unrestricted ballot would lead to "slavery of the masses to political bosses, and a bastard aristocracy of thieves, liquor sellers and gamblers." Of course, it was reasonable in states with mostly white, native-born populations like those of the West, to call for the unrestricted ballot. In the South, however, "illiterate, unconditional suffrage was forced by federal authority on the reluctant South, after the war as a political necessity. In that entire section it would be impossible to secure by voluntary action a similar extension of the suffrage to women." Southern suffragists must call for the education requirement.[10]

Blackwell's friend and colleague William Lloyd Garrison II disagreed. He referred *Woman's Journal* readers to a speech by Frederick Douglass, given in Washington and Boston earlier that year. Douglass pointed out that if an educational test was added, the whites would bar the blacks from getting an education. "I would not make suffrage more exclusive, but more inclusive," Douglass said, calling for the unrestricted ballot. "Much thoughtless speech is heard about the ignorance of the Negro in the South, but plainly enough it is not the ignorance of the Negro but the malevolence of his accusers which is the real cause of southern disorder."[11]

The debate continued almost until the end of the year, with Stanton suggesting that the existing educational requirement be stiffened. "If Mr. Garrison belonged to a disfranchised class he might more keenly feel the humiliation of a foreign yoke," she protested, and later argued that a Kansas suffrage referendum might have been lost to ignorant immigrant voters.

Anna Gardner replied that Stanton "would have class legislation"; Garrison, who had just set a memorial stone at the grave of Wendell Phillips on the tenth anniversary of his death, replied with a quote from Phillips: "The white South hates universal suffrage; the so-called cultivated North distrusts it."[12]

At the heart of the question of universal suffrage was the matter of the social class of the New England suffragists, including the Stone-Blackwell family. This in turn related to their feelings about the city around them. Both Blackwell and Stone were born to humble but enterprising parents and both had known hard work, but not poverty, as children and young adults. By the time they married in 1855, Blackwell had a developing hardware business, and after they moved to Dorchester in 1870 he became interested in real estate and prospered.[13] The once-scorned reform group was celebrated after the Civil War, and Blackwell and Stone inhabited this respectable space. Although Blackwell was then a champion of such unusual causes as the plight of the Jews and Armenians abroad, he also favored a sound currency and Canadian trade reciprocity as conservative financial bulwarks against the encroachments of a populace inclined to inflationary and free trade measures. Blackwell was a social progressive, generally, but, like many other old reformers of his day such as Moorfield Storey or Thomas Wentworth Higginson, an economic conservative.[14]

His class feeling was probably exacerbated by his suffrage views. Boston was a center not only of the suffrage movement, but also of the antisuffrage movement. In 1895, the state legislature rebuffed the annual appeal for women's suffrage by scheduling a nonbinding "mock" referendum on municipal suffrage for women. Both men and women could participate. Only 23,000 women cast ballots, overwhelmingly in favor by a 25-1 margin. Men, however, cast 187,837 nays against 108,974 yeas, and the referendum was defeated. Alice Stone Blackwell laconically noted, "There was the smallest affirmative vote in the most disreputable wards of Boston." To Protestant Bostonians in 1895, "disreputable" meant "Irish" or "immigrant." To the middle-class suffragists, reform projects had to be won against the backward working classes.[15]

The hostility to immigrants that informed the arguments of Stanton and Blackwell in 1894 became interlinked with their paternalistic subordination of black rights to women's rights. The North, Blackwell asserted, was chastened by its exposure to the immigrants. Having imperiously dictated its conception of class relations to the South in the past, it was now ready to see the South's point of view about rule by an intelligent ballot, rather than by mobocracy.[16]

There were limits to this approach, however. The *Woman's Journal* celebrated and upheld the abolitionist tradition, for it was too much a part of the early lives of Lucy Stone, Henry Blackwell, and the older participants in the suffrage campaign. The weekly also approved of the self-organization and uplift campaigns of African-American women. During the encampment of the Grand Army of the Republic in Boston in August 1890, the *Woman's Journal* praised the comradely intermingling of white and black veterans, and when Newburyport unveiled a monument to William Lloyd Garrison, Lucy Stone waxed enthusiastic about her old comrade. Frederick Douglass's 1894 visit to Boston included a warm reception by hundreds of NAWSA members. The *Woman's Journal* reported on various gatherings of African-American women's organizations, and Garrison II and Blackwell addressed the founding meeting of the Federation of Afro-American Women. To uphold the abolitionist tradition was not the same, however, as to uphold Reconstruction. Newly allied with southern women, the northerners granted that the ballot was not a natural right, but a privilege to be earned by education or property.[17]

The family was not unaware of the situation in the South, since they read the newspapers and traveled there themselves. Responding to a proposal to establish a family "settlement" in the South, Alice dissuaded her aunt Ellen from pursuing the idea. "[Uncle George] says when Emma was at Thomasville she gathered a little class of colored children and tried to teach them to read, and this at once caused her to be regarded with suspicion by the whites, who do not like to have the colored people taught," she wrote in 1903.[18]

In a telling communication to her cousin Emma, she confided her delight in Booker Washington's 1901 White House dinner with President Theodore Roosevelt. "I think one has a little physical repulsion from black people until one knows them, but if on acquaintance one finds them nice, it quickly goes off." Compared to any white northerner in 1901, Alice Blackwell was certainly liberal in her racial views, but as the daughter of Lucy Stone, comrade of Frederick Douglass, this sentiment marked a retrogression from the experience of the earlier generation.[19]

To accomplish its reconciliation with the South, the *Woman's Journal* had to maintain a discreet silence about race relations there. In fairness, this might be justified in that the weekly was the organ of the suffrage movement, and the voice of women's wider concerns. It was not bound to address all instances of oppression everywhere. On the other hand, the newspaper did take up the particular concerns of Henry and Alice: fourteen editorials on the Armenian question and many more articles appeared in 1896 alone. These were linked to the newspaper's mission by focusing on the plight of women and child refugees. However, the link between the oppression of Armenians abroad and American women was tenuous, whereas the connection between the oppression of African-Americans and American women was manifest. Nevertheless, when Mississippi disfranchised black men in 1890, Lucy Stone decried its failure to enfranchise women, saying nothing about the African-Americans. The issue was directly raised at the NAWSA 1899 convention at Grand Rapids, Michigan, by an African-American woman delegate. She demanded that the NAWSA pass a resolution against segregated railways—it was the NAWSA's business because the category of "Negroes" included women. Susan B. Anthony squelched the resolution, and the *Woman's Journal* failed to report it.[20]

When the movement scheduled its 1903 convention in the Crescent City, the *New Orleans Times-Democrat* attacked the NAWSA for its allegedly northern-influenced views on the race question. The NAWSA leadership responded with a diplomatically worded statement declaring that the association simply wished to remove the disabilities of gender from the law. On race, the association had no opinion and each state campaigned for women's suffrage as it saw fit.[21] However, in the friendly New Orleans setting, and with the encouragement of the *Times-Democrat* attack, Mississippi delegate Belle Kearney expounded upon "durable white supremacy." She argued the view of politicians like Mississippi's James K. Vardaman that even Booker Washington's project posed a threat to Anglo-Saxon civilization. Kearney borrowed statistics and arguments from Blackwell's 1890 editorial, but concluded that whites should permanently dominate African-Americans. Black women were barred from the convention. Only Carrie Chapman Catt demurred on the part of the northerners, and in defensive tones. The relationship of forces had shifted so that the extreme racist southern view now seemed linked to women's suffrage.[22]

Alice Stone Blackwell received a warm reception from her hosts during the convention and was swept away by a combination of moonlight, magnolias, and modernization. The convention buildup promised a visit to "the old plantation home, the garden . . . the darkies and the darky quarters . . . a touch of romance to everything connected with 'ante-bellum times.'" Her convention coverage in the *Woman's Journal* featured a lengthy report on the atmosphere of the city, with its riverboats, antiques, French and Spanish architecture, bustling commerce and new industry. The Kearney speech was reprinted in full, but not mentioned in the news coverage. The *Woman's Journal* rated the gathering as a whole as an unqualified success from which everyone departed happily.[23]

After the convention, Henry Blackwell blessed the proceedings in an editorial that summarized his current thinking. Reconstruction had been wrongly forced upon the South, but now the injustice was being undone: "the suffrage has been wrenched from the Negro population, thereby eliminating much of the dominant illiteracy and corruption." Foreigners in the North, subservient to "great mill owners, corporations, and capitalists" were similarly degrading the sanctity of the ballot in that section. Educated female suffrage was the remedy. Given Blackwell's conservative economic views, his declamation against "capitalists" should not be interpreted as populism, but as a backward-looking longing for the New England village, free of factories and foreigners and full of native-born artisans.[24]

Blackwell's old friend and collaborator William Lloyd Garrison II was disgusted by the entire performance. It was not "illiteracy and corruption" that was being disfranchised, he wrote, but the Negro people, including the literate and honest. This was accomplished by means of violence. The offending editorial was in line with the "policy of timid silence" adopted by northern suffragists at the New Orleans convention. An imperialist war (this reference was to the Philippines) furthered the atmosphere of racism. At New Orleans, the northerners had fallen under the sway of southern hospitality, and, not wishing to offend their gracious hosts, capitulated. "For the *Woman's Journal* to hold up these blood-stained hands and applaud this degenerate condition is astounding."[25]

To Alice Stone Blackwell fell the difficult task of reconciling the New England conscience with southern reality, in reply to Garrison. The poll tax and educational tests, she argued, were valid measures. It was true that in the South they were often used unfairly to the disadvantage of the Negro, but that did not invalidate the wisdom of the laws. "Speaking simply for myself as an individual, my own view is that when the majority of the people are below a certain point in intelligence and character, democratic government is impossible; and that in the Southern states most of the Negroes (and many of the whites) were below that level." At any rate, Garrison's criticisms of the northern suffragists was unfair. The NAWSA was a single-issue coalition, and while it may have been inappropriate for the southerners to raise the race question at New Orleans, the northerners were under no obligation to state their own views. Besides, Mrs. Catt's diplomatic rejoinder had been sufficient.[26] The contemporary reader should recall the wider context of this debate: Booker Washington was the unchallenged spokesman of the race, so far as any white folk knew in early 1903, and if he accepted segregation at southern meetings, why should suffragists object?

Underpinning the argument of both Blackwells was their nervousness about the shifting class and ethnic relations in Boston. Like other middle-class Protestants, Henry Blackwell viewed with alarm the growing power of Irish voters. In a series of editorials around the time of the New Orleans convention, he hailed the establishment of a good government committee to curb corruption in municipal government. He complained that 70 percent of Boston voters did not pay their poll tax, while the authorities looked the other way. For her part, Alice Stone Blackwell, in her capacity as a state suffrage leader, argued before the legislature that women's suffrage would not increase the foreign vote, as only one-third of the immigrants were women. Women's suffrage in Massachusetts was thus motivated by an appeal to class stability.[27]

Between 1903 and 1920, Massachusetts suffragists never again paid the race question sustained attention. Henry Blackwell died in 1909, and Alice Stone Blackwell steered the paper in a direction more friendly to the working classes, covering, for example, the Triangle Shirtwaist Factory fire of 1911 with great anger toward the ownership. One more suffrage referendum was held in Massachusetts, in 1915, and it lost overwhelmingly, by a 2-1 margin, in every city and town except two. The vote in Boston was also about 2-1 in every ward of the city. This demoralizing defeat took a great deal of energy out of the suffrage movement. Financial difficulties hurt the *Woman's Journal* also, and it published its last number in 1917.[28]

The national suffrage victory in 1920 seemed to liberate Blackwell's personal radicalism. She lived until 1950 and joined an array of reform organizations that included the Women's Trade Union League, the National Association for the Advancement of Colored People, and the American Peace Society. She helped found the League of Women Voters. Her political views shifted leftward even as reform nationally gave out during the 1920s, and she became an avowed socialist. Convinced of the innocence of accused anarchists Nicola Sacco and Bartolomeo Vanzetti, she worked on their defense and corresponded regularly with Vanzetti. The course of her later career suggests that the campaign for women's suffrage, with its attendant coalition with southern racists, retarded the development of her broader sympathies. Only after 1920 could she join the NAACP, and speak out for the rights of labor and immigrants. In a sense, she had come home to the place from which her mother had begun.[29]

AFRICAN-AMERICAN WOMEN CONFRONT JIM CROW

The political rights of African-American women were doubly denied. Female black Bostonians could win votes for women, but their sisters in the South would still be disfranchised. Therefore, they appealed to the natural rights argument to demand an unrestricted ballot. In this, they were more consistently democratic than white suffragists, but women's suffrage was a low priority among their concerns. Boston's leading African-American women necessarily had a different agenda than that of white suffragists. They organized as women to defend their race and gender, but the overwhelming reality of increased racial oppression focused their energy on such issues as lynching, disfranchisement, and segregation.

The two most prominent Boston African-American women of this period consistently supported women's suffrage. Josephine St. Pierre Ruffin and Maria Baldwin organized the Woman's Era Club in 1893 to defend the honor of African-American women, display their accomplishments, motivate the uplift of their poorer sisters, and fight for civil rights as women. Ruffin organized and led this work; Baldwin, as the first African-American administrator of an almost all-white school, exemplified the virtues of intelligence, courage, and modesty that the club movement upheld. In this, they drew upon the city's abolitionist tradition and on the social club model elaborated by Boston's Brahmin elite. Neither woman possessed much wealth, but both were leaders of Boston's black upper class by dint of character and accomplishment. They were affected by the militant versus accommodationist split in black politics, but less so than men were. Probably neither woman joined the Niagara movement, and both were associated with the NAACP, but played minor roles. Ruffin, who did her most important work after her husband's death, and Baldwin, who never married, made their own plans independently of men. Ruffin became famous for attempting to integrate the General Federation of Women's Clubs, and Baldwin was celebrated as an African-American educational leader, not as a woman schoolmaster.

John Daniels, a white social worker and observer of African-American Boston, wrote in 1914 that black women were relatively more powerful within their community than white women were in relation to white men. The reason, simply, was economic. Many more black women were forced to work, relative to the proportion of white women. This conjecture was not entirely borne out by the facts. Of Boston's 350,207 employed workers in 1920, 245,905 were male and 104,302 were female. Of these workers, 9,984 were African-American, 3,224 of whom were female. Thus the proportions were roughly the same. Nevertheless, there is probably a kernel of truth in Daniels's hypothesis: the African-American workers, male and female, were clustered at the very bottom of the job categories, so the proportion of income contributed to the family by black women was greater than that contributed by white women. If Daniels's facts were wrong, his insight into African-American gender relations has merit and contributes to an understanding of the special importance of the African-American women's club movement, in comparison to the white women's club movement.[30]

Daniels estimated a membership of about 750 for these clubs in the Greater Boston area. In 1915, the clubwomen mobilized their own protest against the showing of *The Birth of a Nation*, and the *Boston Globe* estimated that eight hundred women participated, so in the absence of official statistics, Daniels's approximation is probably workable. Boston's total black population was 13,651 in 1910 and 16,350 in 1920; thus a very high percentage (roughly 10 percent, if we use the 1920 figure and assume that half the population was female) of African-American women were affiliated with these clubs either as members or supporters. Clubs existed in Boston, Cambridge, Everett, West Medford, and Salem in the Boston area and nearby in Worcester and New Bedford.[31]

Josephine St. Pierre Ruffin (1842–1924) was the outstanding leader of this movement in Boston, and played a crucial role in bringing together the movement nationally. Her father was racially mixed and her mother was an English immigrant; the children were very light-skinned. St. Pierre was a clothing dealer and founder of the Zion Church. Her parents refused to send her to the segregated Boston schools, so she studied in Salem until the local schools were desegregated in 1855. At sixteen she married George L. Ruffin, a freeborn African-American migrant from Virginia. During the Civil War they contributed to homefront campaigns; afterward George Ruffin became the first African-American to graduate from the Harvard Law School. Ruffin became the most prominent African-American political figure of his day in Boston, serving as city councillor, state legislator, and municipal judge in Charlestown, a position he held until his death in 1886. The Ruffins had five children.

Josephine St. Pierre Ruffin participated in a range of community activities. She organized the Kansas Relief Association in Boston during the exodus of southern African-Americans to that state. She also worked with the Associated Charities of Boston, the Massachusetts Moral Education Association, and the Massachusetts School Suffrage Association. Through these latter activities she met Lucy Stone, Julia Ward Howe, and other leaders of the suffrage movement. In the 1890s she worked as an editor on the *Boston Courant*, the black community newspaper.[32]

She was an imposing woman of fifty when she traveled to New York in October 1892 to hear Ida B. Wells speak against lynching. Earlier that year Wells had written from Memphis about the lynching of three African-American businessmen, and had been driven from that city by threats. Later, probably in February 1893, Wells came to Boston and spoke privately at Ruffin's home, to black women around New England, and publicly to several white audiences, thus laying the basis for African-American women's clubs.

During the same period, African-American women in New York, Chicago, and Washington were also organizing. The Washington, D.C., group was the largest and most important. Led by Mary Church Terrell, the daughter of a Memphis millionaire and wife of a future judge, the Colored Women's League was rooted among the administrators and teachers in the African-American public schools.[33]

The Boston group held a public meeting in May 1893, at which Laura Ormiston Chant of England, and Boston suffrage leaders Lucy Stone, Ednah Cheney, and Abby Morton Diaz spoke. This was Stone's last speech in Boston before her death, and the first issue of the *Woman's Era*, appearing one year later, memorialized her on the first page. The women took her last words, "Make the World Better," as its motto. The club was to be led by African-American women, but was open to all. Its constitution stated broadly conceived goals, pledging to work against lynching, to show the progress of the race, but also to work for oppressed women everywhere, be they Chinese, Hawaiian, or Russian Jews.[34]

Meanwhile, Ida B. Wells entered into a dispute with English reformers that had impact upon America. Wells criticized fellow American lecturers preacher Dwight Moody and Frances Willard, leader of the Women's Christian Temperance Union, for equivocating about lynching. Their presentation of the problem suggested that Negroes might really be inclined to commit rape, and that women, bearers of morality, were generally to be believed when they alleged that their honor had been besmirched. Wells argued that lynching victims were usually not even accused of rape, that lynching and rape were not connected in reality, and that Moody and Willard were obscuring an important issue. Wells hoped that the English would pressure their American associates to take action against lynching, but Willard's host turned against Wells instead.[35]

Ruffin defended Wells throughout this episode. In June 1894, the *Woman's Era* published an open letter to Laura Ormiston Chant, the English reformer who had spoken at the club's first meeting. The *Era* charged that Chant had blocked an antilynching resolution at a Unitarian Church conference. It then reprised the substance of the Wells-Willard debate. In an accompanying editorial, Ruffin accused Willard and Chant of valuing temperance over racial justice, and of apologizing for lynching. Further articles in July and August kept the pressure up. The *Woman's Era* declared a partial victory in December when Willard vowed to resign from her own woman's club if it was found to bar African-American women.[36]

This continuing controversy led to the Boston group's launching a national club movement. In March 1895, a Missouri newspaper editor, John W. Jack, wrote a letter to Florence Balgarnie, the leader of the British antilynching campaign, in which he vilified colored women as habitual liars and sexual degenerates. The *Woman's Era* told the story without publishing the letter, and used the incident as a catalyst to convene a national convention of the proliferating African-American women's clubs.[37]

The idea of holding a national conference had percolated among Washington, D.C., Boston, and Chicago women from at least the time of the Chicago Columbian Exposition in 1892–93. Personal rivalries prevented any positive action in that direction. In the June 1894 *Woman's Era*, Fannie Barrier Williams, a Chicago leader, suggested waiting at least two to three years before convening a national gathering. Meetings among men frequently were a waste of time and the same might be true for women, she wrote. However, the Jack letter crystallized sentiment for the event, and in its May 1895 issue, the *Woman's Era* announced that a meeting would be held. "Boston has been selected as a meeting place because it has seemed to be the general opinion that here, and here only, can be found the atmosphere which would best interpret and represent us, our position, our needs and our aims," Ruffin declared. She did not explain how the actual decision was made to go ahead with the conference. In effect, she had proceeded against the inclinations of Williams and Terrell.[38]

The meeting was held 29–31 July at Boston's Berkeley Hall, with an extra session held 1 August at the Charles Street AME Church. One hundred and four delegates representing fourteen states and the District of Columbia attended. The sessions addressed topics such as "Women and Higher Education," "Need of Organization," "Industrial Training," "Individual Work for Moral Elevation," "Political Equality," "Social Purity," and "Temperance." A secret session was held to discuss the Jack letter. The delegates passed resolutions endorsing the work of Wells, condemning the Georgia convict system, and opposing lynching in general. Ruffin delivered a welcoming address that tied together these various themes in the context of the Jack letter. Slander, she said, had been employed by white southern women to keep black women out of national organizations. "Now with an army of organized women standing for purity and mental worth," colored women were ready to refute their accusations. "We want, we ask the active interest of our men, and too, we are not drawing the color line," she declared. As proof of this last point, white Bostonians Henry B. Blackwell and William Lloyd Garrison addressed the session "Political Equality," as did African-American journalist Timothy Thomas Fortune and educator Dr. Alexander Crummell. The conference launched the National Federation of Afro-American Women, headed by

Margaret Murray Washington, a principal at Tuskegee and the wife of Booker T. Washington.

This meeting represented only a step in the direction of unifying the women's clubs, for the Washington, D.C.–based League of Colored Women still maintained a separate structure. Mary Church Terrell did not attend the Boston meeting. In addition, there were tensions within the federation that reflected differing political viewpoints among the women. The delegates approved a resolution backing the Women's Christian Temperance Union over the objection of the Bostonians. Ruffin continued her editorial barrage against Willard. She objected also to the appellation "Afro-American" in the name of the new group, probably for integrationist reasons. These minor squabbles aside, the two groups successfully merged in 1896, electing Terrell president but retaining the *Woman's Era* as the organ of the new National Association of Colored Women (NACW). The association claimed to unite more than two hundred groups nationally.[39]

In general, Ruffin tended toward more militant views than her collaborators Williams and Terrell. These two women had husbands who later came to depend upon Booker Washington for their positions. Ruffin was always closer to Ida B. Wells, who around this time married a Washington opponent. In 1899, Terrell persuaded Booker Washington to block W. E. B. Du Bois from gaining an assistant superintendency of the Washington, D.C., schools, a position she coveted for her husband. That same year Terrell bypassed the now-named Wells-Barnett as host of the NACW's Chicago convention. Only with Ruffin's assistance did Wells-Barnett address the delegates in her own home town. While nothing suggests that Ruffin was an opponent of Booker Washington (she had worked with Margaret Murray Washington in the short-lived federation) she also wished to include militants like Wells-Barnett.[40]

In Boston community politics, Ruffin sometimes adopted "militant" positions herself. In 1895 the *Woman's Era* attacked the "servile compliance" of African-American state representative Robert Teamoh, who failed to confront the Virginia governor who rebuffed him during an official visit. A few years later, Ruffin protested attempts to remove Isaac Allen, an African-American Republican machine politician of dubious character who was elected to the Governor's Council because his name suggested that he was a white man. On national matters, the *Woman's Era* questioned the advisability of colored people participating in the 1895 Atlanta Exposition. A July 1895 editorial pointed to the disfranchisement of South Carolina blacks and increasing segregation as signs that "our position grows worse" in the South, while northern whites refused to protest. Colored people should leave the

South to improve their lot, Ruffin argued. While the paper sometimes praised Frederick Douglass, it discreetly said little about the ascendant Booker T. Washington.[41]

At the same time, Ruffin and the *Woman's Era* were firmly rooted in Boston's black upper class and did share core values with other upper-class club-women. The *Woman's Era* reported regularly on the teas and social events of its set. Ruffin's daughter Florida, who worked with her mother in the club and on the newspaper, married into the prominent Ridley family; the *Boston Globe* identified "the Ruffins and the Ridleys" as "the centers about which swell society at the West End revolves." Ruffin also presided over a sophisticated discussion group that impressed the young Harvard student W. E. B. Du Bois. Mrs. Ruffin's other children held responsible positions that elevated her status in society.[42]

The *Woman's Era* cleaved to traditional Republican upper-class economic values. Its very first issue, reporting a march of Boston's unemployed, concluded that "labor problems, in a large measure must be left to adjust themselves, 'creating work' for the unemployed can do no permanent good." Ruffin worried that unemployed factory workers were becoming too proud to accept jobs in domestic service. Immigration should be restricted, she urged. Too many immigrants were but "criminals and traitors" in their native lands, and they soon became typical racists after landing on American soil. During the 1896 presidential campaign, the *Woman's Era* feared William Jennings Bryan not as a racist, but as an economic radical whose free silver monetary policy would lead to inflation.[43]

The African-American women's club movement itself embodied many traditional values that fit into the philosophy of Booker Washington. "Lifting as we climb," the national club movement's motto, expressed the educator's philosophy well. The agenda of the 1895 Boston convention, with its sessions on temperance, social purity, and moral elevation made it easy for Margaret Murray Washington to participate. The Woman's Era Club encouraged institution building, and helped sustain St. Monica's Home for Sick Colored Women and Children, an Episcopal project located in Roxbury. Ruffin's worldview thus embraced conservative economic values, black self-help and institution-building on the one hand, and integration, defense of the ballot, and opposition to lynching on the other. Where men might counterpose these values, Ruffin saw merit in various approaches.[44]

She was similarly diplomatic in relation to white suffragists. Ruffin supported women's suffrage and praised the white women who fought for it. Lucy Stone gave the club its motto, and her picture adorned the platform of the 1895 founding convention of the federation. The *Woman's Era* argued that

African-American women in particular would benefit from suffrage rights, which would help them in the battle for full equality. Like white suffragists, Ruffin considered the mock referendum of 1895 a fraud; the legislature ought simply to give women the vote. Ruffin also cautioned white women not to ignore their colored sisters. The *Woman's Era* protested the choice of Atlanta as a convention site for the 1895 meeting, since black women would be excluded. She called on the Association for the Advancement of Women to protest segregation and lynching, and to "cast aside policy and expediency and boldly face this race question."[45]

Significantly, the *Woman's Era*, despite these sentiments, generally kept a distance from the suffrage movement. It did not campaign in 1895 around the Massachusetts mock referendum for municipal suffrage. The *Woman's Era* never directly confronted the racist argument for women's suffrage that the *Woman's Journal* advanced. After the *Woman's Era* stopped publishing, the *Colored American Magazine* appeared in 1900 in Boston as a sophisticated, upper-class literary journal. Pauline Hopkins, the leading writer for that magazine, had her doubts about suffrage. In part she accepted the traditional "anti" notion of woman's place, but in part, she carried the logic of the Blackwell position to its conclusion. If female suffrage would guarantee white supremacy, she then asked rhetorically, "Is it desirable for us as a race to place the ballot in woman's hands?"

It is strange that the *Woman's Era* never posed this question. The likelihood is that Ruffin did not want to start a fight with the white suffragists, and guarded her silence over what was a less important question to her. The NACW did not endorse women's suffrage until 1912, although this was two years before the General Federation of Women's Clubs endorsed it. Women's suffrage was not high on Ruffin's agenda.[46]

This attitude toward suffrage probably reflected the sense that race, rather than gender, was the more important problem in American life. Ruffin was politically close to Ida B. Wells during the 1890s, and Wells was an admirer of Susan B. Anthony. A chapter of Wells-Barnett's autobiography details her admiration for Anthony, and her rejection of the white suffragist's view that votes for women would cure all social ills. Like Wells-Barnett, Ruffin's priorities suggest that she was skeptical of what are today termed "essentialist" views of woman's nature. She hoped to break down the racial barriers between women. Her speech at the founding convention of the federation shows that this goal was central to her concerns. Ruffin wanted to be accepted as an equal among women, and believed that her personal victory would help destroy the color line in society at large.[47]

That project culminated in the most famous incident of Ruffin's career, her attempt to integrate the General Federation of Women's Clubs at its 1900 biennial meeting at Milwaukee. The Woman's Era Club was an affiliate of the state federation, and Ruffin was part of the Massachusetts state delegation. In addition she represented the New England Press Association at Milwaukee. The General Federation, led by Georgian Rebecca Lowe, accepted her credentials from the first two groups, but not as a representative of an African-American club. Unaware of the Woman's Era Club's racial composition, the General Federation accepted its dues, and Ruffin would not take the money back. She demanded to be seated as a representative of her club and race or not at all. However, Mrs. Lowe called the roll when the Massachusetts delegation was caucusing, and by means of this parliamentary maneuver a vote on Ruffin's credentials was avoided. The Massachusetts delegation later protested, and many northern women backed Ruffin as well. During the convention, a prominent Milwaukee society woman demonstratively invited Ruffin to dinner. The debate was marked by hissing and hot tempers, creating an unprecedented scene at the normally genteel federation assemblies. The Ruffin issue dominated press reports of the convention as a whole, at least in Boston.

Despite these impressive shows of support, Ruffin returned to Boston disappointed. "The Southern women proved themselves too clever politicians for the Northern women" she said. In the election for new officers, the more numerous northern women were split by a solid South that blocked with the northern conservatives, and Lowe was reelected president amid a threat by southerners to secede from the federation if the Woman's Era Club was recognized. With characteristic aplomb, Ruffin advised the Massachusetts delegation against withdrawing from the national group. "Our people [African-Americans] are conservative and wish to avoid trouble, yet they do not like to yield a principle," she said. Nevertheless, she retained a lawyer and was considering a suit against the general federation, which never materialized. President Lowe reaffirmed her goodwill toward African-Americans and her support for strict racial segregation.[48]

A few weeks later, the Massachusetts delegation met and passed another resolution condemning the treatment of Ruffin who "demonstrated the splendid possibilities of her race." The *Boston Evening Transcript* patronized all the women by urging them to use their clubs as men used theirs: as an escape from the real world of pressing problems. Ruffin herself claimed not to be angry, but determined to press on. The parliamentary maneuver at Milwaukee had only postponed the outcome, without sealing it.[49]

The question was settled with less attendant publicity two years later at Los Angeles. Probably because an unfavorable recommendation had been accepted by a Massachusetts committee between conventions, Ruffin decided not to attend. In 1902, she would have been sixty years old and the journey may have seemed too arduous or expensive. Ruffin's own interests might have been shifting; in 1902 she helped found a school in Liberia. Because the Woman's Era Club might have sent a younger delegate and did not, it is probable that the women realized that the cause was already lost.

After the convention, the club heard a report from a white woman who attended, Kate Lyon Brown of Waltham. Boston black community leaders were present, as were NACW president Mary Church Terrell, and Woman's Era leaders Agnes Adams and Eliza Gardner. Ruffin was absent. Brown, apparently an outsider in the Massachusetts delegation, decided on her own to present the black women's case at Los Angeles. On the train ride across country, she discovered to her surprise that sentiment among the Massachusetts women had shifted. Sometime prior to the convention, they accepted a "compromise" loaded in the South's favor. State federations could admit whomever they wished, but the national committee on membership must return a unanimous ruling to accept an applicant, thus assuring the rejection of African-American clubs. The Massachusetts delegates en route to Los Angeles felt the question was closed. Brown was ruled out of order when she tried to argue the point on the convention floor, and the Massachusetts women did not protest.[50]

Ruffin lived until 1924 and participated in other civic associations. The last extant issue of the *Woman's Era* is January 1897; it is not clear how long the newspaper or the club actually lasted. Besides the school in Liberia, Ruffin also sponsored a school in Georgia. Along with Maria Baldwin she helped organize a group during World War I that later became the League of Women for Community Service. A rivalry of obscure origin with Butler and Mary Wilson limited her participation in the NAACP, although she allowed her name to be associated with it.[51]

Just before the 1920 suffrage victory, African-American women, led by women of Massachusetts, attempted to integrate the NAWSA. Within the NACW, there was a separate Northeastern Federation of Women's Clubs that was formed after the 1899 Chicago convention. This group reflected the feeling by New England and New York women that the more conservative Terrell and Fannie Barrier Williams had accrued too much power; rather than split the organization they adopted a separate structure but remained within the NACW framework. In 1919 the Northeastern Federation, led by Elizabeth Carter of New Bedford, a longtime ally of Ruffin's, applied to the NAWSA for membership. Ida Husted Harper of NAWSA urged the African-American women to withdraw their request so as not to antagonize needed southern congressional support for the suffrage amendment. If the Northeastern Federation would wait until the amendment passed, then there might be a favorable response to their request, she wrote. Of course, once the amendment passed NAWSA would no longer have any reason to exist. Apparently the Northeastern Federation did not press its case. This final act in the drama of the relation between the races in the suffrage movement owed much to the lifework of Josephine St. Pierre Ruffin.[52]

MARIA L. BALDWIN: A LIFE OF SERVICE

If Ruffin was the central organizer of the African-American women's clubs, her friend and colleague Maria L. Baldwin personified the life of service to which the clubs were dedicated. A more retiring person than her controversial colleague, Baldwin was a universally admired educator who moved easily in both black and white circles. She accomplished in her career what Ruffin tried to win for a wider layer of African-American women: integration into American society and the opportunity for advancement based on merit. Her personal professional success gave the lie to race-based discrimination in the professions and public life in general.

Baldwin (1856–1922) lived almost her entire life in Boston and Cambridge. Her father was a Haitian immigrant who worked as a letter carrier; little is known about her mother. She attended the Cambridge public schools, and rose from grade school teacher to become principal in 1889 and master of the Agassiz school in that city in 1915. The student body was 98 percent white and many students were the children of Harvard professors. This unusual situation—being an African-American master of an overwhelmingly white school—won Baldwin national attention and contributed to the perception of the Boston area as a region of advanced racial views. Her position as a schoolmaster also won her the friendship and respect of Boston's genteel reformers. These included men who supported Booker Washington's perspective, such as Thomas Wentworth Higginson, Edward Everett Hale, and Harvard President Charles W. Eliot. A suffragist, she counted as female friends Ednah D. Cheney and Julia Ward Howe. Because of her work, she was probably better connected in white society than any other Boston African-American of her time.

Throughout her life she participated in the African-American community's civic affairs, apparently without taking sides in the ideological disputes. She joined the Banneker Club, a literary discussion group organized in 1874, that included her friend Archibald Grimké. Like Ruffin, she later organized her own discussion group, which W. E. B. Du Bois attended in 1885. "It was a sort of a salon, unnamed, unorganized, but palpitating with spirit," he re-called upon her death. Along with Ruffin, she helped to initiate the Woman's Era Club. She served on the board of the Robert Gould Shaw settlement house, which aided southern migrants, and during World War I she orga-nized a service group for African-American soldiers that later became the League for Community Service.[53]

Like Archibald Grimké, Baldwin straddled the divide between militant and accommodationist camps, but her associations suggest that she may have been more comfortable with the latter. Her only published works are two very brief essays, one that appeared in the Hampton College magazine, *Southern Workman*, and the other in the NAACP journal, the *Crisis*. The Hampton piece appeared in 1900 in the midst of deteriorating race relations in the South; in keeping with that journal's orientation, her article was appropriately vague and philosophical, demonstrating a determined optimism about a fu-ture that proved to be increasingly bleak. The 1915 *Crisis* essay endorsed wom-en's suffrage in a few paragraphs.[54]

Archibald Grimké wrote two columns about her as Boston correspondent for the *New York Age* in December 1905, at a time when the *Age* was blasting away editorially at the militant Niagara movement. Grimké's biographer sug-gests that he used the pro-Washington newspaper to undermine the Tuske-gean's ideas, which may be true; Grimké broke with Washington less than a year later. The use to which he put Baldwin's career does suggest a subversive intent in regard to the Bookerite paradigm. Grimké extolled Baldwin's char-acter, personality, and perseverance and held up her career as a model for young people. "About herself as a pedagogue there is an atmosphere of breed-ing, the fine manner of a lady," he wrote. She was easily the most popular teacher at the Hampton Institute 1899 summer school, he recalled, yet she maintained an attitude of modesty. Nevertheless, these eminently respectable qualities were repaid with insult when some southern women took up lodg-ings in Boston's Franklin House, where Baldwin also lived. The southerners prevailed upon the management to evict Baldwin; the managers refused; whereupon the southerners left in a huff. Grimké contrasted Baldwin's digni-fied and steadfast behavior through this episode to that of another resident who was "passing" for white, and refused to come to Baldwin's defense. Bald-win's resistance to the southerners, albeit on northern soil, showed the impor-tance of standing up for one's rights.[55]

Baldwin did keep her distance from Washington's critics. Association with Monroe Trotter would have been deleterious to her career, and she seems to have avoided the fiery editor. African-American women did on occasion ap-pear as speakers at Trotter-sponsored events, but not the prominent Baldwin.

There is no evidence of her reaction to the 1903 Boston "riot" but it is difficult to imagine approving of the angry confrontation that Trotter instigated. She did speak at the 1905 centennial celebration of the birth of William Lloyd Garrison, but at the meeting sponsored by the moderate defenders of civil rights. Despite her friendship with Grimké, who later became the president of the Washington, D.C., NAACP, Baldwin did not contribute much to the Boston chapter. In this she probably followed the lead of Ruffin.[56]

It is not clear when the Woman's Era Club dissolved. Its successor was the League of Women for Community Service that Baldwin led from its origination in 1918 until her death four years later. Mrs. George W. Forbes, Mrs. George Lewis, Florida Ruffin Ridley, and Agnes Adams, some of whom were Women's Era veterans, helped with the new group. This began as the wartime Soldiers' Comfort Unit, which planned entertainment and brought food and clothing to African-American soldiers stationed at nearby Fort Devens. Half a year after the Armistice, the group changed its mission to doing social work with young women and girls, and changed its name. The group heard a speaker from the newly formed Urban League, whose settlement-house orientation eschewed civil rights agitation in favor of self-improvement. Baldwin's group replicated the work of the Women's Service Club, founded by Mary Wilson of the NAACP, which taught girls sewing and brought food baskets to the needy. The existence of these two separate groups serving remarkably similar needs suggests the persistence of an old rivalry whose original significance was probably transcended by 1920.[57]

Baldwin supported women's suffrage but devoted little time to it. Her 1915 contribution to the *Crisis* roundtable is titled "Votes for Teachers" and celebrates the contributions to society of her fellow teachers while offering little on the natural rights of women as citizens. Her tone is pensive and hopeful that her colleagues will use their ballots wisely if allowed to vote. "One is warranted in thinking that teachers will transfer to their use of the ballot their habit of fidelity to ideals," she concluded. Although her friends and acquaintances included suffragists, she herself had other priorities.[58]

According to the *Boston Evening Transcript*, Baldwin was "one of the most prominent colored women in the United States" at the time of her death. She expired dramatically, collapsing after a speech to the board of the Robert Gould Shaw House. A well-attended funeral service at the Arlington Street Church attracted mourners from her numerous civic and professional associations. Her pallbearers included four white men from the philanthropic and social-work fields, and four prominent African-Americans, among them Booker Washington's friend from Hampton days, Samuel Courtney, and the NAACP's Clement Morgan.[59]

Although Baldwin did not play a prominent role in the fight for civil rights or women's suffrage, her quiet life of accomplishment refuted the arguments of racists and sexists. At a time when white male theorists were generating ideas of hereditary Anglo-Saxon supremacy, her example suggested to thousands of students that those ideas might be flawed. By serving so prominently in the African-American and white worlds, she fulfilled in her life the goals articulated by her friend Josephine St. Pierre Ruffin when she founded the Women's Era Club and demanded to be seated as an equal among the white clubwomen.

William Monroe Trotter. Courtesy of the Boston Public Library.

FOUR

❧❧❧❧❧❧❧

William Monroe Trotter
Bostonian

WILLIAM MONROE TROTTER was above all else a product of the Boston racial environment: he was born, raised, educated, and married there and rarely left. Intellectually he descended from various strands of abolitionist thought, but he devised his own strategy to win equality for African-Americans during the high tide of white racism. Because the National Association for the Advancement of Colored People had a more appropriate method for winning full legal equality, and perhaps because he never wrote a book, Trotter's importance within national African-American politics is sometimes overlooked. He is best known for the 1903 meeting at which he challenged Booker Washington, the "Boston Riot"; and in a certain sense he can be seen as the bridge over which W. E. B. Du Bois passed to the founding of the Niagara movement. In Boston he was the central leader of the African-American community from 1904 to about 1915, and is perhaps the single most important figure in all of Boston's African-American history.

Trotter's father James was born a slave in Mississippi. His family arrived in Cincinnati around 1854 (whether by escape or manumission is not clear) and the free James Monroe Trotter joined the 55th Massachusetts Civil War regiment, serving under N. P. Hallowell and George Garrison, son of William Lloyd Garrison. As a soldier, James Trotter was a leader in the fight for equal pay for African-American troops. After the war he moved to Boston. Virginia Isaacs Trotter, William Monroe's mother, returned to Ohio for health reasons in 1872 to deliver her only son. Two daughters, Maude and Bessie, were born later. The elder Trotter worked at the post office, and after suffering racial discrimination at the hands of the Republican patronage machine, he turned to the Democrats. During the first Grover Cleveland administration, he rose to the highest appointed post open to African-Americans, recorder of deeds in Washington, D.C. At the end of Cleveland's first term, James Trotter returned to Boston and began a prosperous real estate business.[1]

William Monroe Trotter was an outstanding student, popular with his classmates in the mostly white Hyde Park section, and possessed of a strong religious inclination that he exercised in an integrated Baptist church. Trotter attended Harvard, where he won scholarships and was the first African-American elected to Phi Beta Kappa. He cheered the athletic teams enthusiastically, joined the Wendell Phillips Club, and was president of the Total Abstinence League. He took a wide range of courses, studying with teachers Francis Peabody, Edward Cummings, Albert Bushnell Hart, and Oswald Garrison Villard. He graduated magna cum laude in 1895, having had a positive and happy experience.[2]

Trotter took a succession of jobs after college, planning to enter his late father's business. In 1899 he married Geraldine Pindell, whose uncle had participated in the movement to desegregate the Boston public schools in the 1850s; they were happily married and Geraldine was her husband's main collaborator on the newspaper they would help to found, the *Guardian*, until her death in 1918. The Trotters joined social clubs and helped to organize the Boston Literary and Historical Association in 1901. Trotter's correspondence with his white classmate John A. Fairlie shows much of his sensibility around this time. He writes somewhat condescendingly of playing tennis with his country cousins in Ohio on their large farm. After graduation he eagerly sought tickets for Harvard football games and attended reunions with his white friends. Joining a white real estate firm in 1899 Trotter prospered and acquired various properties in his own name. His sister Maude was married in 1907 to Dr. Charles G. Steward, son of Chaplain Theophilus Steward of the 25th Infantry. According to the *Boston Herald*, "The bride wore a gown of imported embroidered Swiss en train"; the leading lights of Boston's black upper class brought expensive gifts.[3] Trotter inherited culture, wealth, and racial pride.

Yet, Trotter sensed the contradictary nature of his situation. On the one hand, he was born into comfort, was blessed with remarkable gifts of intelligence and self-discipline, had married a woman of similar temperament, and had a promising financial career. On the other hand, he was conscious of the prejudice he faced at home and of the national deterioration of race relations that grew increasingly more ominous. Offered a job as a teacher in Washington, D.C., after graduation, Trotter declined, explaining to Fairlie his preference for a business career, but protesting also that "the place is too far South and the school a separate one." He recognized that there would be obstacles in business as well: "I should prefer to take my chances in an established firm but there is in the way of *high* preferment for me one large impediment that other men do not have to hinder them."[4]

As Stephen R. Fox accurately observes in his biography of Trotter, the combination of renascent racism nationally, the influences of his father, Harvard, and the militant group among the Boston elite pushed Trotter in the direction of political activism. Along with William H. Scott, a minister from nearby Woburn, and George W. Forbes, a writer who worked at the public library, Trotter participated in the Massachusetts Racial Protective Association. In his first address before this group, he spoke against the policies of Booker Washington. With these new friends, he began to publish the *Boston Guardian*, whose first issue appeared 9 November 1901.[5]

This truncated summary of Trotter's early career may be usefully compared and contrasted to that of the preeminent leader of the protest tradition, Trotter's brief ally and later antagonist, William Edward Burghardt Du Bois. Like Trotter, Du Bois was gifted, Massachusetts-born, exposed to white playmates as a boy, and educated at Harvard. Du Bois had even courted Geraldine Pindell. Du Bois, however, as he later revealed in several striking literary passages, was earlier troubled by "the veil" drawn by whites against Negroes, and he grappled more intensely with the problem of the "duality" of the African-American identity. Unlike Trotter, he was not born a Bostonian, nor to a father well-connected to the white world. Unlike Trotter, he made his way south to study at Fisk and teach in isolated rural schools, and later at Atlanta University. He admired Booker Washington throughout his formative years. Four years Trotter's senior, he did not publicly break with Washington until 1903, with the thoughtful volume, *The Souls of Black Folk*.[6]

Du Bois's early career, with a rich experience of the North and South, allowed him a better appreciation of the national relation of forces between black and white. A key to Trotter's political outlook is that he apparently never set foot in the states of the Confederacy. Although the *Guardian* reported every lynching, Jim Crow law, disfranchisement measure, and racist utterance by southern white politicians, it necessarily recorded these developments by clipping the national press. In a sense, Trotter was covering a foreign country. Welcoming conventioneers to his National Independent Political League's Boston meeting in August 1911, the *Guardian* banner enthused, "Welcome to the Home of Abolition," a place "where it is no crime to be black." Trotter urged his guests to "breathe Boston air, spend a short time in its atmosphere, and you will be proud that you are an American citizen."[7] No doubt, a visit to the many shrines honoring the abolitionist heroes could be inspiring. Conversely, exclusive respiration of such a rarefied atmosphere could be limiting. After Trotter's second confrontation with President Woodrow Wilson in 1915, he made a midwestern speaking tour, organized by his ally Ida B. Wells-Barnett. "I thought that he needed to get out in this part of the country and see that the world didn't revolve around Boston as a hub," Wells-Barnett noted.[8]

If Trotter lived in a rapidly changing and increasingly multinational Boston, his imagination was rooted in its abolitionist past. African-Americans nationally regarded Boston with special reverence; even Booker Washington celebrated the abolitionists as heroes. Trotter esteemed the lives of the abolitionists as a rebuke to the commercial spirit of his own age. He sponsored commemorations of their centennials in an almost religious spirit. As the leader of the Boston militants, he was keeper of the flame, a secular priest in a holy city.

Trotter borrowed from the distinct strands of the antislavery impulse. Very early he fashioned his own strategy to win civil rights. He never wrote a book or even a pamphlet, but his métier was the editorial and the indignation meeting. As Fox notes, Trotter was the only African-American editor to make a lifelong career of producing a weekly newspaper and leading a national protest group. In this choice of career, William Lloyd Garrison was the obvious role model.[9]

Ultimately he drove away every strong-willed person with whom he collaborated. "You are finding that it is impossible to work permanently with Mr. Trotter, unless he does the commanding; he is not well balanced enough. . . . He is a splendid fellow in many ways: self-sacrificing and honest, at the same time we cannot afford to let him go ahead and have his own way."[10] Thus Du Bois advised Bishop Alexander Walters of New York, who was then working with Trotter to establish the Negro-American Political League (NAPL). One need not adduce the many harsh judgments of him by his opponents to establish this case. He should have been able to treat with respect militants like Clement Morgan or Butler Wilson with whom he disagreed. This was his tragic flaw: a sectarianism that personalized even tactical political disagreements.

AN INDEPENDENT IN POLITICS

From men like his father, and the editor Timothy Thomas Fortune, he adopted a stance of political independence. Exercise of the suffrage was the linchpin of Trotter's strategy, and the names of his various organizations reflected this: New England Suffrage League, Negro-American Political League, National Independent Political League. On the national level, Trotter supported Theodore Roosevelt with reservations in 1904 (the reservation being that he dump Booker Washington as political adviser). In 1908, the *Guardian* campaigned for Ohio Republican Joseph Benjamin Foraker, then fell just short of endorsing Democrat William Jennings Bryan after the Republican convention. After his 1912 endorsement of Woodrow Wilson, Trotter returned to the Republicans in 1916 and 1920.[11] This particular electoral peregrination was not entirely unique in that all Progressive Era presidents betrayed preelection promises to African-Americans, causing some uncertainty about traditional Republican loyalty. What made Trotter unusual, however, was that he elevated these tactical choices to the level of principle. "Any [Secretary of War William Howard] Taft Negro Is Blood Guilty of Disfranchisement by Taft's Own Speeches," a 1908 *Guardian* headline declared, and beneath it, "The Race Traitor's Column" named names.[12]

Trotter's electoral strategy overestimated the race's power to win its demands through the ballot. "Can Control Presidency," a May 1904 *Guardian* headline declared. "Negroes of North Hold Balance of Power in Next Presidential Election Says New York Sun . . . Chance to Force Demands." The *Sun* article included a table showing the margin of Republican victory in 1900 in California, Connecticut, Indiana, New York, and New Jersey, and contrasted it to the eligible African-American electorate in those states. If these voters threatened to bolt and vote Democratic, the Republicans would have no choice but to act on the civil rights agenda. By and large, African-American voters stayed with the Republicans throughout this period, shifting only during the 1910 midterm election, along with the white electorate. However, it is unlikely that the electoral card could have been played with much effect on a national level by the nation's small number of enfranchised northern African-Americans. Not until the 1920s did black voters figure into the plans of some big-city machines, and Boston, with its small community, was not one of these.[13]

This strategy was made more strict by Trotter's corollary belief that no member of his organization could hold a responsible position in a political party. For this reason, Trotter demanded that Virginia's James H. Hayes resign the presidency of the National Negro Suffrage League in 1904, because he was a member of the Republican national convention.[14] By this logic, Trotter would have banned from membership his father, a Democratic officeholder, or Frederick Douglass. This early dispute with Hayes was a Rosetta stone that explained the pattern of Trotter's career. The important turning point in Trotter's life was his disruption of the Massachusetts branch of the Niagara movement in 1907. This was the national movement founded by Du Bois that stood for the full civil rights agenda. Trotter had no important political differences with Du Bois or Clement G. Morgan, his rival for Massachusetts leadership, yet he clashed with them over minor issues. Trotter and Morgan were among the six New England founding members of Niagara in 1905 and had been closely allied since the Boston Riot of July 1903, after which Morgan represented Trotter in court. In July 1906, Trotter argued with Morgan, who was a good friend of Du Bois, over several issues. He opposed the admission of women to the Niagara movement, in particular Maria Baldwin and Mrs. Archibald Grimké. He distorted a Morgan speech that was printed in the *Guardian*. Finally, Trotter opposed the reelection of Massachusetts Governor Curtis Guild, whom Morgan supported.[15]

Du Bois traveled to Boston in February 1906 and June 1907 to try to reconcile the two men. Trotter agreed to work harmoniously with Morgan and then fired off a letter full of recrimination as soon as Du Bois returned to Atlanta in 1907. In June, the Boston group organized a fundraising play for a challenge to a Virginia Jim Crow law. George Forbes, a *Guardian* founder who broke with Trotter under pressure from Booker Washington, worked energetically on the play. To this Trotter also objected. He and his supporters did not help organize the Niagara movement's 1907 meeting in Boston, but Forbes and his wife did.[16]

The *Guardian* did promote that convention, but with its own particular slant. Trotter ran larger articles boosting his favorite local Republican, Senator Winthrop Murray Crane, and bashing Morgan's favorite, Curtis Guild, who had urged the Massachusetts legislature to fund the segregated Jamestown, Virginia, tercentenary exposition. Eight hundred people attended the public meeting, over which Du Bois presided. It was addressed by Niagara movement stalwarts like New Haven attorney George W. Crawford, the Baptist Reverend Dr. Charles S. Morris of New York, and New York school principal William L. Bulkeley. Trotter and his allies, except the nonsectarian Reverdy Ransom, were notably absent from the speakers' list.[17]

In the aftermath of the convention, Du Bois attempted to address further organizational questions raised by Trotter. Trotter charged that nonmembers of the movement had voted for officers and the election was thus invalid. Du Bois staged another election in Massachusetts and tried to establish who was actually on the membership rolls. In Du Bois's opinion, an exceedingly scrupulous election was then held; the Forbeses and Grimkés were accepted as associate members, and remaining matters in dispute were to be laid before the executive committee. Du Bois concluded: "Is this movement a great movement which invites co-operation from all the race or is it a small clique which is using the movement to settle personal debts and its petty animosities? . . . Finally, I regret to say that while no one has defended Mr. Trotter more than I have or believes more than I do in the worth of his work and the great sacrifices that he has made, nevertheless I am reluctantly compelled to believe that Mr. Trotter is a burden to the Niagara Movement at present."[18] Trotter never worked with Du Bois again, and he went on to build the Negro-American Political League with New York's Bishop Alexander Walters and J. Milton Waldron of Washington, D.C., as allies. Trotter had allowed a series of minor tactical questions to separate himself from Du Bois, who adroitly identified the underlying conceptual differences between the two approaches. Trotter had never been wholly loyal to Niagara anyway, keeping his Suffrage League going during Niagara's tenuous existence.

Working from his Boston base and armed with the *Guardian*, Trotter simply saw himself as the center of the national movement. A few months after the Niagara movement left town in 1907, Trotter organized a centennial celebration in honor of the martyred abolitionist Elijah Lovejoy. Twelve hundred people came to Faneuil Hall to press for a congressional resolution outlawing the Jim Crow railroad car in interstate travel. William Lloyd Garrison Jr. and future NAACP leader Mary White Ovington spoke, Trotter read a bill drawn up by Albert E. Pillsbury, and Moorfield Storey and Thomas Wentworth Higginson sent letters of support. The meeting was held under the auspices of the New England Suffrage League without a mention of Clement Morgan or the Niagara movement; by any measure the meeting was a success. Trotter was back at Faneuil Hall in March 1908 with a meeting of equal size, this time threatening to bolt the Republican Party if Secretary of War William Howard Taft was the nominee. The long list of speakers comprised African-American ministers, some attorneys, and Trotter.[19]

This meeting provided the momentum for a Philadelphia conference that founded the Negro-American Political League in April 1908. Trotter portrayed this event as a complete vindication, claiming a total of four thousand participants at two rallies. One article described in vivid detail an enthusiastic gathering of two thousand that overflowed the packed church. William H. Scott, Trotter, and Bishop Walters presided, and Trotter ally Reverend Byron Gunner, now of Hillburn, New York; nominal chairman J. Milton Waldron; and James Hayes of the Suffrage League delivered the speeches. The new organization pledged itself above all to prevent the nomination of Roosevelt or Taft.[20]

Walters was nervous about the convention before it began and appealed to Du Bois to come to Philadelphia to counter Trotter's influence: "As I told you before, the initiative for the Philadelphia meeting was taken by Messrs. Trotter and Scott and not by myself, I joined in with them with the hope that we might be able to unite all the forces, but I have since discovered that it is utterly impossible to work with Mr. Trotter." Du Bois was through with Trotter and would not come. In the aftermath, both were disconcerted by the convention's outcome. "The convention was a success, in point of numbers and as a sentiment maker: the personnel of the convention was quite representative at least enough so as to disarm the ridicule which the [conservative] New York *Age* had prepared in advance to give it. Hundreds were turned away at the door each evening," Walters reported. Du Bois observed that the convention had simply built a rival organization, further fracturing the race to no apparent purpose.[21]

Trotter fought with Niagara's more potent successor, the NAACP, when after a scheduling mix-up Trotter and the association's Clement Morgan planned separate centennial celebrations for Charles Sumner. The New York office urged Morgan to cancel his meeting but Morgan persisted. Trotter organized a series of meetings on 5 and 6 January 1911, under the auspices of the New England Suffrage League in cooperation with the National Independent Political League, succesor to the NAPL. Five years after the Brownsville incident of 1906, when President Theodore Roosevelt summarily discharged a battallion of African-American soldiers, Trotter was relentlessly firing away at Roosevelt's faction in the Republican Party. Trotter's evening meetings drew a combined total of 2,200, and were addressed by Democratic Governor Eugene N. Foss; Albert E. Pillsbury; Mayor John F. Fitzgerald; George Downing, the son of an African-American friend of Sumner's; Professor Charles Zueblein; Dr. A. A. Berle, a Methodist bishop; and a host of African-American ministers headed by Reverdy Ransom. Governor Foss struck the partisan theme that Trotter desired: Charles Sumner's successor in the Senate, Henry Cabot Lodge (a Roosevelt man) was unworthy of his predecessor. There were daytime celebrations as well, and Trotter had reason to be pleased with the outcome.[22]

Morgan, on the other hand, stumbled badly. His featured speaker was ex-governor Curtis Guild, who painted an unflattering portrait of Sumner before a mostly African-American audience. Abolitionist veteran Frank Sanborn and African-American civil rights lawyer Butler Wilson answered Guild from the rostrum. Trotter turned this tense encounter into grist for his vengeful mill, pointing out in his paper that Lodge himself had been invited to speak; that Lodge's agent had paid for the hall rental; and that some endorsers of the meeting had had their names used without being notified. Trotter covered the NAACP's New York commemoration favorably, but in Boston the damage to the community's unity was serious.[23]

This sequence of events from 1905 to 1910 reveals much about Trotter's national strategy and his self-perception. Simply put, Trotter conceived himself to be at center stage in the North, and he was not entirely without reason. It was he who had challenged Booker Washington in 1901 and set in motion the train of events that led to the Niagara League. He had built large public protests in Philadelphia and Boston, and had allies in Washington and New York. As a Bostonian, Trotter had access to a tradition that New Yorkers or Atlantans, despite the size of those communities, could not match. By mobilizing militant sentiment, it is not surprising that he could challenge Du Bois and regard himself as the real leader of the movement.

Trotter boldly called for protest meetings because he believed that mass action inspired people. Although he stressed the value of suffrage, he never argued that electoral politics was sufficient by itself to effect full equality. Like Garrison and Douglass, he was an activist who thrived on indignation meetings to rouse the conscience of the nation. Almost as a counterpoint to this approach, Trotter showed very little interest in legal challenges or legislative maneuvering to win the day. There is little coverage in the *Guardian* of lawsuits. By contrast, Butler Wilson and Clement Morgan, the African-American leaders of the Boston NAACP, were both attorneys. Trotter did have legal allies: Edgar Benjamin and Emery T. Morris were the outstanding ones, but his chief Boston supporters tended to be ministers. As we shall see in more detail later, Trotter was deeply rooted in Boston's black community and its antislavery tradition.

With this understanding, it is easier to appreciate how Trotter misjudged the potential of the NAACP when it appeared in the 1909–11 period. Trotter attended the New York meeting that presaged the NAACP and he contributed rancorously to the debate over the platform. He advocated adding a phrase on Jim Crow transportation, and more explicit language on lynching, but displayed a skeptical attitude. He was not among the twelve African-Americans on the original Committee of Forty that came out of the meeting. Toward the NAACP nationally he was wary. When the association's 1911 meeting was scheduled for Boston, the *Guardian* welcomed it as a white civil rights organization that colored people should support.[24]

Trotter pointed with local pride to the prominence of Bostonians in the association such as Moorfield Storey, Albert Pillsbury, Maria Baldwin, Francis Jackson Garrison, Horace Bumstead, Archibald Grimké, and, nominally, himself. He editorialized that "such a movement has great power, at least in means, brains, and influence. Its effectiveness depends on the principles the movement espouses, its consistency and the number of white Americans it can win to its program." He urged his readers to participate and help give direction. "This is the home of abolition, of equal rights. It leads in these principles the rest of the country. Reaction is setting in. Any compromise in

Boston will doubly damage the cause. . . . Let's all attend." Eight hundred people came, and Trotter praised the harmonious atmosphere. In a significant editorial, titled "A Great, Important Movement," Trotter regretted that association leader Moorfield Storey had a kind word for Booker Washington and feared that "the wide open door policy of membership pursued has its dangers." However, "we should all wish it success and take part in making it of great benefit to race and country."[25]

Trotter rejected his own advice. As soon as the delegates left town, he announced plans for the convention of the National Independent Political League (NIPL; successor to the Negro-American Political League), to be held in Boston in August. His colleagues in this endeavor included Bishop Walters, Ida B. Wells-Barnett, and local supporters the Reverend M. A. N. Shaw, Emery Morris, I. D. Barnett, M. Cravath Simpson, and writer Pauline Hopkins. Trotter saw two civil rights organizations: a colored one that he led, and a white one. As Fox suggests, a combination of Trotter's belief in the need for a black-led group, and his own inability to work in a team with equals kept him away from the NAACP.[26]

One further dimension of great import also separated the NAACP from the NIPL: their programs. The NAACP was a response not only to the resurgence of racism, but also to the burgeoning progressive reform movements of the day. The white association leaders in particular were concerned about the lack of interest in the Negro shown by Progressives, but they also were influenced by the nonpartisan spirit of the reformers. The association itself did not endorse candidates and adopted "pressure group" tactics. White and middle-class in leadership, its tone was earnest but reasoned, rather than militant. The very topic of the 1911 conference, "Race Discrimination: Its Relation to Segregation, Peonage, Violations of Property and Labor Rights, and Its Ultimate Results," sounded like the title of an academic paper. Its plan of work for 1911 was to study Negro schools, organize a national legal redress committee, establish a bureau of information, publish the *Crisis*, hold mass meetings, form local groups, campaign to reapportion Congress, study national aid to education, and make foreign propaganda. While there existed varying points of view about membership and organization, the association aimed to be broadly based and racially integrated.[27]

The National Independent Political League, by contrast, planned to participate in the elections as the main part of its strategy. Condemning both parties, it resolved to "vote only for congressmen and other candidates for office who pledge themselves to advocate the following measures," including opposition to disfranchisement, peonage, Jim Crow cars, and support for equal education, national legislation against lynching, and the restoration of

the discharged Brownsville soldiers. If the NIPL's agenda overlapped somewhat with the association's, it did have a different focus. Notably absent from
its plans was legal defense or initiative. This may have been for lack of funds,
or because Trotter felt the legal field was best left to the more high-powered
and mostly white lawyers in the NAACP's camp.[28]

During the year, *Guardian* reports on Boston branch meetings of the NIPL
showed the organization's concerns. The national convention would "advise
the race as to the position it should take in the presidential campaign of 1912
and lay plans for the enfranchisement of our people in states where they are
disfranchised." At an August meeting in Boston, New Yorker A. W. Whaley
described a black revolt in the Republican Party when African-American
applicants for clerkships were turned down. Only when the applicants threatened to vote for the Democrats did they get their jobs. The implication for
national political strategy was clear. African-Americans had to play off one
party against the other.[29]

The August 1911 NIPL convention was poorly attended and had a narrow
speakers' list. Not even the outrage over a Coatesville, Pennsylvania, lynching
could swell the delegate size to over 150. Out-of-town orators included Waldron, Walters, S. L. Carrothers, and old ally Byron Gunner. The local speakers were Edward Everett Brown, representing Mayor John F. Fitzgerald;
Albert Pillsbury; and Frank Sanborn. J. R. Clifford, an editor from West
Virginia, was elected president. This weak showing revealed that the initiative had passed to the NAACP.[30]

These two national gatherings, both held in Boston and separated by half
a year, may be seen as turning points in the relation between the two groups.
Over the next few years, the counterposed strategies of the NIPL and the
NAACP would be tested in practice. The failure of Trotter's organization
cannot be traced simply to his difficult personality, although that was a factor.
Certainly, Trotter was overmatched by the wealth and access to power that
the white leaders of the NAACP possessed. However, over the next decade, African-Americans would flood into the NAACP and take its leadership, bypassing Trotter. The main problem was that Trotter's strategy led to
a dead end.

The NIPL emerged from its desultory 1911 convention and wound up arguing for Taft against Roosevelt during the Republican campaign. This was
the same Taft whose supporters Trotter characterized as race traitors in 1908,
and the same Taft that Republican loyalist Booker T. Washington was backing. When Roosevelt formed the Progressive Party after the Republican convention, some civil rights leaders favored Roosevelt. Among those was J. R.
Clifford, president of the NIPL. At a July 1912 meeting, therefore, the NIPL

split. While individual NAACP leaders made their own presidential choices in 1912, the nonpartisan organization did not divide. Trotter, leading one of two groups claiming to be the NIPL, now turned to Democratic presidential candidate Woodrow Wilson. While the NAACP moved forward, the NIPL fragmented over which white presidential candidate to support.[31]

Trotter's group campaigned seriously for Wilson. One week after the inauguration Trotter wired the new president his congratulations. "As editor of the *Guardian*, which alone of the few national Negro newspapers unqualifiedly supported you, as President of the New England Suffrage League which endorsed you from a racial viewpoint, as corresponding secretary of the National Independent Political League . . . I did my utmost to further your election among the colored voters. . . . I greatly desire to have your confidence, and to know and be granted the privilege of consultation on your general policy where we are concerned."[32]

Almost immediately after taking office, President Wilson presided over the segregation of the federal bureaucracy. His decision affirmed Jim Crow as federal policy. Trotter organized two delegations to Wilson, in 1913 and 1914, which brought no changes. Their first meeting was formally correct and Trotter reported it with cautious optimism. In the second meeting Trotter cut off a presidential monologue defending segregation as a boon to the Negro. "We didn't come here as wards of the state," Trotter interjected. Protesting that he had been branded as a race traitor for supporting Wilson (the shoe was now on the other foot), Trotter voiced his disillusionment. "Two years ago you were thought to be a second Abraham Lincoln," he lamented. Wilson was aghast at Trotter's bold manner, reprimanded him while complimenting the other delegates, and curtailed the interview. Trotter then gave his version of the supposedly confidential discussion to the press, further angering Wilson. If ever there was a case of defeat in victory, Trotter's strategy had led to precisely that. The great irony of his career was that he wound up trying to play Booker Washington to Wilson's Theodore Roosevelt.[33]

The effect of Trotter's second interview upon his notoriety was spectacular. The story appeared in the leading national newspapers and in some Boston dailies elbowed aside the news of World War I and the conflict in Mexico. "President Rebukes Boston Spokesman," the *Boston Globe* announced at the top of page one, placing Trotter's picture there for probably the first time.[34]

Trotter tried to capitalize on his new fame. The National Independent Equal Rights League (NIERL; successor to the NIPL) organized a midwestern speaking tour for him, during which he addressed sizable audiences. However, he could not convert these audiences into recruits. Trotter had no talent for building a national organization. Even if he had, it is not clear what that organization could now project. The NIERL replaced the NIPL because the latter organization's support for Wilson was an embarrassment, but Trotter never offered a new strategy or acknowledged the failure of the old one. It should be recalled as well that Wilson was Trotter's second presidential disillusionment. He had backed the winner in 1904 and got Roosevelt and Brownsville, but this time Trotter was notorious as a former Wilson man.[35]

Thus, with no viable strategy to counterpose to the NAACP, toward which Trotter remained neutral, the remainder of his career consisted of a series of isolated episodes. He returned from his Midwest tour to campaign against the film *The Birth of a Nation* when it opened in Boston. He participated in a series of local battles against discrimination in alliance with, but separate from, the NAACP. There was no space on the national stage for two distinct civil rights groups.

Racial Politics, World War, Labor, and Black Nationalism

The death of Booker T. Washington in 1915, the American entry into World War I, the development of a northern black working class and the new rise of nationalism, including black nationalism, presented separate but related opportunities for Trotter to recast his policies. In all four instances he remained an isolated individual, going his own way. The death of his beloved wife and collaborator in 1918 only increased his solitude. Bypassed by larger events to which he could not respond creatively, Trotter apparently jumped (he may have simply fallen) to his death in 1934 on his sixty-second birthday.[36]

Trotter deliberately stayed away from the summer 1916 Amenia Conference organized by the NAACP's Joel Spingarn in the aftermath of Washington's death. While the conference produced no new united organization of Bookerites and militants, it did clear the air and produce a spirit of harmony among race leaders. Trotter aimed simply to recruit to his own (renamed) National Equal Rights League, while a diverse group of Tuskegeans and Niagara men produced joint resolutions and attempted to bury past differences. In a sense, Trotter lost his reason for being with the death of Washington; it was opposition to accommodationist policies that had called the *Guardian* into print. Now he no longer had his opponent.[37]

American entry into the world war provoked a limited opposition by a small group of African-Americans. By a large majority, race leaders supported the war effort and hoped that prejudice would be retarded by the enthusiastic participation of African-Americans in the military. Most leaders agreed to abjure the struggle during the national emergency. Emmet J. Scott served as a special assistant to the secretary of war, essentially charged with organizing

African-American support. Under Du Bois's editorship, the *Crisis* agreed that the special demands of African-Americans could wait. The influential *Chicago Defender* and the *New York Age* led almost the entire African-American press along this line.[38]

Trotter was a reluctant supporter of the war. The *Guardian* dispelled false rumors of pro-Germanism among Negroes and avowed the loyalty of the colored soldier. Unlike other African-American editors, however, he called for the government to fulfill its part of the bargain and grant civil rights. He argued that other aggrieved groups pursued a similar policy. On this issue, Trotter's unique Boston location brought him in touch with another influence that his fellow race leaders did not encounter so directly. "White People Use War as Chance to Secure Redress and Benefits," a *Guardian* headline announced over a story about Irish-American ambivalence regarding the war. "English Moved by Reluctance of Irish-Americans to Enlist Here," ran the next headline. If there was only a germ of truth in this last pronouncement, Trotter was not loath to utilize it. In an editorial, he argued that Negro enlistment should be tied to the demand for justice at home. As the war effort unfolded, Trotter attacked the separate officer training for colored officers that some individual leaders of the NAACP accepted.[39]

This reaction to the war might have brought Trotter into sympathetic cooperation with either those NAACP leaders who opposed the war, or the new young militants like Chandler Owen and A. Philip Randolph who declared their opposition in the *Messenger*. Trotter did sponsor a meeting for Randolph in Boston and Randolph said he "was the only Negro who had the guts to join us on the platform." Trotter had shown some openness to socialist ideas earlier in his career, having invited an African-American socialist to address the Boston Literary and Historical Society. Trotter did invite Randolph to participate in a delegation to President Calvin Coolidge in 1925. Unlike Randolph, however, Trotter did not take an interest in the labor movement. Here again, Trotter was probably influenced by his Boston environment. The number of African-American railroad workers, or white radical workers, was too small to attract him, unlike the situation in New York or Chicago. In addition, Trotter was a Harvard man and Randolph a poor migrant from Florida who had worked in kitchens and studied at City College. Trotter paid little heed to the labor movement.[40]

The last famous episode of Trotter's career was his heroic, quixotic journey to Paris for the National Equal Rights League to represent the cause of African-Americans at the 1919 peace conference. The Wilson administration denied passports to nine NERL representatives but Trotter made his way overseas under an assumed name as a cook's assistant. Arriving in Paris illegally, hungry, penniless, and in rags, he nevertheless deluged the conference with requests for an audience. Ignored, he published articles in the French press on the true condition of African-Americans. When he returned to the United States, he addressed huge audiences in New York and Washington. Then, irony of ironies, he testified before Henry Cabot Lodge's Foreign Relations Committee against the treaty brought home by President Woodrow Wilson. The *Guardian* had lambasted Lodge for his defense of the Brownsville dismissals, but Wilson was the bigger enemy now. Again, Trotter was unable to turn the notoriety of his exploits into a viable organization. This was Trotter's last moment of national attention.[41]

During the 1917–20 period, Trotter developed a new theme in response to the nationalism unleashed by the war. He began to see oppression in international perspective, and to understand the similarities among other dispossessed groups. It was only natural that the ambivalent reaction of Boston's Irish-American population to the peace treaty should cause Trotter to do this. As early as 1915, a representative of the Irish National League began speaking at his meetings. After the war, the *Guardian* covered the Irish-American opposition to the peace terms, pressing the lessons of the Irish struggle on its own constituency.[42]

On the other hand, Trotter was skeptical about Pan-Africanism and black nationalism. He held to the traditional stance derived from antebellum opposition to colonization schemes fostered by whites to banish African-Americans from America. He stressed the Americanism of his people, to whom he referred as "colored Americans," "Negroes," or "Negro-Americans." In 1911 he answered a *Boston Transcript* editorial that wondered at the failure of American Negroes to "civilize" Liberia. He replied that "the colored people here, some of whose very distant relatives were natives of Africa, are Americans, not Africans, not anything else." He stayed away from Du Bois's Pan-Africanist conference in Paris in 1919. When Marcus Garvey's Universal Negro Improvement Association and its "back to Africa" campaign began, the *Guardian* publicly and deliberately dropped the term "Negro" from its columns.[43]

Yet, if Trotter was an integrationist, there is a sense in which he could also be seen as a nationalist. In his insistence upon African-American leadership of the struggle for equality, he foreshadowed the militant organizations of the 1950s and 1960s that bypassed the NAACP. Trotter accepted white members of his organization—the Reverend William Brigham was his lone conspicuous white follower—but the leadership was to be in African-American hands.

LEADER OF BOSTON'S AFRICAN-AMERICAN COMMUNITY

Monroe Trotter played a powerful role on the national stage between 1903 and 1911, when the NAACP began to bypass his political organization. After that, his national influence was episodic. In Boston, he was the leader of the community at least through the struggle against *The Birth of a Nation* in 1915. Unlike the African-American leaders of the Boston NAACP, he earned his living in and depended upon the community for support, as subscribers to and advertisers in his paper. He had crucial backing from the clergy. The *Guardian* championed the cause of local African-Americans and reported on a range of issues important to them. Time and again he built spirited protests in Boston against the oppression of the race in the South. He participated vigorously in local politics, hoping to influence white leaders to act on behalf of the African-American community.

Trotter made an inauspicious start in his relations with the community by promulgating the confrontation with Booker Washington. In Boston, the balance of forces between the two camps may be gauged by the audience at two meetings. Two thousand people came to hear Washington at the AME Zion Church, but not more than a handful of people took part in the disruption. After Trotter's trial and monthlong confinement, he drew some two hundred people to a meeting celebrating his release.[44]

Regardless of the politics of the two antagonists, it is likely that Trotter's tactics only hurt his cause. He might have attempted a dignified and thoughtful critique of Washington's policy from the floor, in the spirit of Du Bois's *Souls of Black Folk*. Had he tried and failed, he would have shown up the controlling and repressive side of Washington's behavior. That he chose to disrupt the meeting with catcalls showed the difference between him and Du Bois, who was ignorant of the event before the fact and disapproved of the tactics afterward.[45]

The white Boston press predictably painted Washington as the victim of an unruly assailant who demonstrated all the emotional qualities of an unstable race, which the wise leader was trying to raise up. The day before, Washington's picture appeared in several newspapers that reported his speech at the nearby Weymouth "Town Day" celebration. Pictured along with the town fathers, Washington paid homage to a locale that had bravely sent its young men forth to the Civil War and its young women south to teach during Reconstruction.[46]

This harmonious scene contrasted sharply with the following day's report of razors, police, tumult, and arrest among "a people quick in anger," as the *Globe* reporter put it. After a description of the conflict, Washington's reasonable speech was reported at length. Urging the Bostonians to learn from thrifty Italian bootblacks who saved their money to go into business for themselves, he held up the wealthy tailor J. H. Lewis as "a great example of what we can do." Washington even gave an anticlerical twist to this appeal to the Horatio Alger myth: "If the colored people of Boston owned as many shoe factories as they owned churches, I suspect that the race in this city would be advanced immensely." He reminded his audience that he did not counterpose higher education to industrial education. According to the *Boston Globe*, Washington received a mighty ovation.[47] Reaction quotations in the *Globe* and *Boston Herald* naturally favored Washington heavily. The *Herald* report began: "One of the most disgraceful scenes ever witnessed in Boston was the deliberate attempt of a few opponents of Booker T. Washington to break up the mass meeting." Edward Everett Brown, an African-American attorney who was on the platform, probably spoke for a wide sector of the community when he said, "Before we can gain the respect of the Anglo-Saxon, we must merit their regard by our own actions." The *Boston Transcript* weighed in with a similar account.[48] This negative press coverage could only have alarmed and embarrassed black Bostonians, regardless of their opinions of Washington's policy of accommodation.

The Washington confrontation also marked a turning point for Trotter in his relations with neo-abolitionists. The Garrison family turned sharply against Trotter, with Francis Jackson Garrison communicating his support immediately to Washington. Others, such as Albert E. Pillsbury, Moorfield Storey, and Richard P. Hallowell, were working in secret with Washington on civil rights cases and/or contributing articles to the pro-Washington *Colored American Magazine*.[49]

Despite this controversial beginning, Trotter took leadership in the community for at least the next decade. The *Guardian* undoubtedly was crucial to his success. The newspaper functioned as a tribune of the people. While it focused on national politics, it also covered the Boston scene to the best abilities of its tiny staff. Sometimes this meant just clipping the Boston press and inserting hortatory headlines; sometimes the Trotters simply covered the activities of their own circle. The *Guardian* denounced police or popular brutality against colored people, maneuvered in local politics, followed deeper issues as they were presented to the Boston Literary and Historical Society, and reported the deeds of outstanding local African-Americans. Like any small-town editor in search of sales, Trotter printed an enormous number of names of ordinary people going about their quiet lives.

The *Guardian* criticized police brutality and racist violence episodically. In general, the *Guardian* praised Boston as a model of what the nation should

126 Boston Confronts Jim Crow

be. However, Trotter was cognizant of police brutality and the concomitant image of the Negro as criminal promoted by the newspapers. The very first issue ran a small article attacking the *Dorchester Beacon*, which demanded a more severe penalty for a colored man who had killed a policeman. The *Guardian* pointed out that the policeman was off duty, out of uniform, and had attacked the man, who proved to be an imbecile. When a Boston patrolman assaulted and arrested an interracial couple, the *Guardian* demanded that the officer be disciplined. Years later, the *Guardian* chastised the police for failing to pursue several incidents in which white thugs, rumored to be a gang called "the Forty Thieves," assaulted colored people. To offset reports of Negro criminality, the *Guardian* countered the hypocrisy of white newspapers by prominently and regularly reprinting reports of white crime with headlines calling attention to the race of the criminals.[50]

In local politics, Trotter campaigned for candidates who promised friendliness to the race, regardless of party. The *Guardian* rarely editorialized on nonracial issues such as the tariff, municipal reform, trust regulation, or foreign policy. This allowed him to support such diverse politicians as Republican Winthrop Murray Crane, and Democrat John F. Fitzgerald.

Trotter first opposed Crane's appointment to fill the Senate seat vacated by the death of anti-imperialist Republican George Frisbee Hoar. With a touch of condescension, Trotter dismissed Crane "even though he is a great friend of the race, although he has on occasion disappointed us," as a poor orator. When Senator Crane resisted the Roosevelt-Lodge-Taft wing of the party after the Brownsville incident, Trotter began to champion his cause. Lodge induced Trotter's disfavor when he gratuitously criticized the African-American regiment. Crane worked in the Senate to facilitate an inquiry into the affair, and Trotter began promoting him for president. He supported Crane's reelection by the legislature in 1912, even though Crane had gone over to the Taft side (which Trotter himself did briefly), explaining that "the only way to have friends in politics is to establish the fact that you will support a friend when he is attacked." If the race turned its back on Crane, "no white man will ever stand up for us in Congress."[51]

On the Democratic side, John F. Fitzgerald was the municipal candidate who most consistently sought black votes as a way of tipping the balance in the factional jungle of party politics. As mayor he did not have to do much to win Trotter's favor. At Trotter's request, Fitzgerald lowered the city flags to half-staff in commemoration of the poet John Greenleaf Whittier's centennial. He appointed Edward Everett Brown to the highest city post occupied by an African-American to that date, assistant health commissioner. At a Faneuil Hall election rally, the highlight of six addressed by the mayor in one day, Fitzgerald condemned the dismissal of the Brownsville troops. Trotter was conspicuously absent from a platform that included Brown, who had testified against him after the Boston Riot, and Archibald H. Grimké, who was working for *Alexander's Magazine*. Nevertheless, the *Guardian* covered the meeting enthusiastically. When Republican George Hibbard ousted Fitzgerald, the *Guardian* noted with derision that his first act was to fire Brown.[52] Trotter was generally in the Democratic camp between 1906 and 1914, from Brownsville to the second Wilson interview.

There is a certain amount of pathos in the energy Trotter extended in these electoral contests. The stakes for African-Americans were small, and in most cases merely symbolic. Such traditional patronage boons as jobs in municipal departments were not even on the agenda in this period. Treatment of African-Americans merited little attention from either politicians or the press. The very parsimony of the promises of white politicians suggests how counterproductive it was for Trotter to allow party loyalties to separate him from Clement Morgan or Butler Wilson, who were steadfast Republicans.

Trotter placed his stamp on the consciousness of the community by acting as high priest of its secular ritual: the Faneuil Hall indignation meeting. Trotter himself usually spoke only briefly at these events, which suggests that his oratorical powers were pale in comparison with the more practiced skills of the clergy. These meetings were organized thematically around a particular outrage, electoral opportunity, or centennial observation. Prominent whites usually spoke along with African-American community leaders to largely black audiences. The meetings were generally well attended and spirited. The *Guardian* would advertise their coming weeks in advance and report them effusively, while the white press would dutifully record the event on inside pages.

One typical meeting, held in May 1902, called for the passage of the Crumpacker Resolution to reduce the congressional representation of those states that disfranchised African-American voters. A speaker from South Carolina denounced a recent lynching there. Trotter used the occasion for a factional attack on Booker Washington. The Reverend William Scott of Woburn, speaking for the Massachusetts Racial Protective Association, read messages of support from the Reverend Johnson W. Hill, a Trotter ally; E. D. Crumpacker of Indiana, sponsor of the resolution; Governor Crane; former governor George S. Boutwell; Moorfield Storey; and others. Edward Everett Brown, Archibald Grimké, Massachusetts Congressman William H. Moody, and former governor John Quincy Adams Brackett spoke. Edwin B. Jourdain of New Bedford presented a resolution that called on the administration to protect the civil and political rights of Negroes, and asked the colored voters of Massachusetts to support only candidates who backed the bill.[53]

Boutwell and Brackett shared the platform two years later when the Boston Suffrage League attacked Republican backsliding on Negro suffrage. The *Guardian* boasted that it was a "monster mass meeting." Clement Morgan was in the chair, and Butler Wilson, the Reverend Francis H. Rowley, and the Reverend Byron Gunner of Newport, Rhode Island, spoke. This meeting showed that within a year of the Boston Riot, Trotter had recaptured the initiative and could still stage significant meetings attracting prominent speakers and large audiences.[54]

In 1905, Trotter celebrated William Lloyd Garrison's centennial, despite the hostility that he had engendered among the abolitionist's children. The Bookerites had the upper hand in that Garrison's descendants were in their camp. Trotter tried to effect at least a truce, seeking a photo of Garrison *père* from *fils* Francis Jackson, who extracted a promise of nonsectarianism from Trotter. "Trotter is inviting [William H.] Lewis to speak as a token of his non-partisanship," Francis Garrison reported to his nephew Oswald Garrison Villard, along with the news of Butler Wilson's inclination to boycott both sides. Wilson was to preside over a united meeting on 10 December at the Joy Street Church, which Garrison decided to address after some hesitation. The moderate group gathered at the AME Zion Church to hear Fanny Villard, Frank Sanborn, Moorfield Storey, Archibald Grimké, James H. Wolff, the commander of the Massachusetts Grand Army of the Republic (who was African-American), and a Tuskegee representative. Trotter held ceremonies at the Garrison gravesite and statue, and at St. Monica's Home for Sick Colored Women. He sponsored two meetings at Faneuil Hall, which heard Garrison family members, *Boston Transcript* editor E. H. Clement, *Boston Herald* editor William Allen, and a host of others. Reverdy Ransom was the keynote speaker, and the *Guardian* reported all events in glowing terms.[55]

These meetings, along with others like the 1907 Elijah Lovejoy and 1911 Sumner celebrations, showed that Trotter had important allies in the African-American community and could build successful community gatherings. White supporters of civil rights generally tried not to take sides, and even after the NAACP's founding they did not universally disdain Trotter's invitations to speak. Moorfield Storey, for example, was particularly sensitive to Trotter's authority in the black community and urged New York NAACP leaders in 1911 not to attack him.[56] During the 1915 fight against *Birth of a Nation*, Trotter was the one who mobilized the community, while the NAACP leaders handled the legal representation before Mayor James Michael Curley, Governor David I. Walsh, and others. That episode will be discussed in the following chapter, and shows that black Bostonians still looked to Trotter for leadership. In other cities, African-Americans were turning to the NAACP, or, a few years later, to nationalism.

While Trotter had needlessly antagonized many people in both the Bookerite and NAACP camps, he had also made and kept many close allies among the African-American clergy, some attorneys, women's club leaders and fraternal lodge men. The church leaders were the most important of this group. Time and again, the Reverends William Scott of Woburn, Reverdy Ransom of the Charles Street AME Church, M. A. N. Shaw of the Twelfth Baptist, Byron Gunner of distant Newport, Rhode Island, and Johnson W. Hill spoke on Trotter's behalf, and probably mobilized their parishioners. Women's club leaders like M. Cravath Simpson and Elks leader Alfred P. Russell probably also brought their sisters and brothers.[57] The movement that Trotter led was rooted in the community, and from it his inspiration sprung.

Trotter's local supporters were activists who made their way to Boston, usually from the South, and were probably overawed by Trotter's Harvard background, driving energy, and principled politics. If they were not necessarily his intellectual equals, neither were they his lieutenants or creations. As community ministers they were talented individuals in their own right.

Scott, Trotter's most loyal supporter, was born a slave in Faquier Co., Virginia, in 1848, ran away during the Civil War and attached himself to the Twelfth Massachusetts Regiment as a quartermaster's boy. After the war he was ordained as a Baptist minister and pastored in Virginia, then Lawrence and Woburn, Massachusetts. Along with George Forbes, he and Trotter founded the *Guardian*, and he appeared at Trotter's side as a key ally until Scott's death in 1910.[58]

Johnson W. Hill, another Virginian, studied in his home state and then at Harvard, Brown, and Newton Theological. In 1898 he became the pastor at the Twelfth Baptist Church, Trotter's favorite venue after Faneuil Hall. He was with Trotter at the Booker Washington confrontation and on the platform at many Trotter meetings.[59]

Mathew Arnold N. Shaw took over at Twelfth Baptist, perhaps after Hill became a medical doctor in 1908, and his name appeared frequently in the *Guardian* until his death in 1924. In 1919, for example, the *Guardian* devoted much of its front page to a Shaw speech calling for self-defense against lynching, contrasting Shaw's address to a more cautious one by Du Bois. Byron Gunner was born in Marion, Alabama, in 1857, educated at Talladega and Oberlin, and became a Congregational minister at Hillburn, New York. For a while he was president of Trotter's National Equal Rights League.[60]

Probably the best orator among Trotter's supporters was Reverdy C. Ransom. Ransom was born in 1861 in Ohio, educated at Oberlin and Wilberforce, and held challenging posts as an AME minister in Ohio, Pennsylvania, and Chicago before coming to New Bedford, and then to Boston in 1905. He was the keynote speaker at the Garrison memorial and other meetings.[61]

Taken as a group, these ministers generally came from lower socioeconomic origins than the Boston elite African-American community leaders. The activists with whom Trotter could not work included people like attorneys Clement Morgan, Archibald Grimké, and Butler Wilson. These three had abilities equal to Trotter's and important ties to white people. George Forbes and William Henry Lewis, southern migrants of humble origin like Trotter's allies, worked briefly with Trotter, but had professions that carried them away from the community—Forbes as a librarian and literary man, Lewis as an attorney. Neither those people who gravitated toward Booker Washington (like Grimké for a few years between 1904 and 1906) nor those who like Wilson, Morgan, or later Grimké, joined the NAACP, were so rooted in the community as Trotter's clerical supporters.[62]

Trotter's influence declined during the 1920s. The apex of Boston's influence within the national African-American polity was over as the Great Migration established Harlem, Chicago's South Side, and Washington, D.C., as the population and power centers of the New Negro of the 1920s. The NAACP grew and attracted new African-American leaders; newspapers like the *Chicago Defender* swamped the *Guardian* in circulation and resources. Trotter was heard from less and less, and in 1934 he apparently jumped to his death, although the newspapers said that he fell. He left no note, but he was obviously in despair. Two thousand mourners came to the funeral, including city and state officials, Harvard classmates, and Elks lodge men, to hear more than a dozen clergymen eulogize him.[63] He was the intellectual child of his militant father, Harvard, elite African-American society, abolitionism, and most of all, the wider Boston African-American community. Always out of step on the national stage, but the central leader in his own city, Trotter's life highlights the uniqueness of Boston's contribution to the African-American struggle.

Francis Jackson Garrison. Courtesy of the Massachusetts Historical Society.

❧❧❧❧❧❧

FIVE

White Into Black
Boston's NAACP, 1909–1920

THE NATIONAL ASSOCIATION for the Advancement of Colored People was born in the aftermath of the August 1908 riot at Springfield, Illinois, that drove thousands of African-Americans from that city. This particular race riot, although part of a wider national pattern, was especially symbolic because it transpired in Abraham Lincoln's hometown one year before the centennial of his birth. After the Springfield violence, a small group of white liberals in New York called for an interracial conference to discuss the status of African-American rights. This National Negro Conference was ostensibly scientific in nature, and refuted the claim that the Negro race was inherently inferior to the white. More significant, the conferees also launched an activist political organization that later became the NAACP, which dates its beginning to the 1909 meeting.[1]

The new association grew out of and was a response to the failure of Progressivism to address the Negro problem. The political movement that sought to regulate the corporation and purify the electoral process generally shared the racial views of the wider society. Many NAACP leaders agreed with the goals of Progressive reform and wanted to apply the movement's methods to American race relations. The outstanding example of this type of leader was Oswald Garrison Villard, a chairman of the association in its pioneer decade. As the grandson of Boston abolitionist William Lloyd Garrison, son of a railroad tycoon, and publisher of the *New York Evening Post* and the *Nation*, he represented the fusion of the old New England antislavery tradition with the Progressive impulse.[2]

Although white reformers began the association, African-Americans organized in William Edward Burghardt Du Bois's Niagara movement joined the new group and thousands of others did as well. By 1920 the association had its first black national secretary in James Weldon Johnson. "This is the only Association in the world where white and colored members work together for the rights of colored people," the organization's literature proclaimed. By 1915 the association had almost five thousand members of whom 80 percent were African-American, organized in thirty branches, and 150,000 readers of its monthly journal, the *Crisis*.[3] Massachusetts-born and Harvard-educated Du Bois, editor of the magazine, played the central role in transforming the association from a group *for* black people to one primarily *of* and led by them. When the NAACP was founded, the accommodationist Booker T. Washington was just past the peak of his national authority, and William Monroe Trotter's activist National Independent Political League was a significant organization. By 1920, no viable national organization represented either's ideology, and the NAACP was the leading civil rights group in the country. The NAACP cooperated with the Urban League, which helped find jobs and housing for black people in the North, and was just beginning its rivalry with Marcus Garvey's Universal Negro Improvement Association. Although many national board members were white, almost all of its branches were led by African-Americans.

Four strategic conceptions were central to the success of the NAACP. Programatically, it pledged to achieve full equality of opportunity in all aspects of life for African-Americans. Second, the NAACP utilized the Progressive approach of educating the public as a means to win legislative and legal battles. A corollary to this strategy was that the association remained nonpartisan and, while it might champion local candidates, it made no lasting pledge to either major party. Third, despite enormous difficulties engendered by the pervasive racism of American society, the association tried to build a biracial organization. Finally, it focused on civil rights, leaving aside wider questions of economic policy, upon which the members disagreed. The leadership included some socialists like William English Walling and Charles Edward Russell, and while Du Bois and Mary White Ovington shared some of their views, they were in a distinct minority. More typical were liberals like Villard, the Reverend John Haynes Holmes and the brothers Joel and Arthur Spingarn. Many branch leaders were committed Republicans, some of whom had traditional party economic views.

The NAACP thus differed from its competitors in the field of representing the interests of African-Americans. The most obvious differences were with Booker T. Washington, who relegated the achievement of equality to a distant future. The association also differed with Boston's William Monroe Trotter, who campaigned aggressively for white politicians, built an all-black movement, and generally eschewed the patient strategy of legislative lobbying and court challenges that were hallmarks of Progressivism. Nor did the NAACP entertain notions of separatism that won Marcus Garvey a following in the early 1920s.[4]

By early 1919, after ten years of existence, the association claimed 56,345 members organized in 220 branches, and the *Crisis* had a circulation of 100,000. By the end of that tumultuous year, the association had 91,203 members organized in 310 branches, about 90 percent of whom were black. This phenomenal increase was facilitated by the Great Migration northward starting around 1915; the raised expectations of African-Americans as a result of their participation in combat during the world war; and the dashing of these hopes by the aftermath of both experiences. A wave of violence greeted the migrants in East St. Louis, Illinois, in 1917. African-American soldiers were provoked into a confrontation in Houston that year that resulted in long prison terms or capital punishment for dozens. Whites attacked blacks in Chicago and Washington, D.C., in 1919 and tenant organizers were massacred in Elaine, Arkansas. The NAACP campaigns against these outrages won it new adherents. It also achieved minor but significant legal victories against disfranchisement and residential segregation. What began as a project of northern white liberals, among whom Bostonians were prominent, had become a national African-American organization.[5]

"DESCENDANTS AND RELATIVES"

Despite the small size of Boston's African-American community, only 13,564 in 1910, Bostonians played a disproportionately powerful role in the new movement. The Boston branch of the NAACP was the largest in the country until 1918, reaching 2,553 members that year, when Washington, D.C., leaders organized energetically among the capital's vast black population. The Boston leaders, mostly white men who descended from the abolitionists either literally or intellectually, drew upon the antislavery tradition of the city to promote the cause. Chapters in New York, Chicago, and Philadelphia faltered as Boston's grew.[6] No city in America had an intellectual and abolitionist history like Boston's and the NAACP crystallized the disparate elements of this past into a new solution.

Initially, the Boston branch was singular in the whiteness of its leadership. When the NAACP held its third annual meeting in Boston in March 1911, the *Boston Globe* noted that "descendants and relatives of William Lloyd Garrison, Parker Pillsbury, Lucretia Mott and representatives of the Channing, Clarke, Bowditch, Atkinson and other families" were in attendance.[7] However, the Boston NAACP was a product of not only the white families identified by the *Globe*, but also of the work of William Cooper Nell, Frederick Douglass, Maria W. Stewart, Charles Lenox Remond, Louis Hayden, and other African-American activists of earlier generations. Fifty years after the Civil War, Boston's antislavery tradition still lived in the actions of the founders of the NAACP.

The leaders of the Boston branch were also remarkably old. They represented the last vigorous defenders of the antislavery tradition in Boston; during the politically quiescent 1920s no new generation, black or white, came forward with like energy. When the Boston branch was formally launched in 1912, Butler Wilson was 52, Moorfield Storey was 67, and Francis Jackson Garrison was 64. They gathered around them a group of abolitionist descendants and aging reformers with distinguished careers and long political histories. Unlike the New York founders of the NAACP, there were no socialists among the Bostonians, perhaps because the Boston labor movement was more conservative and Irish than New York's. The New Yorkers also included secular Jewish-Americans like Henry Moscowitz and the brothers Joel and Arthur Spingarn; the Bostonians were largely Yankee Protestants.

The Bostonians weighed heavily in the councils of the national organization. They included powerful legal figures like Storey, Albert E. Pillsbury, and Butler Roland Wilson. Wilson and his wife Mary Evans Wilson were the most prominent African-American leaders; attorney Clement Morgan was less active. Francis Jackson Garrison, youngest son of William Lloyd Garrison, was the president of the branch until his death in 1916 and he corresponded at least weekly with his nephew Oswald Garrison Villard, plying him with ideas and information. Horace Bumstead, Civil War veteran and former president of Atlanta University, was an early influence upon Du Bois when the latter was a faculty member at Atlanta University. The branch treasurer from 1911 to 1920, businessman George G. Bradford, corresponded with several national leaders regarding the association's policies, as did Joseph Prince Loud, branch president after Garrison's death in 1916.

Although most of the leadership was white, the Wilsons directed much of the association's activity. Butler Wilson was the original secretary of the branch and a national board member from 1913 onward; Mary Wilson was a traveling organizer who recruited thousands of new members in several northern states. In the 1920s Butler Wilson became the official branch president. He moved to Boston in 1881 after growing up near Atlanta and attending Atlanta University. After receiving a law degree at Boston University he worked with Archibald H. Grimké on the *Hub*, an African-American weekly, in the mid-1880s. As an attorney he was pronounced a master of chancery by the governor, and his clients were mostly white people. Early in his career he represented William Henry Lewis in an 1893 case that culminated in a legislative expansion of the state's civil rights law. As an upper-class militant he presided over an anti–Booker Washington meeting at Young's Hotel on 24 April 1899. He was one of the original signers of the call for the Niagara movement, but was probably not very active in it. Wilson also kept his distance from Monroe Trotter in the pre–NAACP years, but was friendly with Francis Jackson Garrison.[8]

Mary Evans Wilson was also a transplanted southerner. Like most women of her day she played a less prominent public role than her husband, but a nontheless indispensable one in building the organization behind the scenes. She did speak publicly, and in 1915 she toured Ohio, western New York, and Pennsylvania, laying the groundwork for new branches in those states, meeting with church and community leaders and recruiting them to the NAACP. She made similar tours in New Jersey, and led the recruitment of two thousand African-Americans to the Boston NAACP after the world war.[9]

More than anyone else, the Wilsons convinced African-American Bostonians to join the NAACP. They did this in a community divided among supporters of Booker Washington, Monroe Trotter, and probably a majority who saw some merit to each approach. The Wilsons linked the black community and an organization that many African-Americans at first probably saw as an elite white ally. The NAACP wooed moderate African-American Bookerites like Maria Baldwin, Josephine St. Pierre Ruffin, James H. Wolff, and Edward Everett Brown with varying degrees of success. Like most white NAACP leaders, Butler Wilson was a middle-class integrationist. In a revealing moment, he once told Mary White Ovington as they passed some dice-throwing black youth that if they would not go to an integrated YMCA they could "rot." He was light-hued enough that, on a visit to Du Bois's office in New York, he was mistaken for a white man, and, arriving without an appointment, never got in to see the editor, who was, ironically, of similar color. In politics, Wilson was a regular Republican, but he got along socially with political independents in the NAACP like Archibald Grimké, Moorfield Storey, and Francis Jackson Garrison. This suggests that Wilson, like other prominent African-American NAACP leaders, lived at the junction of several intersecting racial, professional, class, and political worlds.[10]

Storey was the first national president of the association and its most respected legal strategist. A corporation lawyer, as a young man he had been a secretary to Massachusetts Senator Charles Sumner during Reconstruction. He crafted the organization's Supreme Court cases against the "grandfather" clause in an Oklahoma case, another against a residential segregation order in Louisville, Kentucky, and he was an architect of the campaign against lynching. The association honored him by naming its first recruitment drive for him. Storey was also a prominent leader of the anti-imperialist movement, and his protean career is the subject of three biographies. Because he acted more upon the national than the local scene, his contribution will be more fully discussed in a subsequent chapter on law.[11]

Another prominent attorney in the Boston NAACP was Albert E. Pillsbury, a nephew of the Garrisonian abolitionist Parker Pillsbury. He served as Massachusetts attorney general between 1891 and 1894 and had been a lecturer in constitutional law at Boston University Law School. In 1901 he counseled Booker Washington on how best to challenge Louisiana's disfranchisement law, but the case did not come to court. Testifying to Pillsbury's difficult personality, Moorfield Storey advised Villard that he "is very much in earnest, but his manner and attitude are such that most of us here find it impossible to work with him. I have a very sincere respect for him, and I get along with him, but it is not always easy."[12] Pillsbury's generally gloomy assessments of the prospects for change never destroyed his own commitment to the cause. "Candidly, and between ourselves, the movement has turned out a disappointment to me," he wrote to NAACP leader Mary White Ovington as early as January 1912. He had hoped for a movement of "commanding national influence and authority . . . especially to develop a counteracting and nullifying influence to the pernicious activities of Booker T. Washington." He later warned Archibald Grimké testily against beginning an agitation for voting rights in the aftermath of American intervention in the world war. Nevertheless, he was a frequent public speaker for the Boston branch and a legal adviser nationally.[13]

Clement Morgan was not especially active in the branch's work, but his membership on the executive committee suggested that the leadership wanted to encourage African-American participation. Morgan (1859–1929) was a Virginia-born son of slaves. He moved to Boston around 1885, worked his way through Harvard and was chosen as Class Day orator in 1890. He attended Harvard Law School, and practiced law in Cambridge for the rest of his career. As a student he was a friend of Du Bois, and later was his closest ally and the key leader of the local Niagara movement. The antipathy of Morgan and Du Bois toward Trotter carried over into the period of building the NAACP. Against the wishes of whites in the fledgling group, Morgan counterposed his own Charles Sumner memorial meeting to a similar Trotter-sponsored event in January 1911.[14] During Du Bois's conflict with Villard in the NAACP national office, Morgan backed Du Bois, which further alienated him from some of the white Boston leaders. May Childs Nerney, attempting to mediate the national office dispute, wrote to Archibald

Grimké of a "Morgan-Hare" clique in the Boston branch that was opposed to the local leadership, probably for its failure to support Du Bois. The "Hare" to whom Nerney referred was the pianist Maud Cuney Hare, with whom Du Bois had fallen in love while at Harvard. There were probably some racial tensions within the Boston NAACP as well as tensions between the white-led group and more moderate or radical African-American activists. The Boston NAACP leaders were acutely conscious of these problems and did what they could to broaden the leadership base.[15]

Beside these lawyers the Boston NAACP had other prominent national leaders. Francis Jackson Garrison, discussed earlier as a supporter of Booker Washington, was a loyal son of his famous father and typified the second-generation abolitionist. Born in 1848, he set the type on the last issue of the *Liberator* with his father, and wrote William Lloyd Garrison's biography with one of his brothers. For most of his adult life he worked as an editor at Houghton Mifflin, and served as a curator and chronicler of the abolition movement. He had been an enthusiastic supporter of Booker Washington, but became the first president of the Boston NAACP and held the post until his death in December 1916. Joseph Prince Loud, an architect, succeeded Garrison as branch president upon the latter's death. He married May Hallowell, of the Quaker abolitionist family. (Richard Price Hallowell had recruited troops for the Massachusetts 54th and 55th Regiments; Colonel Norwood Penrose Hallowell commanded black troops during the war; May Hallowell Loud and J. Mott Hallowell were NAACP activists.) Adelene Moffatt, a social worker originally from Kentucky, and Rolfe Cobleigh, the assistant editor of the *Congregationalist*, complete the picture of NAACP leaders with successful careers and/or some abolitionist heritage.[16]

A RECORD OF LOCAL ACTIVISM

The NAACP made its first major impact on Boston when the third national conference was held at the Park Street Church in March 1911. This was a particularly difficult moment for the new group. It had on its board many contributors to Tuskegee Institute, and some of its members, especially Trotter and his allies, might attack Booker Washington. The principal was then particularly vulnerable. A few weeks before the meeting, a white New Yorker physically assaulted Washington, accusing him of peeking through a keyhole at a woman. The police arrested the white man, but Washington could not explain why he was at the building, and he refused to press charges. The Boston NAACP leaders explored a variety of responses to the highly publicized incident, and ultimately passed a resolution condemning the assault without commenting on Washington's mysterious behavior. Trotter also came to Washington's defense, although a few months later he insisted that Washington should charge his attacker. Not even Washington's judicious biographer can explain the affair, which marked a deterioration of Washington's position.

Between eight hundred and one thousand people attended and the local press reported the conference favorably. Moorfield Storey presided at the opening session, insisting that the Civil War amendments be revived and that Negroes be guaranteed full rights and the equal protection of the law. Mayor John F. Fitzgerald greeted the conferees warmly, and Villard, Du Bois, Adelene Moffatt, and Rabbi Charles Fleischer took up separate themes calling for full equality. Pillsbury chaired the next session, which heard from reformers Florence Kelley, John E. Milholland, and Mary Church Terrell. The following day Samuel J. Elder, Rabbi Stephen S. Wise of New York, and the Reverend G. R. Waller of Baltimore spoke. Monroe Trotter praised the meeting, encouraged Boston African-Americans to attend, and ignored its results. Neither the daily press nor the *Crisis* reported on the racial composition of the assembly. Clearly, the prominence of the speakers, the press coverage, and the attendance augured well for the new association.[17]

The following May, fifty-eight people came to an organizational meeting that addressed the question of separate black community institutions by insisting upon the rights of African-Americans to participate in all aspects of American life. When the Boston Floating Hospital refused to employ African-American nurses and the YMCA discriminated against black members, the NAACP sent protest letters to each offending board of directors. At a time when white ethnic groups were establishing their own social institutions, the local NAACP never publicly expressed itself on African-American efforts to build separate medical or recreational facilities. Later in the month, the NAACP intervened on behalf of a woman denied a diploma from the Boston School for Domestic Science, and had the decision overturned.[18]

In November, Trotter and the NAACP showed they could peacefully coexist during the Wendell Phillips centennial celebration. This occasion was the last citywide celebration of the life of a once-scorned abolitionist now safely deceased. One hundred thousand public school students participated in various ceremonies throughout the metropolitan area. At the NAACP's meeting, Wendell Phillips Stafford, an associate justice of the Washington, D.C., Supreme Court and grandson of a Massachusetts abolitionist, gave the keynote address. Stafford eulogized not only Phillips's abolitionism, but also his fight for labor reform. Moorfield Storey decried the denial of justice to Negroes in the courts, and the increasing sadism of lynch mobs. Recalling the August lynching of a colored man at Coatesville, Pennsylvania, he said there would have been a greater storm of protest had the victim been a dog.[19]

In January 1912, Du Bois toured Massachusetts reporting on the 1911 Races Conference in London. He spoke in Boston at the Twentieth Century Club, and at Braintree and Brockton. This sojourn helped lay the basis for the 8 February meeting of fifty-six people that formally founded the Boston branch. Joel Spingarn of New York gave the main address. Garrison was elected president; Wilson, secretary; and George Bradford, treasurer. The executive committee consisted of Maria Baldwin, Horace Bumstead, Joseph Loud, May Hallowell Loud, Adelene Moffatt, and Clement Morgan. Thus three of the top nine leaders were African-Americans, but only Wilson was consistently active. Also, three of the nine were women.[20]

The Boston NAACP fought against the American Bar Association when it attempted to draw the color line against three African-American attorneys. The ABA admitted Bostonians Butler Wilson and William Henry Lewis and Minnesotan William R. Morris without realizing that they were black. Lewis was by far the most prominent of the three, and the ABA's executive committee voted to expel him in 1912. The ABA discovered the race of Wilson and Morris after its 1912 executive committee meeting and before its annual convention; they were asked to resign by mail.[21]

As the ABA conference approached, Albert E. Pillsbury and five other members of the Massachusetts Bar Association solicited the opinion of the Massachusetts members by circular letter, finding that a huge majority of respondents opposed the expulsion of Lewis (220-4) and the introduction of the color line into the ABA (218-6). Pillsbury and Boston Juvenile Court Chief Justice Harvey Humphrey Baker carried the fight to the floor of the convention. Attorney General George W. Wickersham stood up for Lewis, but did not oppose barring African-Americans in the future. The ABA had no formal policy at the time, but it did have an unspoken tradition of racial exclusivity. Henceforth, the ABA decided that applicants would have to declare their race.[22] Morris, the Minnesotan, thereupon withdrew from the organization as the only way to maintain his self-respect. Wilson vowed to stay and fight. Storey drew up a circular letter to all ABA members that was signed by leaders of the Massachusetts Bar Association, and by 1914 the ABA retracted a section of its Milwaukee resolution which stated that the admission of blacks had never been contemplated by the Bar Association. This cleared the way for African-American attorneys to join the ABA.[23]

The irascible Pillsbury fired off an angry letter of resignation to the ABA in 1913. "A handful of southern colorphobes, with the help of the usual northern majority, have captured it and turned it into a sort of Bourbon club. . . . The

Association is no longer a Bar Association in any proper sense," he declared. The northern press generally supported the NAACP position, the Boston press especially, and despite Pillsbury's gloomy prognostication, the NAACP opened the doors of American life a bit wider through this episode.[24]

The year 1913 marked the fiftieth anniversary of the Emancipation Proclamation, and if the event was celebrated by the various Boston factions separately, the spirit of factionalism was missing. The Wendell Phillips Memorial Association held a meeting at the Park Street Church, addressed by Trotter and future governor Samuel W. McCall, and a smaller meeting sponsored by the Lincoln Memorial Society was chaired by Butler Wilson. Former Harvard president Charles W. Eliot gave a Booker Washington–like speech, and Trotter ally Reverdy Ransom was also on the platform, suggesting that factional tensions were diminishing. Garrison reported Trotter's meeting favorably to Villard.[25]

On Lincoln's birthday Pillsbury spoke for the NAACP at its commemoration, declaring that the president would always be remembered as "an emancipator of a race and martyr of freedom." He praised Lincoln as a man of complete sincerity, who lived by his antislavery sentiments. Thus, the generation of abolitionist descendants rejected the criticisms of Lincoln by their antecedents. Uncle Parker Pillsbury had once vowed that, "by the grace of God and the Saxon tongue," he would fight the "hypocrisy and cruelty" of Lincoln. Wendell Phillips saw Lincoln as "a huckster in politics," but the NAACP leaders wisely projected themselves as legitimate heirs of Lincoln, implying that those who sought to curtail civil rights were violating his legacy.[26]

Among these violators of the Lincoln legacy was Woodrow Wilson, the newly sworn president of the United States, whose postmaster-general, Albert S. Burleson, initiated the segregation of the federal departments as early as April 1913. Not only were civil service workers segregated, but black political appointees were generally let go and replaced by whites. Southerners were more dominant in the administration and in Congress than at any time since the Civil War, and Wilson's election put wind in the sails of Negro-haters everywhere. One by one the federal departments were segregated, and opponents of the new policy dismissed. Segregation was now national, and integration local.[27]

The irony of this situation was that Villard, Du Bois, Storey, and Trotter had all supported Wilson in the election of 1912. The Progressive Villard had been an enthusiastic backer of Wilson. Du Bois had first hoped for a Theodore Roosevelt victory, and several NAACP leaders acting as individuals urged a civil rights plank on the Bull Moose convention, only to be rudely rebuffed. Du Bois then turned to Wilson, who signed a vague statement promising "justice" for African-Americans. The Boston NAACP leaders, perhaps because they lived in a city dominated by Irish Democratic politicians they considered corrupt, were more chary of Wilson. Moorfield Storey reluctantly voted for him, but six months into the new administration he reminded Villard that the president "was a man of southern antecedents, and I have never really believed that he did not share the race prejudice which is today the fashion." Francis Jackson Garrison warned against any overture to Roosevelt, whom he hated as a proven racist and imperialist. Garrison warned Villard that "someday you will have to train your guns on Wilson." Butler Wilson, a lifelong Republican, probably stayed with Taft. Unlike Monroe Trotter's movement, which divided over the 1912 contest, the NAACP did not endorse presidential candidates as an organization, and suffered no internal crisis over the election.[28]

At the national level, Villard attempted to persuade Woodrow Wilson to establish a Race Commission, which in true Progressive fashion would study the problem and solve it. The president led Villard on for a while, but backed down, sacrificing black rights on the altar of wider reform for which he needed southern support. By August 1913, just as Garrison predicted, the NAACP rebuked the president, issuing a public letter of protest that was widely reported in the national press.[29]

In Boston, Trotter sought the advice of Storey, a fellow Woodrow Wilson supporter. He invited the NAACP leader to appear before a September meeting of his organization. Storey declined, but replied that "we should approach the President as his friends and supporters, presenting to him our views with courtesy. . . . This is no time to abuse him, to cast doubt upon his motives, to assume that what his subordinates have done will be sustained by him." Trotter duly followed Story's advice, and found himself left behind as the national black press vented its anger upon the president.[30]

The Boston NAACP, despite Storey's caution, joined in the nationwide attack that the association launched against segregation in the capital. Whatever his reservations, Storey chaired a 20 October meeting at the Park Street Church at which Minnesota Senator Moses E. Clapp, Pillsbury, Butler Wilson, assistant editor of the *Congregationalist* Rolfe Cobleigh, and the Reverends Theodore A. Auten and Samuel A. Crothers hotly arraigned the president's segregation policy. Governor Eugene Foss, Congressman A. P. Gardner, and other prominent citizens sent messages of support, and the assembly dispatched a sternly worded telegram to the White House. "With the meeting as a whole, Pillsbury, who had been very lukewarm and hesitant, was thoroughly delighted, and Clapp's speech he thought extraordinarily good," Garrison reported to his nephew.[31]

This was followed by another meeting at Faneuil Hall on 1 December. Butler Wilson appealed to the African-American community's church leaders to attend. "My only regret is that the brunt of labor for our meetings falls on Butler Wilson, who is overloaded. He is going now to go personally to all the Masonic bodies of colored men to stir them up," Garrison informed Villard. The Odd Fellows responded to Wilson's appeal by marching to the meeting from the West End, led by the Reverend (Congregationalist) Samuel A. Brown. A second march came from the South End, and many African-American clergymen sat on the NAACP's platform. Among the speakers were Storey, Villard, Bumstead, and Rabbi M. M. Eichler.[32]

This meeting was clearly a triumph for the association, and for Butler Wilson personally. For the first time the NAACP worked in tandem with African-American church and fraternal groups. The budding relationship was facilitated by Trotter's more cautious approach toward Woodrow Wilson. He was still pursuing an inside track, not wishing to burn his bridges to the president. His supporters gathered signatures on a petition that they presented to him at the White House. Meanwhile, the Boston NAACP was openly mobilizing the black community to protest in the streets. Butler Wilson's lifelong Republican loyalties probably made this an emotionally satisfying task. Trotter and the NAACP were working on "parallel lines" as Trotter's biographer Stephen Fox notes, but the NAACP's officially nonpartisan stance left it more free to attack the Democratic president.[33]

The association helped prepare these inroads by participating in local battles against race prejudice, usually by exerting the authority its leaders possessed as attorneys or distinguished citizens. For example, when a light-skinned African-American child was removed from a private kindergarten after her race was discovered, the NAACP objected, arguing that the school was in part public and tax-supported. The teacher relented and a small victory was gained. The YMCA barred an African-American member from its swimming pool, so Wilson and Garrison spoke before the board and won a reversal. "I know Arthur Johnson, the president, and . . . I think the Directors will hardly care for the advertising I assured them the institution would receive if they drew the color line," Garrison wrote. When a high school graduate was kept from a dental school because of his color, the NAACP overturned that decision as well. These important individual victories helped establish the NAACP as a fighter for African-American rights.[34]

The NAACP launched social service agencies such as the Committee on Industrial Opportunities and a legal aid bureau. The former drew up a list of businesses that employed African-Americans, thus providing a refutation to the common argument of prospective employers that white workers would always object to black co-workers. The committee also intervened on behalf of workers who suffered employment discrimination, defending in one case a civil service employee released from her job. The legal aid bureau reported helping thirty-three people in 1913 and the same number in 1919.[35] In 1916 Jane R. Bosfield, an African-American stenographer at the Medfield Asylum, was fired for insubordination when she refused to eat apart from the white employees. Although the newspaper accounts do not say that her attorney was an NAACP lawyer, the association's mere existence certainly encouraged African-Americans like the nineteen-year-old Bosfield to stand up for their rights.[36]

In November 1914 the association convinced the Boston School Committee to dispense with the songbook "Forty Best Old Songs," which included objectionable lyrics. An integrated group of protesters attended a School Committee meeting and Storey, Wilson, the Reverends Montrose W. Thornton of the First AME Church and Samuel A. Brown of St. Mark's Congregational testified to the harm done to children by lyrics about contented "darkies" on the old plantation. NAACP member Elizabeth Putnam presented a protest petition with the names of eminent Boston citizens, and the case was quickly won. The books cost $1,500, but the committee agreed after an hour of hearings to dispose of them. "The colored ministers made an admirable protest to the School Committee," Garrison noted with satisfaction. When southern school boards, hearing of the clamor in Boston, requested the books for their districts, the publisher replied that the entire edition had been discontinued.[37]

Having taken on the Wilson administration and local discrimination, the Boston NAACP next turned to congressional attempts to legislate against intermarriage. The dominance of southerners in Wilson's cabinet emboldened legislators who sought to limit civil rights. They moved first against a practice of which most people of both races probably disapproved. Garrison wrote to Massachusetts Senators Henry Cabot Lodge and John W. Weeks and several congressmen to ascertain their views. Weeks supported the bill, and Lodge condemned intermarriage as harmful to both races, but was not sure that legislation banning it was appropriate. Garrison replied that Booker Washington and Frederick Douglass, as the products of interracial parentage, proved that there was nothing wrong with intermarriage.[38]

The centerpiece of the local campaign was a large public meeting held on 7 March, "Daniel Webster's Day," Garrison sarcastically noted. For Garrison, the present was always inextricably linked with the antislavery past and his father's battles with conservatives like Daniel Webster, whose Seventh of March speech justified the Fugitive Slave Act. The meeting was attended by 3,200 people, by far the largest event the association had staged. Congressman Martin B. Madden of Illinois was the featured orator, and Mary Wilson and New Yorker Joel Spingarn spoke for the association. The congressman attacked the disproportionate number of southern committee chairmen in Congress due to the seniority system and the single party dominance of the South. As for intermarriage, he probably voiced the sentiments of most northerners by opposing both the practice and the laws against it. Perhaps because intermarriage was so unusual anyway, Congress never passed the bill.[39] The meeting also marked further progress for the NAACP within the African-American community. "All the papers gave fair reports and we feel we have strengthened our grip here," Garrison wrote. "The colored ministers cooperated splendidly and rally their people to us."[40]

Nevertheless, Garrison's letter reveals a clear distinction in his mind between "them" and a white "us," a theme that was to assume more importance as the black community continued to mobilize. During the 1915 campaign against the film *The Birth of a Nation*, the NAACP served as spokespeople to the powerful, while Trotter served as spokesman for the community. We shall consider this struggle in a separate section. Boston NAACP members, especially Moorfield Storey, also helped craft the national campaign against lynching, which will be discussed in the chapter on law.

Until the 1960s, a significant amount of the NAACP's energy was devoted to opposing the extradition of accused felons from northern to southern states, by arguing that the accused might be lynched. The Boston branch defended John Johnson, who fled Charleston, West Virginia, after being accused of a crime against a white woman. In late 1917, Massachusetts governor Samuel McCall refused to extradite Johnson, accepting the NAACP argument. West Virginia, a relatively liberal border state, took the issue to federal court the following spring and Butler Wilson, William Henry Lewis, and Richard W. Hale argued the case and won. The lawyers worked without pay for ten days, and the Boston branch and national office of the NAACP covered the legal expenses.[41]

As African-American troops fought and died in the world war, their consciousness was transformed by the experience of combat, and the contradiction of fighting a war for democracy when it was denied to them at home. The Boston branch defended the men of the Thirteenth Battalion, 151st Depot Brigade of African-American troops, who were waiting to be demobilized in October 1918 at nearby Fort Devens. The problem arose when white New England officers were replaced by southerners. The new officers began cursing, hitting, and humiliating the troops by assigning unnecesary labor details. The officers expressed openly racist sentiments, and the soldiers, unaccustomed to such treatment and in no mood to endure it, complained to the War Department. Emmet J. Scott, the former aide to Booker Washington who oversaw race relations in the War Department, dispatched an envoy who apparently reported that the problem had been resolved.[42]

This hasty conclusion proved to be overoptimistic. Private Harold W. Coleman of the 151st wrote to the NAACP in New York that "they are now issuing to our sergeants, who are white men, revolvers. Since they choose to regard us as so many dogs or slaves we have lost interest in it all." This was the voice of the New Negro, who in civilian dress was joining the NAACP or the Marcus Garvey movement and changing the face of racial politics. Coleman's implication was that the small arms issued to the sergeants were designed to be used against the black soldiers. "Officers have told men that they would court-martial them if they caught them using a white man's latrine again," wrote Nelson Dukes of the 443rd Reserve Labor Battalion a few months later. Besides the usual gripes about food and pay, Dukes reported that a soldier who complained to the War Department had been busted in rank from corporal to private.[43]

Butler Wilson went to Fort Devens to investigate, and found that the Dukes allegations were true. Wilson tried to find noncommissioned officers who would swear out affidavits, but the situation was resolved without legal action. At its annual meeting at the end of 1919, the branch reported that it "used its influence for the discharge of these men with varying degrees of success; the men being discharged here and there, but not in large numbers." That the soldiers had turned first to the NAACP for aid indicated the authoritative position the association occupied, nationally and locally, by the end of the decade.[44]

THE NAACP VERSUS *THE BIRTH OF A NATION*

During the fight against the David Wark Griffith movie *The Birth of a Nation* the NAACP was still in transition to achieving this prominence. It functioned with the community's support as legal and public relations advocate, but Monroe Trotter was still the spokesperson for the black community when it gathered together. The two groupings conducted separate but related activities, keeping their factional rivalries hidden from view.

Griffith's masterpiece opened in Los Angeles in February 1915 and the battle to ban the film began immediately. Based on Thomas Dixon's novel *The Clansman*, the motion picture portrayed robed nightriders as saviors of the white South, a land ravaged during Reconstruction by debauched African-Americans and cynical northern politicians. Brilliantly innovative in its cinematic technique, the film depicted African-American males as rapacious, ignorant, and corrupt. Dixon showed the film to his old schoolmate Woodrow Wilson, who allegedly declared the new medium to be "like writing history with lightning." Lynching increased during 1915, and during one showing of the film in Indiana, a white man shot a black youth. Shortly after the film came to Boston in April 1915, Jewish factory manager Leo Frank was lynched in Georgia after his death sentence was commuted to life imprisonment. Racial tension nationally was simmering, and the Griffith film raised the temperature.[45]

The NAACP by this time had the advantage of being a biracial national organization with a directing center. When Butler Wilson notified headquarters that the film was scheduled to open in Boston on 10 April, requesting "all facts you have against the abomination," May Childs Nerney could furnish the branches with the necessary details. A voluntary board of censorship in New York had approved the show, but only after being apprised by the producer that $100,000–$200,000 had been invested in production and advertising. One viewer reportedly vowed to "kill every nigger I know" after seeing the film, Nerney wrote.[46]

Advocates of banning the movie had to make the difficult case, however, that the film in fact inspired racist violence. It was one thing to argue that the film slandered black people, or that it was historically inaccurate, but those problems did not meet the test posed by legitimate advocates of free speech. Censorship was practiced widely in the early twentieth century, usually on the Victorian ground of restricting lewdness, and Boston of course was already famous for its puritanical squelching of the theater. The challenge for Griffith opponents was to stick to the only valid reason to ban the film: that it posed a real danger to African-American physical safety.

This was difficult to do in Boston. Unlike most other northern cities, Boston still was relatively free of racist violence. Besides that, there was a real temptation to argue for suppression on puritanical grounds. Mayor James Michael Curley and Brahmin Boston, through its Watch and Ward Society, shared an abhorrence of public reference to sexuality. Curley had even censored barefoot dancing on the Boston stage. *The Birth of a Nation*, with its theme of black male lust for white women, was, by Boston standards, suggestively pornographic.[47]

Curley assented to the association's request that a public hearing be held on the film, and Mary White Ovington came up from New York to appear before the mayor. Although she was determined to press the case that the film might encourage racist violence, when she confessed to being shocked at the film's eroticism, the wily Curley suggested that Shakespeare could be banned on the same ground. Ovington, still hoping for positive action by Curley, found him to be "a democratic and kindly Irishman." Trotter made a direct, political appeal to Curley, in language that he might be expected to understand: colored people had voted for him; he, Trotter, had endorsed him, and now it was time to pay his political debts. Curley, to the consternation of his mostly African-American audience, requested Griffith to cut some scenes that might be construed as lewd, to which Griffith agreed, and the film was shown as scheduled.[48]

One week later, Trotter, the Reverend Aaron W. Puller and nine others were arrested at a Saturday night melee at the Tremont Theater where the film was being shown. On Sunday, Trotter and Frank Sanborn, a surviving member of John Brown's Secret Six financial backers, hosted a Faneuil Hall meeting attended by fifteen hundred people, mostly African-American. Trotter was the featured speaker, and he arraigned both Curley and two members of the National Negro Business League who allegedly had defended the movie (both later denied doing so). A host of African-American ministers also spoke.[49]

The next day a throng of about the same size descended on the statehouse. Attorneys Butler Wilson, William Henry Lewis, and three others met with Governor David I. Walsh, who issued a statement of sympathy and support, promising to press for new state legislation if no redress could be gained at an upcoming court hearing. While Trotter was not in the small group that met with the governor, Walsh called upon him to address the crowd. During the next week, Storey, Wilson, Lewis, Adelene Moffatt, J. Mott Hallowell, and other leaders testified either in court for a restraining order against the theater manager or in a state legislative committee on behalf of the Lewis R. Sullivan bill, which would establish a new censorship board. The judge effectively consented to restrain lewdness rather than racism; the legislature debated transferring Curley's power to a state committee, composed of Boston's mayor, the police commissioner (then a state appointee), and the chief justice of the municipal court.[50]

The association backed the bill, which would prohibit "any show or entertainment which tends to excite racial or religious prejudice or tends to a breach of the public peace." The motivation for the state board was that 85 percent of the movies shown in the state were shown in Boston. NAACP leaders Storey, Wilson, Moffatt, and J. Mott Hallowell testified for the bill along with moderate attorney William Henry Lewis and a group of Congregational and Unitarian ministers.[51]

The language of this bill was excessively broad, even for 1915, and the theater owners made the most of it. They ran large ads in the newspapers, urging legislators to "Kill the Sullivan Bill." The ads reprinted editorials from the Boston dailies, all making free speech arguments. "Were such a statute in operation today our citizens of German sympathies could prevent by resolutions of protest or threats of violence the exhibition of any film showing the devastation in Belgium," read the excerpt from the *Boston Transcript*. The *Boston Journal* approved the contents of the film as "patriotic" and "true Americanism." An editorial entitled "The Throttling of the Theater" in the *Boston Globe* took a neutral view of the film but rejected the increased powers of censorship granted to the state by the Sullivan bill. The newspapers may have been influenced by their advertising budgets, according to Rolfe Cobleigh, NAACP member and editor of the *Congregationalist and Christian World*. Decrying editorial support for the movie, he pointed out that the *Boston Post* had at first denounced the film, but changed its tune when it began running advertisements for the movie. Cobleigh opposed the film as "un-Christian" and agreed that it should be banned.[52]

Beside the newspapers, other voices opposed banning the film. Rabbi Charles Fleischer, who had earlier supported the NAACP, testified against banning the film on the ground that it would force the country to face the race problem. As a Jew, he said, he did not enjoy Shylock, but he argued that the Jews had been strengthened by persecution. "The Negroes have made splendid progress in the last fifty years but the large majority of them are still children, and this statement is proven by their action in Boston." Writing in the *Boston Herald* Fleischer defended the film's portrayal of Reconstruction as accurate. Moorfield Storey replied to Fleischer, correcting his version of Reconstruction history and condemning the film as a corrupter of public morals.[53]

In its campaign to defend African-American character and accurate Reconstruction history, the association was as successful as print and speech could be against the new medium of film. The *Boston Post* and the *Boston Traveller* proved to be the friendliest outlets for the NAACP. The *Traveller* ran a long article contrasting the actual record of the Ku Klux Klan in the Carolinas, the setting of the film, to the Griffith version. These papers also printed letters from NAACP members and supporters. During the public meetings before the mayor, the state legislative committee, and the municipal judge, the NAACP leaders were the most prominent spokespeople against the film. Nevertheless, while the debate raged, thousands of Bostonians flocked to the theaters.[54]

On 26 April, the African-American community mobilized in two more shows of determination against the film and Mayor Curley. In the afternoon, eight hundred women formed a protective league, led by Mrs. Olivia Ward Bush-Banks, Minnie T. Wright, and Dr. Alice McKane. Clement Morgan, Trotter, and his ally the Reverend M. A. N. Shaw, at whose Twelfth Baptist Church the meeting was held, spoke along with the women leaders. That night, Trotter's National Independent Equal Rights League overflowed the same AME Zion Church at which he had confronted Booker Washington twelve years earlier. Key Trotter allies attorney Emery T. Morris, the Reverends Shaw and Puller, and other speakers prepared the crowd for the struggle to come. The next day five hundred "mostly colored" people packed the state Judiciary Committee hearings on the Sullivan bill, making their feelings known by a disciplined presence.[55]

The groups held separate protest meetings on Sunday, 2 May, the NAACP at the Tremont Temple and Trotter's group immediately afterward, outside on the Common. The meetings were roughly equal in size and probably drew overlapping constituencies. The press described the NAACP's audience as largely "colored." Its speakers' list was equally white, featuring former Harvard president Charles W. Eliot, Dr. S. M. Crothers, an African-American clergyman, Dr. Francis Rowley, Adelene Moffatt, Rolfe Cobleigh, and Susan Fitzgerald. Judge Phillip Rubenstein and Rabbi M. M. Eichler effectively rebutted Rabbi Fleischer's argument about race discrimination as a character-builder. Eliot received a standing ovation when he was introduced but delivered an ambivalent speech that questioned whether the film was in fact racist. Cobleigh made the most important and dramatic point when he revealed that Thomas Dixon, author of the book upon which the movie was based, had confessed to him that the purpose of the book was "the achieving of white supremacy and the getting rid of the colored people." However, by presenting this virtually all-white speakers' list before a largely black audience, the NAACP showed that it was still an organization for the African-American people, but not yet of them.[56]

By contrast, the rally on the Boston Common was addressed by several African-American ministers, including the Reverend M. W. Thornton of Charles Street Methodist, Walter McLean, Benjamin Swain, D. O. Walker of Chelsea, and M. A. N. Shaw of the Twelfth Baptist. The daily newspapers did not bother to record their words, as might be expected, but the Crisis did worse by suggesting that the rally on the Common was also an NAACP-sponsored event. William Brigham, a white follower of Trotter's, protested to Du Bois that he had further neglected to credit the earlier Faneuil Hall protest to Trotter. Brigham argued that there was room for both the NAACP and Trotter's group, both of which he supported. "I try to be fair," Du Bois replied. "On the other hand I do not propose to burden the columns of *The Crisis* simply with names and particularly with names of small organizations." Du Bois would rather ignore Trotter than give him credit where it was due.[57]

Later in May Governor Walsh signed into law a bill with more narrow language than the Sullivan bill, and establishing the three-person committee. Two weeks later the committee met, the members having viewed the film individually. They heard from Wilson, Lewis, and J. Mott Hallowell, but Trotter was not admitted. The three attorneys presented 6,181 signatures on a petition requesting that the film be banned. After a brief closed-door session the committee ruled to permit the film's showing, and it enjoyed a run of unprecedented length. Curley biographer Jack Beatty suggests that the mayor was paid off by the film's distributors, his prudishness overruled by his pecuniary instinct.[58]

BIRACIAL COOPERATION AND AFRICAN-AMERICAN LEADERSHIP

The relation of African-Americans to the national and Boston NAACP underwent a powerful transformation during the association's first decade. If white NAACP leaders projected a biracial organization, Monroe Trotter saw, not without some justice, a white organization—an ally perhaps, but also a potential rival within the black community. In Boston, the NAACP remained largely white until the aftermath of the world war, when about two thousand African-Americans took out membership cards for the civil rights organization. While these were largely paper memberships, the composition of the organization was transformed. This process was unique to Boston, which alone had a preponderance of white members and leaders in the association's first decade. As the older white abolitionists died or retired, African-Americans made the organization their own. This was probably the first time in American history that a white-initiated organization became largely African-American. The process reflected at once the new postwar assertiveness of African-Americans, and the continuing retreat of whites from the civil rights movement. Broader developments such as the Great Migration and postwar disillusionment contributed to this process nationally. In Boston, African-Americans were attracted to the NAACP because of its consistent hard work on behalf of civil rights. Nevertheless, for the first decade of its existence, race relations between the NAACP and the black community, and within the NAACP, were a vexed question that challenged the members and leaders as they sought to forge an organizational identity.

Underlying this dilemma was the notion shared by many NAACP leaders of both races that before long the association must be led by African-Americans. Nevertheless, there was disagreement over what this meant and at what pace it should develop. In the national office, W. E. B. Du Bois's insistence upon the autonomy of the *Crisis* magazine crystallized the conflict over this problem. Backed by a minority of board members and championed within the office only by Mary White Ovington, he clashed with the supercilious Oswald Garrison Villard during 1915 and 1916. While the dispute focused upon organizational matters, the deeper question was over how to achieve African-American leadership. This was no simple matter: Du Bois was the obvious candidate, yet he was temperamentally ill-equipped as an organizer. May Childs Nerney and Joel Spingarn saw the need for black control of the organization, but they too were mindful of Du Bois's weaknesses. The NAACP was not polarized strictly along racial lines, but disputes between social radicals and conservatives, staff members and board members, journalists and administrators, could carry racial overtones. The tensions produced frayed nerves and staff turnover.[59]

Boston NAACP leaders tried during 1915 to resolve the problems in the divided national office. Butler Wilson and his friend Archibald Grimké, leader of the Washington, D.C., branch, urged reconciliation upon the disputants. Boston and Washington were the largest branches throughout the decade. Wilson and Grimké, attorneys who worked together as editors of the *Hub*, Boston's black community newspaper in the mid-1880s, lacked the unique brilliance of Du Bois, but did possess the diplomatic skills necessary to build an organization. Both grappled with the question of black leadership of the association without yielding to sentiment or personal ambition.[60] Grimké was elected to the national board before Wilson, and then proposed his friend for board membership in 1914. Joseph Prince Loud, the vice president of the Boston branch and another national board member, favored Grimké for national chairman. So did May Childs Nerney, who wrote weekly confidential letters to Grimké, apprising him in anxious terms of the leadership crisis in New York.[61]

When Du Bois alluded to the leadership problems in a public speech in Boston during December 1914, Butler Wilson worriedly related this to Grimké. Du Bois, "in an otherwise very able speech," Wilson complained, had virtually accused the national board of acting undemocratically. "These remarks have caused much concern here and people are talking now about the division in our ranks. . . . Du Bois may be courting public favor preparatory to the annual meeting in February. Certainly he is without tact and at times does some very stupid things."[62]

Wilson was likely reflecting a variety of pressures. The NAACP was still a new enterprise, not old enough to be sure of continued existence. It faced the

Scylla of Booker Washington's opposition and, in Boston, the Charybdis of Monroe Trotter; both camps hoped to see the new vessel smash upon the rock of failed biracial cooperation. Du Bois's airing of dirty laundry might be seen as admirable frankness; Wilson apparently thought it gave comfort to the association's rivals. Additionally, Wilson was a longtime friend of Francis Jackson Garrison, whose alliance with his nephew against Du Bois was manifest. These considerations aside, Wilson and Grimké were organization men who knew that compromise and discretion were the necessary oils for a smooth-running machine.

May Childs Nerney feared some sort of coup within the organization and advised Grimké that the "Morgan-Hare" clique of malcontents in the Boston branch were echoing Du Bois's charge that the association was not run democratically. "How many Boston people can Wilson get to come [to the 1915 annual meeting] to counter-act the [Clement] Morgan–[Maud Cuney] Hare clique?" she anxiously pressed Grimké. Morgan and Du Bois were indeed on good terms. Du Bois remembered Morgan fondly in his final autobiography but omitted Wilson. Morgan was clearly out of favor with branch president Garrison. During the *Birth of a Nation* controversy Garrison wrote with disgust about Morgan's speech during Mayor Curley's hearing. It is not likely that he was merely being factional, for in the same letter he praised Trotter, whom he heartily detested.[63]

One year later when Villard and Joel Spingarn proposed to resign their leadership positions, Wilson urged Spingarn to stay on. He also appealed to Du Bois to patch up his differences with Villard and grow into the role that history seemed to have destined for him. "It is now possible for you to have the power and great influence of both the Association and *The Crisis* with you. . . . Everybody concedes your mental equipment. Not so many concede your ability to lead men. Why has not your time come? . . . The colored people are ready to follow a big man." Du Bois knew himself better. Thanking Wilson for his kind words, he regretted that he and Villard could not even speak to each other. "There is no use of me trying to be a leader of men. I am a writer and a critic, but I do not easily make friends."[64] The leadership crisis in the organization during 1915–16 was not fully resolved until James Weldon Johnson became the first African-American national secretary in 1920. Throughout the decade, members of the Boston branch grappled with the question of what sort of organization they were building. Was the NAACP to be a biracial organization, or should it appeal to the growing sentiments of racial pride among black people and become a "race organization?" This problem has appeared in almost every civil rights organization since then, and the Boston NAACP members were among the first to grapple with its implications. From 1909 to 1920, when blacks and whites virtually never met as equals, the question was even more overwhelming than it is today. As the white Boston NAACP members noted the increasingly black composition of the national and local organization, they wondered what it meant. The most troubled of the members was George G. Bradford, the branch treasurer throughout the decade, whose resignation in 1920 may have been motivated by this concern.

Bradford's wider views were informed by his analysis of the South. He saw the region in a schematic but long-term perspective, viewing it as still demoralized by the devastation of the Civil War. The South, as the defeated party, could usefully be compared to France after her defeat in the Franco-Prussian War. Bradford thought there was a "Law of Deferred Results": that is, the defeated party in war required a generation or two to recover itself, during which time it turned to recrimination and hatred. "The low point for the French was the Dreyfus case," he wrote to Archibald Grimké. Just as the French had recovered their vigor, he suggested hopefully, the South was due to recover its senses in a few years.[65] Without saying so directly, he implied that as the French had seen their error, restored Dreyfus, and rebuked the anti-Semites, so too would the South restore full rights to African-Americans.

This optimistic outlook regarding the ability of white southerners to halt their racist practices framed Bradford's concern that the NAACP not become strictly a race organization. When the American entry into the world war unleashed a storm of chauvinism that cast suspicion upon any loyalties to one's ethnic origins, Bradford's apprehension grew. "The American people are not going to have much patience now or later with hyphenated Americans—whether German-Americans or Irish-Americans or colored-Americans," he wrote to James Weldon Johnson during an NAACP membership drive. "Appeals to race loyalty are going to be looked upon with increasing suspicion. In making our great membership drive therefore it becomes increasingly important to make our appeals to the principles of American citizenship—of civil liberty rather than to the racial sympathies of colored people and their friends."[66]

Were these principles genuinely counterposed or could they be made to work in harmony? James Weldon Johnson did not see a contradiction between these two impulses. Granting Bradford's point in a general way, he reminded the Bostonian that if colored people organized on the basis of racial pride, it was only for the purpose of winning full citizenship.[67]

Bradford was somewhat unsatisfied with this explanation one year later, but his awareness of the role for racial self-organization had grown. In a letter to Du Bois he contrasted "race organization to develop racial self-respect, self-confidence, capacity for leadership and organization," to "organization for civil liberty for promoting just and friendly relations between races and classes." Both were necessary, but the NAACP, he averred, should stand for the latter principle, although it would be "very difficult . . . to prevent the NAACP becoming a race organization."[68]

How to do this in an America that was relentlessly hostile to black aspirations? Bradford raised this problem with John Shillady, a white staff member in New York. A few months later Shillady was brutally beaten by Texas racists in front of the state capitol at Austin while on assignment for the association, and when he resigned shortly afterward it underscored the problem. Bradford proposed that branches strive for at least a 10 percent white membership. "As our organization is now made up racial in name and preponderantly racial in membership and purpose—its growth in numbers will inevitably arouse and intensify race distrust and race prejudice—not allay it. . . . Mr. Storey and I argue that we should have branches in states having few if any colored people for the principles for which we stand are national not racial." Later he was careful to qualify his argument by insisting that it was based "not on any theory that *one* race is more important than the other but on the theory that *both* races are important and should cooperate."[69]

Storey in general concurred with this approach, albeit without the numerical schema that accompanied much of Bradford's thinking. In October 1918 he wrote the national office that more organizing should be done in primarily white states. To Storey, though, this was not a bad problem to have. "I think the situation is improving, and is nothing more than the growing self-confidence of the colored people and their willingness to assert their rights."[70]

To a certain extent, Bradford's frame of mind reflected the paternalist impulse uncomfortable with the independence of its prodigy. This sensibility was shared by other whites in the association and can be seen in Garrison's confidences to his nephew. In a particularly revealing passage, Garrison expressed his hope for a large attendance at a meeting: "Tonight another meeting will be held at the West Newton colored church. . . . I believe the colored people will yet wake up and help us." Incredibly, Garrison seemed to have reversed in his own mind who was giving "help" to whom. Nine months later, he expressed similar frustration: "I hope we shall be able to muster a respectable audience, but one can never count upon the colored people in such matters. Trotter understands them when he gets up a dancing entertainment to raise funds to send him to Washington!" It is easy to condemn such paternalism today, but Progressive Era attitudes should not be judged ahistorically. Almost everyone at the time believed that racial characteristics, either inherited, learned, or both, determined behavior. And the NAACP activists were the most advanced whites on racial matters; no one else's ideas better pointed to the future. Even Trotter sometimes expressed the impatience that Garrison showed; frustration is an occupational hazard for leaders of protest movements, which ebb and flow in tidal currents that no individual leader can control. The irony of Garrison's concern is that within a few years his colleague Bradford was worried about the opposite phenomenon—that too few whites participated in the movement.[71]

As previously noted, the transformation in the racial composition of the Boston NAACP and the association nationally was rooted in the Great Migration northward beginning around 1915, with its concomitant urbanization and proletarianization of the race. The participation of African-American troops in the world war and the death of Booker Washington in 1915 further undermined the accommodationist perspective. These interrelated phenomena raised great hopes in the African-American population and quickly dashed them as migrants and returning troops were met by a blizzard of white violence. The "New Negro" who appeared at the end of the war built not only a cultural Harlem Renaissance, but also a new political organization to defend black people against these attacks.

Action would not mean much to the association unless the sentiment behind it was organized, and it launched two membership drives toward the end of the decade. The success of these campaigns was facilitated not only by the deterioration in race relations, but also by the collapse of the association's competitors for membership. Booker Washington's following gradually dissolved after his unexpected death in November 1915, facilitating a transfer of loyalties to the NAACP by such prominent individuals as James Weldon Johnson. Trotter by 1919 was disoriented; in that year he was pursuing his quixotic one-man crusade at the Paris Peace Conference while the NAACP was mobilizing the huge antilynching campaign.

The Boston NAACP leaders had always been diplomatic in their approach to Washington's milieu. As early as June 1910 they convinced Bookerite law partners James H. Wolff and Edward Everett Brown to serve on the national board. Josephine St. Pierre Ruffin and Maria Baldwin, leaders of the African-American women's movement, at various times were members of the local executive committee but still maintained their distance from the NAACP, in part for obscure personal reasons. At one meeting, Ruffin insulted Butler Wilson so severely that he threatened to resign. "It is the old story of jealousy . . . against Mr. and Mrs. Wilson, who have been the real life of our organization," Francis Jackson Garrison mournfully reported to his nephew.[72]

While Ruffin and Baldwin have been properly remembered by historians,

Mary Evans Wilson has unfortunately been forgotten. She was undoubtedly the central recruitment organizer for the NAACP in New England, and probably the most important individual in the transformation of the Boston branch from a white-led organization to a black community institution. In the fall of 1914 and the winter of 1915 she delivered a speech entitled "Race Discrimination and Segregation at the Capitol" in Providence, New Bedford, several Ohio cities, and in western Pennsylvania. She would meet in parlors or churches with local activists and leave town, hurriedly writing requests that one hundred membership cards be sent to a new member in Columbus, that some white supporters had come to the meeting in Dayton, or that Joel Spingarn's speech in Pittsburgh was being well publicized. Her brief missives, probably written aboard a bouncing train, are reminiscent of traveling abolitionists working the same territory eighty years earlier. In the fall of 1915 she spoke in Springfield, New Bedford again, and Maine and New Hampshire. Butler Wilson complained humorously to Archibald Grimké that he introduced himself to his wife on her occasional returns home. Mary Wilson was the unsung heroine of the Boston NAACP, rarely taking center stage in Boston (although she did speak at the huge 1915 meeting) but quietly winning thousands of new recruits to the organization.[73]

By the winter of 1918, the Boston branch was still the largest nationally, with 753 members; St. Louis was next, with 615. After the NAACP won a residential segregation case in the Supreme Court in the fall of 1917, Moorfield Storey called for a membership drive to capitalize on the victory. By the summer of 1918, the Boston branch had won 1,800 new members, for a total of 2,553. In 1920, Boston's African-American population was only 16,350, which meant that Boston had approximately one NAACP member for every six black people. The Washington, D.C., branch grew to 6,906 but its black population in 1910 was 94,446. Boston's NAACP was still second in absolute size. New York was third with 1,237 members with a black population roughly equal to Washington's. By 1919 Boston issued its own branch bulletin and reported 3,300 members, "and this drive is due to add another 1,000." Undoubtedly the vast majority of this number were only paper members, but the recruitment drives did show that the NAACP had a great deal of support.[74]

The NAACP did not keep racial statistics on members, but the likelihood is that locally and nationally these members were overwhelmingly African-American. Mary Wilson and a Dr. John J. Smith headed the recruitment committee and won new members by going door to door, and visiting church and club meetings. A furniture salesman turned in 95 membership cards, and Wilson's knitting classes produced 300 new female members. A Christian endeavor society yielded 43 recruits, and a Methodist Sunday school 176. By

1920 there were separate committees in the neighboring towns of Cambridge, Everett, and Lynn. "There are two score race groups in Boston, 17 are represented in the Branch," the local bulletin reported.[75]

One sign that the association was taking root in the African-American community was the participation of a new group of ministers in its leadership. The Reverend Samuel A. Brown was briefly a member of the branch executive committee before moving to Ohio in 1919. Brown was pastor of St. Mark's Congregational Church. In 1912, the pastorate of the Columbus Ave. AME Church, scene of the 1903 Trotter-Washington confrontation, went to Benjamin W. Swain, an NAACP member. Branch president Joseph Loud spoke at a testimonial for Swain in 1918. At People's Baptist, Aaron Puller, who was arrested with Trotter during the *Birth of a Nation* controversy, was replaced by David S. Klugh, who participated in the NAACP recruitment drive.[76]

Over the course of a decade, the NAACP had transformed itself from an organization of white people linked to the antislavery crusade to an institution within the African-American community. If it could not maintain itself as a genuinely biracial organization after 1920, it did a better job of achieving that goal than any other American organization. As the Garrisons, Storeys, and Pillsburys died out, they were replaced by African-American activists who kept the struggle alive until the significant victories of the modern civil rights movement. Thus the unique historical tradition of Boston contributed powerfully to crafting the national response to racism during the nadir of African-American history.

John Boyle O'Reilly. Courtesy of the Boston Athenaeum.

SIX

❧❧❧❧❧❧

Irish-Americans and the Legacy of John Boyle O'Reilly

THUS FAR, we have considered the efforts of various reformers to focus the attention of Boston and the nation upon the race question. To understand more fully why their successes were limited, we need to consider the wider context in which they operated. Boston changed dramatically from 1890 to 1920, and the major transformation was the shift in power from the Protestant Yankee elite to the rising Irish-Americans.

Toward the end of our period, James Michael Curley was mayor, the militant Catholic William O'Connell was cardinal, and in 1919 Boston's largely Irish police force was on strike. Confrontation between the sons of Irish Catholic immigrants and the declining Brahmin aristocracy was the order of the day. In addition, the city and the country were modernizing, and the institutions of party, church, and union were becoming more centralized, as were all American institutions.

What this meant for the race reformers was that the matter of civil rights for African-Americans now seemed to belong to another time and another place. The city was turning inward upon itself, struggling over how and by whom it should be ruled, how the religious denominations would regard each other, and what the relation between labor and capital would be. By 1920, the Boston that once thought of itself as the Hub of the Universe was increasingly a provincial center whose Puritan past now was evoked not against a sinning slavocracy, but against apparently corrupt Irish politicians, assertive priests, and rebellious workers.

While the Yankee-Irish conflict was at center stage, the picture was complicated by a significant influx of "new immigrants" from czarist Russia and southern Europe as Poles, Lithuanians, Jews, and Italians were setting down roots. There were, for example, 40,000 Jews in Boston by 1910, as compared to only 16,000 African-Americans in 1920. The Catholics among these new immigrants competed within the church for resources and autonomy; the non-Catholics were busy building their own institutions. Nor was the city a roiling mass of hostile European tribes. The new immigrants were working long days (sometimes together), learning English at night, and becoming fellow Bostonians by cheering for the World Series champion (1903, 1912, 1915, 1916, and 1918) Red Sox and their promising pitcher Babe Ruth at Fenway Park, which opened in 1912. Jim Crow was not much on the minds of many white people.

Indeed, to many Bostonians of our period, the "race question" might mean what to do about the Irish, the Italians, or the Jews. Yet, the position of the Irish was clearly different. By 1920, four Irishmen had served as mayor for a total of sixteen years. They were well integrated into the body politic nationally, and they alone of the immigrants had an important voice in a national political party. Black Bostonians had to wonder what this meant for them, and their people nationally.

Northern Irish-Americans did have a particular antipathy to reform in general that went back to the antebellum period. They had been hostile to African-Americans and to abolition, seeing it as a middle-class reform movement aimed in part at their own behavior. However, that Boston's Irish-American political, clerical, and trade union leaders would be unresponsive to African-American aspirations was not a foregone conclusion. Two interrelated aspects of the Irish and Irish-American experience suggested that Boston's Irish-American leaders might be particularly interested in the fate of African-Americans. In Ireland before the famine, the central leader of Catholic Emancipation, Daniel O'Connell, was enthusiastically antislavery. In both Ireland and America, the Irish were, like black Americans, oppressed because of their nationality (or "race" as people of that time said) and consequently were thrust to the bottom rungs of the economy. Both groups had been scorned; both were poor.

Historians of Irish immigration describe three periods of that experience: the pre-famine Irish, who were not necessarily Catholic and whose presence was not especially problematic; the famine Irish of 1846–51, who were the poorest of the Catholics; and a postfamine migration of the late nineteenth century by more traditional economic migrants. The experience of national oppression in Ireland, under which Catholic rights were severely curtailed, coupled with the knowledge that the famine was in part man-made by British policy, dominated the Irish-American memory for at least a century and lingers to this day. Like Boston's African-Americans, the Boston Irish were refugees from another land, where the bulk of their people lived under the domination of an alien nationality.

In addition, the Boston Irish of 1890 to 1920 had the recent memory and sometimes the current experience of economic discrimination at the hands of Boston's Brahmins to remind them of the plight of others. Similarly, they suffered the indignity of nativist cultural or physical assault. The large Irish-American and the small African-American population occupied the lower and lowest rungs of the working class. Boston advertisements read "No Irish Need Apply" and factory managers and store owners refused to hire black workers. Was there not some ground to anticipate a commonality of interest, given these partial similarities of experience?

More than any other Irish-American of his day, John Boyle O'Reilly expressed these possibilities. During a life forged in the Irish revolutionary struggle, he came to Boston in 1870 as a political exile and poet. He gradually reclaimed Daniel O'Connell's vision, but when he died in 1890, the light of "green" and black unity flickered and died. The earlier hostility toward African-Americans by the Boston Irish became a generalized indifference.

Boston's African-Americans, however, were not indifferent toward the Irish. In part, the black community modeled itself on the cultured Brahmin establishment. On the other hand, William Monroe Trotter, the central leader of the black community from about 1904 to 1915, held up the example of Irish revolutionary struggle in Ireland as a model for black militance. In addition, Trotter was a political independent who often voted Democratic, thus removing an important barrier between himself and Irish-Americans. Trotter, as editor of his own newspaper, appealed to the Boston Irish to remember Daniel O'Connell and John Boyle O'Reilly, but with little success. Boston's Irish-Americans forgot the lives of these antiracist campaigners as they achieved institutional power in the city.[1]

IRELAND'S ANTISLAVERY TRADITION AND THE BOSTON IRISH

Viewed retrospectively, Daniel O'Connell was the Martin Luther King of Irish politics. Born in 1775 to a Catholic small landholder, he employed the tactics of peaceful mass mobilization, eloquent rhetoric, and parliamentary struggle to remove legal disabilities from an oppressed people. He lived to see his cause triumph when in 1829 Britain repealed many anti-Catholic laws. O'Connell did not question the fundamental underpinnings of British society; he wanted Englishmen to live up to the promise of their history by permitting Irish self-government under a constitutional monarchy. Like King, he died during a time of profound economic upheaval (the famine years) when the deeper relations between oppressed and oppressor exploded into the open; both moved at the end of their careers to address those more fundamental problems. The support by Americans of Irish descent for O'Connell's program was the first political movement by Irishmen as such in America, and this shaped their identities as newly made "Irish-Americans."[2]

O'Connell was a nationalist who detested oppression everywhere, including that of black slaves. In Parliament, West Indian planters offered O'Connell a bloc: Irish support of slavery in exchange for their support of Catholic emancipation. O'Connell turned them down. New England antislavery activists sent Charles Lenox Remond, an African-American, to Ireland, and he returned with 60,000 Irish signatures on an antislavery petition addressed to the American Irish.[3]

To this appeal the Irish-Americans were notoriously cool. Historian George Potter argues convincingly that cultural factors underlay this response. Irish-American opposition to antislavery was located in their general hostility to the wider Protestant crusade to change individual behavior. Irish-Catholic leaders especially saw Protestant reform as a rebuke to Catholic belief and to Irish cultural values. Temperance, women's rights, the encroachments of an all-powerful state upon the individual's domain, and antislavery became linked in the Irish mind with nativist outrages against themselves. The loyalty of the Irish to the Democratic Party as champion of the working-man meshed with "anti-abolitionist" sensibilities. Potter assigns to a secondary place Irish competition with blacks for jobs, suggesting that this victory the Irish had decisively won virtually upon arrival. Finally, Catholic "fatalism" viewed slavery as a natural disaster about which little could be done but to trust in God.[4]

The antipathy of Boston's Irish-Americans toward abolitionists carried over to the Negro. Francis R. Walsh traces the unfolding of this sentiment in a study of the *Boston Pilot*. This was an Irish immigrant journal from its founding in 1829 by Patrick Donahoe, until 1908, when it became the organ of the Catholic archdiocese. Potter described it as the "best of the [unofficial] Catholic Irish weeklies and the most representative of Catholic Irish thinking" in the antebellum period. He suggests that the *Pilot* was more anti-abolitionist than proslavery, but Walsh more convincingly shows that its "steady course in opposing the abolitionists, a designation of seemingly inexhaustible elasticity" reflected racist and proslavery sensibilities.[5]

The *Pilot* viewed slavery as an institution having biblical sanction and therefore not as an evil in and of itself. How to make slavery a workable institution, or to let it die of natural causes, was best left to the slaveholders who understood the problem. Antislavery advocates were hypocrites who countenanced the oppression of the Irish and the workingman in America generally. American abolitionists were dupes of the British, who freed their Negro slaves while allowing Irishmen to perish in the famine. As the Civil War approached, the *Pilot* supported slavery in the nation's capital, the rendition of fugitive slaves Thomas Sims and Anthony Burns, the Kansas-Nebraska Act, the Dred Scott decision, and Stephen Douglass in the 1860 election. On occasion, the newspaper referred to black people as "niggers."[6] The *Pilot* essentially presented the argument of the slavocracy and sugar-coated it with Irish nationalism.

When the Civil War broke out, the *Pilot* reluctantly condemned secession, blaming the abolitionists for provoking the crisis. Donahoe supported the war to defend the union, and backed Irish-American participation as a demonstration of patriotism. He soured on the war effort with the Emancipation Proclamation, predicting that the slaves would not leave the plantation, for "they love their masters as dogs do." Faced with this ultimate test, the *Pilot* showed that it supported slavery in practice, and now turned against President Abraham Lincoln. The *Pilot* declared Negroes to be an inferior race, and the draft to be an anti-Irish measure. When officials enforced the draft law, an Irish mob attacked the armory and seven rioters were killed.[7]

In the aftermath of the war, the *Pilot* stressed the positive contribution of Irish-American soldiers to victory, and celebrated the outcome of the war. The unity wrought by mutual participation on the battlefield carried over for a while, diminishing the local Brahmin-Yankee antagonism. Within a few years, however, the *Pilot* denounced Reconstruction as a project of Republican nativists. It dismissed claims of antiblack violence in the South as fraudulent.[8]

Meanwhile, relations between Boston's Irish- and African-Americans were influenced by internal developments within the Irish national struggle. The O'Connell tradition alternately competed and coexisted with the revolutionary Irish Republican movement, typified by such martyrs as Wolfe Tone and Robert Emmett. These leaders favored the establishment of an independent republic by methods of physical force, eschewing parliamentary struggle. The Irish Republicans also spoke less than the O'Connell tendency did about slavery, in part because their movement was shaped more from American exile. Further, the American "Fenians" were militarized by their experience as Civil War combatants. This contributed to their reckless decision to "invade" Canada in 1866 and 1870, and the subsequent collapse of their movement.[9]

1870 was also the year that John Boyle O'Reilly, a famed Irish Republican political prisoner and budding poet, arrived in Boston. Born in 1844 to educated parents, he became a revolutionary by age nineteen, and joined a plot to infiltrate the British Army and spark a mutiny. He was captured, court-martialed and sentenced to death, but the sentence was commuted to hard labor and Australian exile. O'Reilly made a daring escape, came to Philadelphia and then New York, and decided that Boston was the place for him.[10]

With the aid of fellow Fenians Dr. Robert Dwyer Joyce and Patrick A. Collins, O'Reilly became a writer for the *Pilot*. He covered the 1870 Canadian expedition and then the "Orange" riots in New York. These public-relations disasters for the Irish-American community, and the assumptions underlying Irish-Catholic militance that they displayed, caused him to rethink the course of Irish-American nationalism. Shortly thereafter the Great Boston Fire of 1872 and the depression of 1873 reduced the *Pilot*'s owner financially, and Archbishop John J. Williams and O'Reilly became owners of the *Pilot*.[11]

O'Reilly began to wonder if some rapprochement with the O'Connell tradition was now in order. A complex process of reevaluation carried O'Reilly and his colleagues through various organizations such as Clan na Gael and the Land League, but it generally moved them toward the parliamentary struggle for Home Rule that Charles Stewart Parnell would advance in the 1880s, in problematic alliance with the English Liberal leader William E. Gladstone. O'Reilly and his friends were now moderates under the broad philosophical influence of O'Connell.[12]

Closer to home, O'Reilly was living in the same city as Wendell Phillips, one of the few abolitionists who also cared about the Irish and labor questions. Backed by militant shoemakers, Phillips ran for governor on an Independent ticket the year O'Reilly arrived in Boston. These two revolutionaries were men of similar spirit who had known scorn and isolation, but by the 1870s were enjoying respectability. On O'Connell's centennial in 1875 they addressed four thousand Bostonians, celebrating the Liberator in prose and poem. Along with them were Governor William Gaston, General Nathaniel Banks, Father James A. Healy (an African-American), Archbishop Williams, and others. Ethnically and politically this was an ecumenical gathering rather than an Irish Catholic celebration. Phillips was the main orator, and O'Reilly recited his "A Nation's Test," a hymn to Ireland and its heroes, and to the brotherhood of all the oppressed. The *Boston Evening Transcript* praised the "fiery young Boyle O'Reilly, as good a representative specimen of pure Celtic stock as Wendell Phillips is of straight English lineage." This public celebration thus ratified the coming together of the Irish and Brahmin antislavery traditions, with the blessing of the archbishop and the staid *Transcript*.[13]

O'Reilly was shaped by the currents of working-class radicalism that gained ground in the turbulent late 1880s. Although he generally described himself as a "Jeffersonian Democrat," he was also attracted to notions of

Christian socialism. He flirted with Edward Bellamy's Nationalism, wrote a sympathetic obituary for Karl Marx, and argued for the militant union the Knights of Labor. He supported Single Taxer Henry George's New York mayoralty campaign in 1886, but turned against him when George later attacked the Catholic Church. This broader radical framework informed his outlook on race relations.[14]

He was also a committed Democrat. This posed an obstacle for his relations with Boston's generally Republican black community. Some black Bostonians, however, were Independents, such as Archibald Grimké and James Trotter, father of future editor William Monroe Trotter. In December 1885, O'Reilly addressed the Massachusetts Colored League, which had recently resolved in favor of political independence. O'Reilly looked for points of commonality between the Irish and black struggles. "I don't care whether you vote the Republican or Democratic ticket," he said, "but I know that if I were a colored man I should use parties as I would a club—to break down prejudices against my people." O'Reilly, however, remained a Democrat, and the differing orientations could not entirely be wished away.[15]

In this speech O'Reilly sounded themes that no Brahmin abolitionist, not even Wendell Phillips, could match. O'Reilly was himself born to a people suffering national oppression. He had been a revolutionary, a soldier, a political prisoner, and he was an exile. Perhaps more important, he was a poet. Even as he gained respectability in Boston, these experiences gave him an empathy for the black struggle that was unique among whites. Ultimately, O'Reilly said, the white man's bigotry was at the heart of the race question, and that would only break down as the colored people built their own culture. Therefore the Negro must be true to his African roots, rather than a student of the white people. This flew in the face of progressive white teaching, which was generally paternalistic and stressed that the Negro was making great strides by emulating white society. "In his heart still ring the free sounds of the desert," O'Reilly enthused about the Negro. "In his mind he carries the traditions of Africa. . . . Inside he is a new man, fresh from nature." O'Reilly, a Byronesque Romantic, celebrated the Negro as "the only American who has written new songs and composed new music," who would soon bring forth poets and philosophers whose accomplishments would break down the barriers of prejudice.[16]

A few months later, Boston's African-American leaders again invited O'Reilly to speak at a protest meeting after a massacre of unarmed blacks in Mississippi. A large audience gathered at the Twelfth Baptist Church, and the black leaders drew their conclusions about what to do from the lessons of the Irish struggle. Attorney Edwin G. Walker, son of abolitionist David

Walker, declared that progress in the Irish movement came only through violence, and that the colored people in America should learn from that. Lewis Hayden, who had warded off slave catchers with threats of explosives, noted the Irish use of dynamite and suggested its possible employment by black people. O'Reilly was introduced as the successor to Wendell Phillips (who had died the year before). By now, however, O'Reilly's urgings were more cautionary. He agreed with the right of self-defense, and said that Mississippi blacks should "meet lawless violence with legal violence." However, he advised that the struggle might take one or two generations before achieving victory, and drew a rather different conclusion from the Irish example. He had just come from a meeting at Faneuil Hall, where Irishmen had assembled to honor an English statesman (probably Gladstone). As a youth he could not have imagined such a development. Now he urged the protestors to maintain their dignity, culture, and African roots. These remarks, slightly out of step with those of the African-American speakers, reflected the differing tempos of the Irish and black struggles, the new mood of an older man, and the growing respectability and power of the Irish in Boston.[17]

The dedication of the monument to Crispus Attucks and the other victims of the Boston Massacre of 1770 brought together the leaders of the black community, O'Reilly, and Boston's first Irish-born mayor, Hugh O'Brien. At this 1888 commemoration, O'Reilly's poem "Crispus Attucks" linked the American struggle against the British with the Irish and black struggles in the person of Attucks, whose sacrifice showed, "There never was separate heart-beat in all the races of men!" The "blood of the people" wherever they might be, confronted the same "Patrician, aristocrat, tory—whatever his age or name," who was loyal only to his own privileges.[18]

By 1890, the importance of the African-American vote in the South took on national significance as Republicans, possessing the presidency and both houses of Congress, attempted to pass a Federal Elections bill that would send federal officials into states where voting irregularities were alleged. Boston's Democratic press, especially Boston's other Irish newspaper, the *Republic*, campaigned vigorously against the bill. O'Reilly, by marked contrast, spoke out for civil rights in this period, mentioning his opposition to the measure only in the most muted of terms. For example, after the murder of eight black men at Barnwell, South Carolina, he urged the residents to take up an economic boycott of town merchants, among other tactics. He chastened an Alabama senator who called for the expulsion of blacks from the United States. When South Carolina newspapers challenged the tenor of these pieces, the *Pilot* replied that lynchers should be hanged, and that segregation could be turned against northern working-class people. Later that year he defended Clement Morgan, an African-American class orator at Harvard, from suggestions that Negroes should be barred from such roles. O'Reilly's opposition to the Federal Elections bill was limited to two brief editorials, and one of these stressed his support for Fourteenth Amendment remedies instead of the Republican bill's approach. At a time when the Democratic press was haughtily deprecating the voting rights of African-Americans, O'Reilly's record was impressively steadfast in its devotion to the civil rights cause.[19]

O'Reilly died accidentally in August 1890, when he took the wrong medication for insomnia. He was universally mourned in moving and generous tributes in Boston, around New England, and by Irish and church leaders. Mayor Thomas Hart presided at the Boston memorial meeting, and leaders of the clerical, journalistic, educational, and literary professions spoke. Edwin G. Walker represented the African-American community, and Patrick Collins, later a mayor and O'Reilly's earliest Boston friend, delivered the final speech.[20] While O'Reilly was widely remembered for his vision and largeness of spirit, his commitment to the civil rights movement was quickly forgotten. In fact, his very prominence as an advocate of civil rights suggests that his Irish-American contemporaries simply ignored this part of his character while he lived. The next generation of Irish-American leaders, having less connection to Ireland and less still to the Irish revolutionary movement, played more central roles in the history of the city. The southern question receded, while black people in Boston gradually disappeared from the view of Boston's Irish-Americans.

IRISH-AMERICAN DEMOCRATS

A copious historiography discusses the development of Boston's Irish-American political culture and its relation to Brahmin Boston in this period. Very little is written about Irish- and African-American relations within Boston, or Irish-American attitudes toward the national race question, because little occurred. Irish-Americans built a rich political culture that sustained three newspapers, and captured the mayoralty for a century after. This section examines what two of those newspapers said about race relations, and selects two politicians, John F. Fitzgerald and James Michael Curley, to see how their policies affected the black community. Finally it explores the factors that diminished O'Reilly's influence.[21]

James Jeffrey Roche was O'Reilly's contemporary, disciple, and successor at the *Pilot*. However, his early life experience was radically different from O'Reilly's, his notoriety much less, and the time of his editorship less hospitable to liberal views on race. He led the newspaper until 1904, resigning after endorsing Republican Theodore Roosevelt for president.

Like O'Reilly he was born in Ireland, but he grew up on Prince Edward Island and had no direct connection to the Irish struggle. He was a writer and journalist rather than an activist. Again like O'Reilly, he was a Catholic, but he labored under the influence of a more conservative papacy than did his mentor. Roche remained true to O'Reilly's vision, but the passion was missing from his prose. He was one of the best Irish-American spokespersons for civil rights in this period, but in comparison to O'Reilly his voice was more restrained.[22]

Roche took over the *Pilot* in the middle of the Federal Elections bill dispute, and his editorials in opposition to the bill were forceful where O'Reilly's had been muted. He described it as a "monstrous scheme" that would "rob the states of their electoral freedom." When the Democrats swept to victory in November, he saw that more as a repudiation of Henry Cabot Lodge and the "Force Bill" than of William McKinley's protective tariff. Two years later, when the Democratic Party began to revive the dead issue for partisan purposes, Roche wrote more evenhandedly. When Congressman William C. P. Breckenridge of Kentucky spoke in Boston in February 1892, he urged northerners to let the South work out its own race problem. He called for "No Force Bill" and "Home Rule" (for the South)—an appeal to Irish sympathies, for the latter slogan was that of Charles Stewart Parnell for Ireland. Roche replied that the *Pilot* had opposed the bill too, but reminded the congressman that southern violations of Negro voting rights had given the bill's proponents their opportunity. Roche conceded that Negroes were inferior to whites, but not inherently, only because of the legacy of slavery. The colored people could be raised up by "the missionary, the teacher and the free ballot." This tepid defense of African-American voting rights provided no means to enforce those rights.[23]

Roche also departed from O'Reilly's view that African-Americans would find their own way, by positing the standard white paternalistic model in this editorial. O'Reilly said little about missionary work, and stressed the new culture that black people would create on American soil. Roche was enthusiastic about missionary work, a position he defended against bigots who argued that the church should not waste its time or money on an unteachable race. This was "un-Christian race prejudice," the *Pilot* declared when a South Carolina Catholic paper voiced this opinion. Roche was a liberal on the race question who nontheless lacked O'Reilly's advanced understanding of black pride and militance.[24]

He wrote against racist violence, condemning the Virginia legislature for

proposing a public whipping post in 1898, and two years later against urban
mobbists in New York and New Orleans. He linked the imperialist adventure
in the Philippines and Puerto Rico to the spread of lynching sentiment. At
the same time he condemned "the professional 'friend of the black man'
[who] is the same now as he was in carpet-bag days, on the look-out for
number one first, last and all the time." This editorial suggested that Reconstruction and imperialism were linked Republican projects that equally promoted white racism. Again, however, Roche suffered only in comparison to
his predecessor, who bluntly called for the hanging of lynchers and generally
supported black self-defense.[25]

Behind this retreat from O'Reilly's militance was the new spirit of the
times and the ascension of Booker T. Washington. Roche's views were as
compatible with those of Washington as O'Reilly's were with the ideas of
Wendell Phillips. He sounded the same themes of education, self-help and
accumulation of property as the Tuskegean, without the latter's public accommodation to segregation and disfranchisement. Roche wrote little about segregation and, in opposing the grandfather clause, allowed that literacy tests
were reasonable. He praised the National Negro Business League, and Theodore Roosevelt for inviting Washington to dinner at the White House. When
Monroe Trotter criticized Booker Washington in Boston, Roche naturally
took the educator's side.[26]

As O'Reilly's disciple and *Pilot* editor from 1890 to 1904, Roche's evolution
is most instructive. Historian Thomas N. Brown suggests that O'Reilly's insomnia, and finally his death, was caused by the tension in his life between
his roots in Irish nationalism and his growing toward Brahmin respectability.[27] Roche competeled this trajectory, calling for a Republican victory in
1904 and abandoning the editorship. He wound up writing remarkably like
E. H. Clement, editor of the gray and sober *Boston Evening Transcript*.

By contrast, the *Republic*, founded in 1882 by the leader of Boston's Irish
Democrats, Patrick J. Maguire, was unconcerned with black rights. Maguire
was born in 1838 in Ireland, arriving in Boston in 1850 by way of Prince
Edward Island. He learned the printer's trade, developed interests in real
estate, and apprenticed himself in politics to Michael Doherty, leader of the
Irish Democrats in his day. Maguire prospered, and in the twenty-five years
before his death in 1896 was the most powerful Irish-American leader in
Boston. Except for a minor exception, he did not seek public office, but
worked as a behind-the-scenes manipulator. A self-made man, he followed
Doherty's strategy of alliance with Yankee Democrats and engineered the
election of Hugh O'Brien, Boston's first Irish mayor in 1884. The Irish-
American leaders of the Gilded Age provided the votes for Mayors Frederick

O. Prince, Nathan Matthews, and Josiah Quincy, Governor William E. Russell, and President Grover Cleveland. The framework for this arrangement lasted until the 1893 crash broke Maguire's power and inaugurated the era of the less tractable ward bosses Martin Lomasney, John F. Fitzgerald, and James Michael Curley.[28]

For a backroom politician of humble origin, Maguire produced a sophisticated and literate newspaper that covered Ireland and Irish America closely. His columns carefully dissected complex party alignments in the British Parliament and their meaning for Ireland. Editorials on American or local questions invariably included some denunciation of state encroachment upon Irish-Catholic rights, especially during the anti–parochial school campaign of the late 1880s and early 1890s, immigration restriction, or high tariffs. These stories carried the theme of the all-powerful national or local state against the individual. Democratic opposition to the Federal Elections bill of 1890 fit neatly into this conceptual framework. Of all Boston's Democratic papers, Maguire's campaign against the bill was the most shrill. The contrast with the *Pilot* was stark. After 1890, civil rights disappeared from the pages of the *Republic*.[29]

The *Republic* added one new note to the Democratic campaign against the Federal Elections bill, which was to argue for more liberal voting rights in the North for immigrants. As long as Irish or other prospective immigrant voters had to contend with property requirements in Rhode Island, for example, or residency requirements in Massachusetts, it was best to remember the proverb about those who lived in glass houses. "Let us settle our race differences in New England before we would undertake to lecture our Southern brethren," concluded one editorial. Other than that, the argument was similar to that of Democratic dailies like the *Globe* or *Post*. Republicans did not care about Negro rights, wished to centralize power, acted only for partisan purposes, violated the Constitution, threatened sectional reconciliation and normal commercial relations. As for the Negro himself, he was treated better in the South than in the North anyway, and was being used as a tool of cynical Republican politicians.[30]

These arguments were no better or worse than those of Yankee Democrats against the bill. All suffered from the same simple problem: they ignored the disfranchisement and attendant violence suffered by the southern African-American. Maguire's editorials on this subject show a profound contrast to those of the *Pilot*, which told the truth about events in the South, even if it did not accept the Republican remedy. Maguire did not polemicize with O'Reilly, and upon his rival editor's demise the *Republic*'s mourning was heartfelt.[31] The difference in approach to the race question showed the contrast between the life experience and outlook of O'Reilly and Maguire. The latter was entirely concerned with his own rise and class standing with his Yankee allies, and the Irish nationalism of his paper was narrow rather than universal. His focus was on Boston and its ever-shifting political alliances, a setting in which African-Americans played a small role. Finally, his lack of concern for black civil rights was rooted in a conservative worldview that feared an independent labor movement, new immigrants, women's suffrage, and other reforms.

The trend of development in Boston's Irish newspapers complemented that of the city's Democratic politicians. Maguire has been considered here as an editor, but his death in 1896 and the election that year also mark a turning point in the institutional life of the Democratic Party. Power now began to devolve toward neighborhood ward leaders. Josiah Quincy was the last Yankee mayor to serve more than an interregnum; Patrick Collins was the last Irish mayor of the Maguire mold (that is, a respectable Cleveland Democrat). John F. Fitzgerald, who served from 1906 to 1907 and 1910 to 1913, and James Michael Curley (1914–17), the first mayoral native-born sons of immigrant fathers, set the confrontational tone that would now dominate Boston politics.[32]

That tone was matched by William Monroe Trotter, who emerged as the leading figure in Boston's African-American politics around the same time that Fitzgerald became mayor. Temperamentally, the two men were opposites: Fitzgerald, the merry ladies' man, showy politician, and singer of sentimental songs; Trotter, the unsmiling abstinence man for whom the smallest question could be elevated to a matter of principle. There were, however, similarities. Both were second-generation Bostonians consciously representing a sometimes scorned group; both were editors of weekly newspapers (Fitzgerald took over the *Republic* in 1900 and Trotter launched the *Guardian* the following year); and while Trotter was the more uncompromising about his views, Fitzgerald at least had a sense of decency and fair play. Trotter campaigned for Fitzgerald every time he ran for mayor. The most important difference between them was that Fitzgerald represented Boston's rising Irish-Americans and Trotter represented Boston's activist black community during the nadir of the African-American experience.

Fitzgerald proved to be the most responsive Irish-American politician of his day toward black aspirations. However, it is difficult to determine to what extent his actions represented mere vote-getting and to what extent they represented genuine sentiment. Boston's black population was too small to merit much attention, and too unimportant to warrant pandering to racist sentiment—the very language for that did not yet exist in northern big cities until the Great Migration. Nevertheless, votes were votes, and Fitzgerald was the most energetic campaigner the city had ever seen. He attained political prominence in 1894 by defeating Joseph O' Neill, Maguire's man in the U.S. Congress, thus opening a split in Irish Democratic ranks. To win future elections, he would need the support of voters of every nationality, and these he aggressively pursued throughout his years. At the same time, he did take a few controversial, if little-noted stands that showed a genuine streak of concern for black equality.[33]

As a congressman, he was one of only three members to support an amendment to a bill on the size of the House that would reduce southern representation by twelve seats. Republican Edgar D. Crumpacker of Indiana proposed to reduce the Mississippi, South Carolina, Louisiana, and North Carolina delegations because those states disfranchised black voters through specific constitutional revisions; Crumpacker would marshal the Fourteenth Amendment against them. Clearly, these would be Democratic seats lost to the Solid South. Of Crumpacker's three backers (there were then 356 House members) Fitzgerald was the only Democrat to speak. He defended the Massachusetts election law from unfavorable comparison with the new southern laws, contrasting the racial bias of the grandfather clause with race-neutral restrictions in Massachusetts (these were English literacy and one-year residency). Denouncing race chauvinism, he praised the valor of black soldiers in the Spanish-American War, arguing that their sacrifice should count toward their political rights. As with many legislative attempts to aid African-Americans, the Crumpacker amendment never even came to a vote. Nevertheless, this unpopular stance by New England's lone Democrat in Congress suggests a certain commitment to principle.[34]

As mayor of Boston, Fitzgerald took one other difficult stand. His leading African-American spokesperson in the crucial 1909 campaign was Edward Everett Brown, an attorney who supported Booker Washington against Trotter. Along with his law partner James Wolff, Brown organized a colored rally for Fitzgerald at St. Paul's Church just before the election. In April, the victorious Fitzgerald appointed Brown head of the department of weights and measures; Brown had been Fitzgerald's assistant health commissioner in his first term. No black person had been head of a city department before. Eleven employees at weights and measures now threatened to resign, explicitly because of Brown's race. Fitzgerald threatened to fire the employees, and they backed down. A few months later, Wolff delivered the city's Fourth of July address.[35]

In smaller, symbolic ways, Fitzgerald responded to African-American initiatives for recognition. He routinely sent letters of support to Monroe Trot-

ter's protest meetings at Faneuil Hall. When Trotter asked that the city flags
be lowered to commemorate the centennial of abolitionist poet John Greenleaf Whittier, Fitzgerald complied. Heeding the protests of black citizens, he
convinced a theater manager to withdraw an offensive play, *The Clansman*,
from the stage (without actually banning it). He spoke at the NAACP's national convention in Boston in 1911. By these small measures he showed a
regard for fair play and decency.[36]

There is much less to be said about the record of James Michael Curley.
His most public act regarding municipal race relations was to disappoint the
black community by refusing to ban *The Birth of a Nation* from a Boston
movie house. Later, as American entry into the world war approached, he
proposed a segregated unit for local civil defense, to the consternation of
some black Bostonians. On the other hand, he did protest Woodrow Wilson's segregation of the federal departments, pushed to allow a black veteran
to be buried in Arlington National Cemetery, and supported an antilynching
bill; his 1930s mayoralty included other accomplishments.[37]

Boston's Irish-American politicians, in the period 1890–1920, did not have
a worse record on the race question than Boston's Yankee politicians, whether
Brahmin Republican or Yankee Democrat. Nor did they lag behind or stand
out from the record of other urban political leaders in the North or Midwest.
That they fell away from the vision of John Boyle O'Reilly is not surprising;
O'Reilly was a dreamer and poet. If these political leaders failed to confront
the southerners on the race question, or failed to include Boston's small African-American population in the patronage distribution, this was par for the
national course.

Nevertheless, Boston had been different from the rest of the nation, and
to a certain extent remained so until 1920. Boston generated a group of race
reformers who supported African-American education in the South, and later
built the NAACP. Certainly, few prominent white people populated these
movements. Just as certainly, however, none of them were Irish-Americans.
After O'Reilly, there was no Boston Irish analogue to the Yankee reformers,
or to the Jewish NAACP leaders of New York such as Joel and Arthur Spingarn. What broader factors limited the development of an alliance, even if a
limited and temporary one, between Boston's Irish- and African-American
political leaders and activists?

By far the major reason for the separation between these groups was the
marginality of African-Americans to city politics. Comprising about 2 percent of Boston's population throughout much of the period, they could not
claim to represent a balance of power between contending Irish-American
factions. That role fell to the city's "new" European immigrants, such as

Italians in Fitzgerald's North End, or Jews in Lomasney's West End. African-Americans clustered increasingly in the South End, led by a lesser figure, James Donovan.[38]

A second factor was the implosion of the national, state, and local Democratic Party in the 1890s. In Massachusetts, the party began the decade with the victory of William E. Russell, a moderate Democrat who served as governor from 1890 to 1893. Russell's unifying political influence collapsed under the impact of the depression of 1893. By 1896, George Fred Williams led the Yankee Democrats behind William Jennings Bryan, while the Grover Cleveland Democrats and Independents scattered. The Irish leaders followed Williams and Bryan out of party loyalty, but split into a separate faction that was itself split between Maguire's supporters and the younger ward bosses. The question of civil rights was never important in a party based on unity with the South. It completely disappeared in this blizzard of factions.[39]

Third, after 1896 the Democratic Party nationally closed down even to Irish politicians. Bryan's radicalism was well larded with fundamentalism; his successor as party leader was the stern moralist Woodrow Wilson; and after 1915 the Ku Klux Klan raised its head within the party so that later conventions hinged on anti-Klan resolutions. The entire atmosphere of the country turned against black people and part of the backlash extended to the rising Irish Catholics. Wilson's racism drove the few blacks in the Democratic Party back toward the Republicans. After supporting Wilson in 1912 and suffering a brutal betrayal, African-American Democrats had no more room to maneuver inside the national Democratic Party.[40]

Fourth, the rise of Boston's ward bosses occurred in a period of economic prosperity. Boston enjoyed a building boom as the nation recovered at the end of the century and through most of the next three decades. The economic radicalism of the mid-1890s disappeared. Local politics in general became increasingly sterile after 1896. Tariff, currency, civil service reform all mysteriously disappeared as issues and municipal reform and regulation of trusts emerged. The ward bosses rose not as spokespersons for particular issues, but as deliverers of jobs and services to the immigrant poor. Nothing of substance separated Lomasney, Fitzgerald, and Curley politically except the unending struggle for power. The civil rights question was above all one of principle. The politics of the ward bosses, especially in an era of prosperity, was unprincipled.[41]

A fifth conservatizing influence on Boston's Irish-American political life was the decreasing importance of the Irish national struggle for American-born Irish immigrants. The ward bosses lived in a more narrow world than did their predecessors. Ireland was farther away. One sign of this was the fate of the *Republic*, which Fitzgerald acquired a few years after Maguire's death. In Maguire's day, the paper was polemical, complex, and full of news from the struggle in Ireland. Fitzgerald greatly expanded the paper's circulation by neutering it. The next generation preferred the women's pages, words for young people, and bland homilies to sainted figures that graced Fitzgerald's family magazine. The Irish problem was losing its urgency to people who were building a new culture in America.[42]

Finally, American entry into the world war on the side of Britain rendered Boston's Irish-Americans more conservative. Curley, for example, was at first hostile to American participation. Irish nationalism directed against Britain, such as that expressed in the Easter Rising of 1916, became a complex matter for patriotic American Irish. As the preparedness bandwagon cranked up, the uniformity of thought that was ultimately to contribute to the postwar Red scare closed down the space for social change of any type. O'Reilly could unite with black Americans behind the figure of Crispus Attucks in his day, and perhaps find a sympathetic ear among Brahmin American nationalists intent upon asserting American prerogatives against the British. By 1917, Ireland's enemy was America's ally, and the cause of rebellion suffered. Irish-Americans returned from the war as patriotic members of the American Legion, but black soldiers came back as embittered New Negroes ready to fight for their rights. The war widened the cultural gulf between Boston's Irish- and African-Americans.

O'REILLY'S FADING INFLUENCE IN THE CATHOLIC CHURCH

John Boyle O'Reilly's influence was felt in the religious sphere as well as the political. He was a practicing Catholic all his life, and he enjoyed the support of Archbishop John J. Williams of Boston. His radical message of racial tolerance went out to thousands of Catholics who read the *Pilot* especially for its reports of developments within the church. During O'Reilly's lifetime, the American Catholic Church was rent between liberal and conservative factions. O'Reilly and his successors gave voice to the liberal group. Archbishop Williams stood between the two camps, probably favoring the liberals. When he died and William Henry O'Connell succeeded him in 1908, the *Pilot* fell into his hands and the conservative faction won. O'Connell consolidated his power and bureaucratized the church during his long tenure.

The civil rights question played little part in this important process, which nontheless affected Boston's race relations. The Catholic Church was different from the Protestant denominations in that it was organized on interracial lines; there was no independent black Catholic Church. It might have been a point of contact between Irish- and African-Americans through which the broader aspirations of black Bostonians might have been expressed. As in politics, the small size of Boston's black Catholic population, combined with the small number of Catholics in the South, together worked to prevent the Catholic Church from promoting racial equality in civic life. Again, it was not a foregone conclusion that events should transpire as they did.

The Church liberals wanted to "Americanize" Catholicism in the new world. They believed in American democracy and did not fear its influence on church life. They embraced the doctrines of separation of church and state, believed that Catholics should freely enter into associations with their Protestant brethren, and felt that American soil was favorable to the growth of their religion. They favored Catholic education with a secular tinge and opposed official condemnation of the militant union the Knights of Labor. Their leaders were the diplomatic James Cardinal Gibbons of Baltimore, whose early career included service in the South, and the more outspoken Archbishop John Ireland of St. Paul, Minnesota. The conservatives were led by John Cardinal McCloskey of New York, Michael Corrigan, his successor, and Bishop Bernard McQuaid of Rochester. They simply put a minus where the liberals placed a plus, favoring the Roman, top-down style of organization and preferring the classical European arrangement in which the state and church were mutually interdependent.[43]

Archbishop John J. Williams (1822–1908), Boston-born son of an Irish-immigrant blacksmith, was educated in Boston at Bishop Fenwick's school, Montreal, and Paris, and ascended the ecclesiastical ladder, becoming archbishop in 1866. Modest and retiring by nature, he counseled prudence when Boston's Catholics were assailed by nativists in the late 1880s and early 1890s. Williams's restraint won him the approbation of Boston's Brahmin leadership. In a sense, this relationship paralleled that between Boston's Irish Democrats and their Yankee allies. Williams thus showed a confidence in the promise of American life that inclined him toward the church liberals. As a liberal, he feared that if the church banned the Knights of Labor, the church's influence would be weakened among workingmen. On the other hand, Williams would not go too far to countenance radicalism. When the conservative New York leaders chastened Father Edward McGlynn, who supported radical Henry George in the 1886 mayor's race in New York, they had Williams's support. His sentiments were generally Americanist, but he gave no offense to the conservatives. Upon Williams's silver jubilee as a priest, Cardinal Gibbons praised him effusively.[44]

In this protective space, O'Reilly, Roche, and Roche's successor Katherine Conway infused their readers with modern social opinion. The archbishop had acquired three-fourths interest in the *Pilot* when founder Patrick Donahoe relinquished control in the 1870s. Williams left the editorial policy to the lay journalists, who featured the progressive church leaders in the weekly. On race relations, Cardinal Gibbons was a liberal paternalist who believed in Booker Washington's patient approach. Like Washington, he also worked behind the scenes to foster racial equality; in 1909–10 he helped defeat a scheme to disfranchise Maryland's black voters. Archbishop Ireland was more outspoken. When the national Afro-American League met in his St. Paul diocese, he condemned segregation, disfranchisement, and all color prejudice. He opposed proscribing interracial marriage. "I would say let all people in America be equal socially and politically," he concluded. In this spirit the *Pilot* instructed its readers. Years later, Roche wrote editorially that "Catholics must give the Negro practical proof of their own faith in the brotherhood of all for whom Christ died."[45]

Williams himself showed little tangible interest in the question of civil rights, certainly nothing to match Ireland's rhetoric or Gibbons's deeds. He was a spiritual man who was apparently free of any racial prejudice himself. Williams promoted the remarkable careers of three black priests: the brothers Healy, who were born to a Catholic Georgia planter and a former slave. These three served as Jesuit (Patrick), administrator (Sherwood) and as bishop of Portland, Maine (James). James achieved the highest rank and notoriety, but his service in Maine effectively isolated him from other black people. He exchanged only a few letters with Archbishop Williams, and none on racial matters within the church. Upon his death, the *Pilot* did not mention his race, or any contribution he made on race relations.[46]

Black people, mostly from the Caribbean, had been part of the Catholic community at least since 1789, praying in separate pews. In Williams's time, they worshiped at the cathedral, Immaculate Conception, and St. Joseph's, located in the integrated communities of the West and South Ends. Among the worshipers was the outstanding civil rights attorney Robert Morris, whose clientele included many Irish-Americans. According to his biographer, Williams "arranged for a special mass at the Cathedral and gave one of his own priests full charge of this portion of his flock." This was probably the Reverend Thomas J. McCormack, chancellor of the archdiocese, who, according to the *Pilot*, "has long had charge of the little Negro congregation." In the summer of 1906, Boston's black Catholics requested a separate congregation, and apparently began to pray in segregation. There is no evidence that any of the brothers Healy, or Boston's black Catholics, tried to influence church policy on civil rights matters between 1890 and 1920.[47]

Williams died in 1908, and his coadjutor, the Lowell-born William Henry

O'Connell (1859–1944) succeeded him. Associated with a conservative papacy, his leadership marked the eclipse of the liberal "Americanist" wing of the church; his biographer James O'Toole shows that he was imposed upon a hostile New England priesthood. O'Connell launched a highly visible counterattack against perceived secular and Protestant indignities, contributing to the polarized atmosphere of the city. He fought vigorously against modernism in the broad sense: secularism, women's rights, sexual expression, and for the notion of a "triumphant" Catholicism, whose implication was that the church taught the one and only true way. His elevation to cardinal in 1911 showed that he had the backing of Rome. He centralized church power in his own hands, and personalized the struggle against his opponents in a manner analogous to James Michael Curley's course in politics. In a broad sense, O'Connell revived the old, antireform thrust of antebellum Irish Catholicism.[48]

Like Williams, O'Connell paid little attention to American race relations or to Boston's few black Catholics. His policies had a chilling effect on reform of any sort, and his tight control of church institutions shut down the *Pilot* as a liberal organ. On the other hand, he promoted the Sisters of the Blessed Sacrament, a national group of missionaries to racial minorities, whose Boston endeavors he underwrote. The intentions of this latter project must be viewed with a certain ambivalence, however.

O'Connell effectively stilled the echo of O'Reilly's voice at the *Pilot*. Roche resigned as editor in 1904, and Patrick M. Donahoe, a descendant of the founder, gained financial control with the acquiesence of Williams, who regarded himself as a trustee. Katherine Conway, an associate of O'Reilly, became the new editor, and continued in Roche's genteel tradition of liberal reform. For example, an April 1906 article, "A Model Parish of Colored People in Washington, D.C.," praised the piety of St. Cyprian's parishioners. Later that year, the Atlanta race riot brought a stern rebuke against white malefactors. In 1908, O'Connell gained financial control and the *Pilot* became the official organ of the archdiocese. David J. Toomey, a priest, assumed the editorship, and the paper fell silent on race matters.[49]

The tenor of the *Pilot* during the controversy over the showing of *The Birth of a Nation* in April 1915, is instructive. During the most visible African-American protest in Boston's history to that date, the *Pilot* simply ignored the matter. In March, the paper advocated stopping one stage play, and decried playwrights George Bernard Shaw and Charles Rahn Kennedy as blasphemous. Culture in general was on the *Pilot*'s agenda, but only as it affected Catholics directly. Most telling of all was an editorial memorializing U.S. Supreme Court Justice Roger Brooke Taney, whose "sterling Catholicity puts him at the very forefront of the Catholic American laity." While proudly celebrating Taney's long career, including his regard for the souls of his slaves, whose freedom he "set about to establish," the editorial could only say about the Dred Scott decision that it was his most famous. Protests against the racist film then showing in Boston went unnoticed.[50]

O'Connell actively promoted the work of the Sisters of the Blessed Sacrament, the Mission to Indians and Negroes, founded by Philadelphia heiress Katharine Drexel. He facilitated the group's establishment in Boston and contributed financially to the order, something he did not do for other orders. At the same time, he limited the group's right to raise funds on its own. The Sisters came to Boston in 1914, locating their convent in the South End where they proselytized and comforted the poor. With the aid of Reverend Father [Michael?] Doody of Cambridge, they opened a "colored" Sunday school in that city as well.[51]

As with missionary work by any denomination, the business was heavily invested with paternalist rhetoric and attitude. "Yet, in Boston, these dark skinned children are not forgotten and missionaries are busily engaged in bringing the consolations of religion to the colored people who live hereabouts," the *Pilot* effused in 1916. By that time, this sensibility was at odds with the emerging militancy and race-proud consciousness of Boston's African-Americans and the paternalistic approach was bound to cause some resentment. O'Connell may have been especially interested in the Sisters as part of his struggle against Protestant denominations, for as the *Pilot* noted, "zealots of another fold" were hard at work in the same neighborhood.[52]

THE LABOR MOVEMENT: INDIFFERENCE IN BLACK AND WHITE

Boston's Irish-Americans gradually assumed the leadership of the city's Central Labor Union between 1890 and 1920, as they did with the Democratic Party and Catholic Church. The union movement grew more bureaucratic and conservative, as did the American Federation of Labor under the leadership of Samuel Gompers. The bureaucratization of Boston's unions cannot be attributed to Irish leadership. If they failed to organize Boston's African-American workers, who toiled for the most part at menial jobs, so did other white trade unionists.

Boston's labor movement was more ethnically diverse than either the Democratic Party or the Catholic Church. Yankees such as George E. McNeill and Frank Foster were guiding lights for part of this time, and Yankees and British-Americans constituted an important part of the workforce. Dominic D'Alessandro, leader of the Hodcarrier's Union, represented an

Italian immigrant group that competed with Irish workers for jobs. Henry Abrahams led the Cigarmakers Union, and thousands of Jews belonged to the Hebrew Trades Association. African-American workers fared no better where these leaders had influence than they did in the construction trades, transportation, municipal unions, or teamsters, where Irish leadership was strongest. The ethnic diversity of the labor movement also meant that the competition between white ethnics for jobs, predominance of ideas, or organizing jurisdiction, pushed the possibility of black equality further down on any white leader's agenda.[53]

John Boyle O'Reilly did write about labor questions, but he exerted no leadership in this field. His equivalent in Boston's labor history was of Scotch-Irish descent, George E. McNeill (1837–1906) who, along with Ira Steward, championed the eight-hour movement throughout the state. McNeill helped lead the Knights of Labor, a more militant forerunner of the American Federation of Labor. After McNeill lost an idealistic campaign for mayor in 1886, his protégé Frank Foster became editor of the *Labor Leader*, the official journal of several unions. Foster steered the labor movement into the camp of the AFL, an entirely different course than the universal reformer McNeill had imagined. Along the way, Foster had to beat down the attempts of Marxists and other radicals to gain control of the AFL; this job was mostly done by 1894. The Irish-American labor leaders rose in the context of waning radicalism and waxing conservatism and prosperity.[54]

Boston's labor history followed the national trend. The implications of this were largely negative for African-Americans. The Knights of Labor helped to organize black workers, sometimes separately and sometimes in integrated locals. The AFL's record was much worse in this regard. Structurally, it was a federation of organizations, not a membership organization. As such, it officially discouraged whites-only unions, but in practice it tolerated them and did little to organize black workers. In the construction trades, metalworking unions, railroad brotherhoods and other organizations, blacks were effectively barred from membership.[55]

There is a paucity of material on Boston's Irish-American labor leaders of this period, who include relatively obscure figures such as Cornelius Shea of the Teamsters, Frank H. McCarthy of the Cigarmakers, John F. O'Sullivan of the Typographical Union, and many others. Probably the best known is Daniel Tobin, who rose from a poor Cambridge background to national leadership of the Teamsters in 1907. He retained an iron grip on the union until 1952, fighting against every progressive trend in labor history throughout his career. He was never above vilifying his opponents because of their ethnic background; he sided with anti-Semites like radio priest Father Charles

Coughlin during the 1930s. If he was more extreme than other Boston labor leaders, he was not entirely atypical.[56]

One of the best records of Boston's labor movement in this period was Foster's *Labor Leader*. The columns were filled with engaging articles on contemporary problems such as the eight-hour workday and the relation of the labor movement to cooperativism and socialism. In contrast to the high level of this discussion, Foster drew a complete blank on race relations. Over a ten-year period, he almost never wrote about black workers. In December 1891, Foster traveled to an AFL convention in Alabama. From his railway car he gaped at the segregated waiting rooms and listened to stories of disfranchisement as if learning about these practices for the first time. This was the southern way of doing things, he observed, and if he disapproved, he did not say so. Earlier in the year he mused about Frederick Douglass's reception in Haiti: "How can other races have faith in the Negro when he has none in himself?" Lynching, he noted briefly the following year, would cease only when black crime did. Foster's eyes were simply closed to the real problems.[57]

John Daniels's *In Freedom's Birthplace* is both an impressionistic account of African-American Boston in this period and a statistically driven sociological study. Daniels clearly demonstrates the marginality of black labor to the union movement. Relying upon the census return of 1900, he found that in Boston 13 percent of white males, 30 percent of white females, 61 percent of black males, and 76 percent of Negro females worked at "menial" jobs. Of the 2,930 black men in this category, 1,676 were servants or waiters, 404 were porters, and 665 were day laborers. Of the 1,739 black women in this group, 1,222 were servants and 492 were laundry workers. In the next highest black male industrial group were 150 teamsters, 75 construction workers, 30 masons, 19 printers and a scattered remainder. Of 367 black women in this group, 114 were dressmakers; the rest divided among various other occupations. Writing in 1914, Daniels observed that the workers in the menial group were socially segregated, while more in the skilled group worked in racially integrated settings. "Probably not much more than one union in twenty has any Negro members at all, and of those which have, probably not over one in ten counts half a dozen or more of this race on its rolls." While Daniels thought the race prejudice of union leaders was exaggerated, "it nevertheless remains true that a considerable number of the unions are averse to admitting members of the Negro race. The Negroes themselves complain that such is the case." Daniels concluded that "few, if any [unions] have shown any interest in the Negro's industrial welfare." He knew of only one black union, the Boston Colored Waiter's Alliance, AFL Local 183, and this was more of a social club and hiring hall than a labor organization. There were also a few black longshoremen and teamster members. The latter worked mostly as coal-wagon drivers, and one of these locals had a black majority.[58]

Two visual images of Boston's labor history dramatize this reality. On 20 February 1894, radical labor leaders led a protest of unemployed workers at the statehouse. Among the throng of mostly immigrant workers reporters noticed only a handful of colored faces. Fifteen years later, AFL members demonstrated against the imprisonment of President Samuel Gompers, and in a crowd of about a thousand, not one black face can be seen.[59] Irish-American workers and their leaders, like other whites, insisted on excluding African-Americans from their workplaces, unions, and struggles in Boston just as they did in the rest of the country.

John Boyle O'Reilly dreamed a vision of the brotherhood of all the down-trodden; he saw the fate of the African-Americans and the Irish as one. By 1920, that dream had vanished. As the Boston Irish built a powerful political party, church, and union apparatus, they forgot John Boyle O'Reilly and the notion that no group is free while another is oppressed.

Moorfield Storey. Courtesy of the Massachusetts Historical Society.

SEVEN

❧❧❧❧❧

Life Experience and the Law
The Cases of Holmes, Lewis, and Storey

"THE LIFE OF THE LAW has not been logic: it has been experience. The felt necessities of the time, the prevalent moral and political theories, intuitions of public policy, avowed or unconscious, even the prejudices which judges share with their fellow-men, have had a good deal more to do than the syllogism in determining the rules by which men should be governed."[1] Thus wrote Oliver Wendell Holmes in *The Common Law*. This chapter seeks to discover the "experience" and "felt necessities of the time" that informed the work of Moorfield Storey, William Henry Lewis, and Holmes himself as they acted in the field of American race relations. All three lawyers had to confront Boston's antislavery heritage, and test its relevance against the evolving new racial codes of the South.

As with Henry Cabot Lodge and George Frisbie Hoar in the political arena, these Boston jurists exercised great influence in the courts of law and public opinion between 1890 and 1920. Holmes, who paid little attention to race relations, nevertheless wrote about a dozen important Supreme Court opinions on voting rights, segregation, peonage, and due process of law during his tenure on the Court. His reluctance to overturn state judges or legislatures influenced his inclination to accept the new laws of the South. Lewis began as a militant, but abandoned his principles to become an assistant attorney general of the United States, the highest appointed position ever held by an African-American at the time. Moorfield Storey was probably the country's leading civil rights lawyer during the second decade of the century. He consciously carried forward the civil rights legacy of Charles Sumner, whose secretary he had been as a young man.

All three lived during a period in which the mores and laws of society, North and South, turned increasingly racist. In the legal field, few developments symbolized this more than the U.S. Supreme Court ruling in *Plessy v. Ferguson* (1896) and the reaction to it. This 7–1 decision affirmed that the state of Louisiana could mandate segregation in public transportation. The case became an important precedent and facilitated the segregation of the South. The North did not seem to care. The northern press paid the decision almost no attention, and even in Boston the verdict went unnoticed in the newspapers.[2]

OLIVER WENDELL HOLMES AND THE INVISIBLE MEN

Oliver Wendell Holmes, who lived one of the richest intellectual lives in American history, and was one of the country's most influential jurists, wrote nothing at all about African-Americans. He did not see them, either as individuals or as a group with special concerns. In this, he reflected the narrowness of the Brahmin world, of which he was an outstanding and thoroughbred example. This aspect of Holmes's worldview is the more remarkable because of the enormity of his intellectual and even social reach. At a time when Jews faced significant hostility, particularly in Boston's legal community, Holmes was conspicuously friendly with such Jewish thinkers as Louis Brandeis, Felix Frankfurter, Harold Laski, Lewis Einstein, and Morris Raphael Cohen. He even sought out Boston labor leader Frank Foster during the labor turmoil of the 1890s. Yet he corresponded with no African-American intellectuals or activists, and almost never referred to the race problem in his correspondence.[3]

Consequently, he contributed little of positive value to American law regarding race relations. By the time of Holmes's elevation to the Supreme Court in 1902, African-American problems had disappeared from the white American agenda. The Boston Brahmins, who now championed the cause of Booker T. Washington, found in the Tuskegee educator the willing recipient of their noblesse oblige. Holmes was not even prepared to accept Washington's vision of race relations. In two opinions on cases brought to the court by Washington (who was working in secret), Holmes voted to reject the pleas of black plaintiffs.[4]

Holmes's Civil War service was the defining experience of his life. He fought for four years and was wounded three times, rejoining his regiment after each convalescence. His Civil War letters suggest that he fought primarily from a sense of duty to his country and loyalty to his regiment. As an intellectual, Holmes never seems to have confronted the central question of the war: slavery and the place of the freedpeople in a reconstructed union.

Holmes wrote to family and friends of the dull horror of war. He wrote without idealism or sentimentality, and with only occasional reference to the grander issues of the conflict. The North was "vainly working to effect what never happens—the subjugation (for that is it) of a great civilized nation. We shan't do it—at least the Army can't." He wrote nothing of the Emancipation Proclamation, and made only one cryptic reference to the black troops. One biographer suggests that emancipation meant little to Holmes. When his friend Norwood P. Hallowell accepted an invitation to lead African-American soldiers, and urged Holmes to join him, Holmes declined. From his letters, one surmises that Holmes saw no African-Americans at all during the war, only once glimpsing what he called a "nigger hut."[5]

Holmes spent the Reconstruction years studying at Harvard Law School and practicing corporation and admiralty law with a conservative Brahmin firm. His social circle included William and Henry James, Moorfield Storey, John Ropes and John Grey, Henry Adams, and Henry Cabot Lodge. As editor of the *American Law Review* he evinced skepticism about the movement to codify the law. This early inclination toward legal scholarship led him to edit the twelfth edition of Chancellor James Kent's *Commentaries* at the youthful age of 32; within a few years he was at work on his masterpiece, *The Common Law*, published in 1881.[6]

At the heart of *The Common Law* is the conception that the law is a dynamic attempt to regulate human behavior by a society in flux, rather than a static body of natural laws discovered by legal scientists. The text is informed by a rich historical discussion of the origins of law. He finds that "laws devised for specific purposes often survived for centuries after their original purpose had been served."[7]

This was a revolutionary notion in a profession whose mental world derived from a medieval cosmology of fixed laws and principles. At the same time, there is a fatalism in Holmes's conception, embodied in the passage quoted at the beginning of this chapter. His attitude toward "the prejudices which judges share with their fellow-men" was that these should be respected. The "first requirement of a sound body of law is, that it should correspond with the actual feelings and demands of the community," wrote Holmes.[8] This necessitated judicial conservatism, and, on the surface, a liberal respect for the democratic practice of the community. The problem with this approach lay in how to accommodate the rights of those excluded from the body politic, such as the blacks in the South.

This judicial conservatism lay at the heart of Holmes's philosophy. He was reluctant to strike down legislation from the bench. In Massachusetts this earned Holmes a "Progressive" reputation: during Holmes's tenure on the state's high court (December 1882 to December 1901), Massachusetts legislatures passed a series of Progressive regulatory measures that Holmes let stand when challenged. This did not imply Holmes's sympathy with any particular law, or with the cause of labor. When Holmes was in doubt, he preferred to find a law "not unconstitutional" rather than "constitutional," a less emphatic formulation that nevertheless allowed the legislature considerable leeway. Holmes's loose construction of the state constitution employed a less stringent test than many of his brethren used.[9]

This tolerance of progressive legislation, Holmes's Civil War record, and his impressive scholarship recommended him to the new president, Theodore Roosevelt. Henry Cabot Lodge, Roosevelt's friend, advanced the nomination, for Holmes had befriended Lodge during 1884 when the future senator stood fast for Republican presidential nominee James G. Blaine. Some Massachusetts businessmen opposed Holmes for his occasional pro-labor rulings, and Senator George Frisbie Hoar preferred his own favorite, but Holmes was easily confirmed in the Senate.[10]

In two early decisions on grand jury composition, Holmes wrote cautious opinions, the first of which set legal formalities above social realities. This was a unanimous opinion that reflected the spirit of the times. In *Brownfield v. South Carolina* (1903), the plaintiff, convicted of murder, argued that "the grand jury was composed wholly of white persons, and that all negroes, although constituting four-fifths of the population and of the registered voters of the county, were excluded on account of their race and color." Holmes found that John Brownfield had failed to prove that blacks were intentionally kept off the jury. Brownfield had merely moved to quash the indictment based on the alleged discrimination, but brought no evidence. "The case involves questions of the gravest character," Holmes concluded, "but we must deal with it according to the record, and the record discloses no wrong."[11]

While Holmes's opinion was restricted to the procedural question, the state supreme court decision shows that Brownfield had killed an arresting officer, alleging self-defense. Brownfield argued that a plainclothes officer unknown to him had assaulted him with a pistol, and that he, Brownfield, was in terror of his life.[12] It is difficult to imagine that a jury four-fifths black would have heard this case in the same way as an all-white jury, or that an all-white jury could have been assembled without recourse to deliberate discrimination. Brownfield's attorneys bungled the case, relying on prima facie evidence to prove intentional discrimination in jury selection. However, even with adequate representation, intent to discriminate would have been hard to prove.

Presented with a stronger case the following year, Holmes found in *Rogers v. Alabama* that deliberate exclusion of black people from grand juries did violate the Fourteenth Amendment. Dan Rogers was convicted of murder in Montgomery County, Alabama, and the case came to the attention of Booker T. Washington. Acting in strict secrecy, Washington raised money for the case and saw that Rogers was represented by the able Wilford H. Smith.[13]

This time, Holmes found that the case was properly argued by the defendant but wrongly judged. The newly revised Alabama constitution did intend to exclude blacks from the voting and grand jury lists. The Alabama court threw out this motion on the grounds of prolixity: the defense attorneys had argued an irrelevant point at too great a length. Relying upon the opinion of Justice Grey in *Carter v. Texas*, Holmes reversed the decision of the lower court, upholding an already established precedent.[14]

Holmes failed to grasp the reality of American race relations in *Giles v. Harris*, which he wrote for a six-judge majority. Alabama amended its constitution in 1901 for the purpose of disfranchising black voters. Under the new law, prospective voters might be asked to write an article of the Constitution, show proof of employment during the past twelve months, or demonstrate ownership of forty acres. Prospective voters might also have to answer, under oath, questions about where they had lived and worked for the last five years. However, war veterans, or merely "persons of good character," might also vote. "As we have said," Holmes wrote, "according to the allegations of the bill this part of the constitution, as practically administered and as intended to be administered, let in all whites and kept out a large part, if not all, of the blacks."[15]

Although Booker T. Washington and the faculty at Tuskegee Institute were allowed to register, all over the state black men were turned away. Governor William D. Jelks wrote frankly to an Alabama senator that "the spirit of the constitution . . . looks to the registration of all white men not convicted of crime, and only a few negroes." A Colored Men's Suffrage Association of Alabama was formed and Washington secretly underwrote the legal expenses of the suit brought by the association. Jackson W. Giles, a leader of the group, lost his challenge in the state court, and the Federal Circuit judge, a Theodore Roosevelt appointee recommended by Washington, decided that he had no jurisdiction.[16]

Holmes agreed that the circuit judge could not hear the case, "because the bill did not aver threatened damage to an amount exceeding two thousand dollars." Holmes decided instead that the Supreme Court had jurisdiction, and could properly rule on the case. Two problems brought Holmes to decide against the plaintiffs. First, Holmes asked rhetorically, if the Alabama constitution was unlawful, "how can we make the Court a party to the unlawful scheme by accepting it and adding another voter to its fraudulent list?" The second problem was that the Court had no authority to dictate political policies. "Apart from damages to the individual, relief from a great political wrong, if done as alleged, by the people of a state and the state itself, must be given by them or by the legislative and political department of the government of the United States."[17]

Holmes's opinion placed technicalities over substance and employed circular reasoning. His finding that the circuit court did not have jurisdiction validated the evasion of responsibility by the lower court. On the substantive matter, Holmes's logic was circular: if the constitution was invalid, the plaintiffs could not get relief by appealing to it. The implication was that there was no way to register blacks through an appeal to the court, as the remainder of the opinion made explicit. The Fourteenth and Fifteenth Amendments disappear from this cold reasoning. The political reality, that henceforth black voters would be barred by white registrars, was lost on Holmes. He also ignored the consequences of disfranchisement—further segregation and economic oppression—upon African-Americans.

Three justices dissented from the ruling in *Giles*, an odd combination of the liberal John Marshall Harlan and the normally conservative David Brewer and Henry Brown, author of *Plessy*. Harlan restricted his argumentation especially to the question of the circuit court's jurisdiction, but disagreed emphatically with Holmes on the substantive issue, concluding that "the plaintiff is entitled to relief in respect of his right to be registered as a voter." Brewer agreed that the circuit court had jurisdiction, and that the plaintiff was wrongfully denied his rights. Brown did not write. The opinion of these dissenters throws into more sharp relief Holmes's blindness on racial matters.[18]

The decision was deeply demoralizing to the plaintiffs. Washington's lawyer refused to press the case further through the slim window of opportunity left open, that damages might be collected. He withdrew, telling Washington's aide that the ruling had given him a bad case of the blues. Jackson Giles, however, persisted, only to be rebuffed in the Supreme Court the following year.[19]

Further insight into Holmes's views on race can be gained from his rulings on cases involving lynching. Lynching was anarchy, and it flew directly in the face of the rule of law. Holmes moved energetically to suppress it in three dramatic cases that appeared before the Court: *Shipp* (1906 and 1909), *Frank v. Mangum* (1915), and *Moore v. Dempsey* (1923). In February 1906, Ed Johnson, a Tennessee black man, was convicted of raping and murdering a white woman and sentenced to hang. Johnson asked for a writ of habeas corpus at the U.S. Circuit Court, arguing that the exclusion of Negroes from the jury and the threat of violence at the trial deprived him of his right to due process of law. The petition was denied, Johnson appealed to the Supreme Court, Harlan issued a stay, and the sheriff was notified. That night Chattanooga Sheriff John F. Shipp withdrew the guard from Johnson's cell and the prisoner was lynched by a mob.

The Supreme Court ordered an investigation into Shipp's conduct, and the Justice Department subsequently charged Shipp with contempt of court. Holmes wrote a strong opinion for a unanimous Court that, contrary to the defendant's claim, the Court did have jurisdiction in the case and was not a party to the suit. Three years later, when the substantive matter came before the Court, Chief Justice Melville W. Fuller wrote the opinion himself, and finding Shipp in contempt, ordered a ninety-day prison term. Holmes thought a one-year sentence more appropriate.[20]

The Leo Frank case, in which Holmes and Justice Charles Evans Hughes dissented from a majority opinion, contributed to the image of Holmes as a "great dissenter." The important issue to Holmes was, as in *Shipp*, subversion of the rule of law by mob violence. Although no black people were involved in this case, Frank, a Jew, served as a surrogate Negro and outsider to the mob. As in *Shipp*, the core of the case was a charge of rape and murder. The decision of the Court would clearly affect the ability of mobs to intimidate judges and juries, especially in criminal cases against black people.

During Frank's trial in 1913, angry mobs threatened to kill the judge if the verdict was not guilty. Inside the courtroom the crowd hooted and cheered during the trial. Frank was convicted and condemned to die. After one appeal failed, Frank turned to Justice Joseph Rucker Lamar of Georgia, who turned him down on the ground that the issue was a state matter. Frank next appealed to Holmes, who reluctantly agreed with Lamar, but expressed his doubts to his fellow justices. Frank again approached Lamar, who, perhaps influenced by Holmes, changed his mind and the case went to the Court, which ruled 7–2 against Frank.

Holmes wrote a bitter dissent, in collaboration with Hughes. He described "a court packed with spectators and surrounded by a crowd outside, all strongly hostile to the petitioner." The judge urged Frank and his attorney to stay outside the court when the verdict was read, lest the mob attack in the event of acquittal. Leaving aside Frank's right to be present when the verdict was read, Holmes found that "mob law does not become due process of law by securing the assent of a terrorized jury." The atmosphere of the trial entered Holmes's opinion. "Any judge who has sat with juries knows that in spite of forms they are extremely likely to be impregnated with the environing atmosphere." After Frank's defeat in the Court, the governor commuted his sentence to life in prison, and Frank was lynched. If ever subsequent developments suggested the validity of an opinion, the grisly conclusion of the Frank case vindicated Holmes and Hughes.[21]

Eight years later the Court effectively reversed itself and accepted their argument in the Frank case. After a meeting of Arkansas tenant farmers was attacked by white men in 1919, a violent confrontation ensued and a large number of blacks were arrested. By 1923, a remnant of these were condemned to death in a brief trial before which witnesses had been beaten and mob rule prevailed. Holmes, this time writing for a 7–2 majority in *Moore v. Dempsey*, ruled that the Arkansas court violated the due process of law, and the convictions were overturned.[22]

Holmes was much more reluctant to interfere with state courts on economic matters. In the case of Alonzo Bailey, an Alabama black man convicted of a criminal charge for running out on a fifteen-dollar debt, Holmes dissented from a majority opinion finding the Alabama law unconstitutional. This was another case engineered secretly by Booker Washington. Attorney General Charles J. Bonaparte filed a friend of the court brief. Dismissed at first on a technicality in 1908, the case returned to the Court in 1911. The Court found the Alabama debt law to sanction peonage (that is, involuntary servitude) and thus to violate the Thirteenth Amendment.[23]

Holmes wrote the majority opinion in 1908, sending it back to the lower court for lack of evidence. He ruled that Bailey was seeking a "short cut" by coming to the Court without exhausting other remedies. Harlan disagreed. The "short cut" Bailey sought was merely to be released on a writ of habeas corpus from jail in Alabama, pending the final decision, Harlan wrote. The Supreme Court had the responsibility to determine the constitutional question, and ought to do so at once. Delay was cruel and "unprecedented," Harlan angrily concluded.[24]

The case went back to the Alabama courts, and Bailey was found guilty. When Bailey appeared again before the Supreme Court, Hughes struck down the Alabama law as a violation of the Thirteenth Amendment, not considering Fourteenth Amendment arguments brought forth by plaintiffs. Hughes also rejected the notion that the case involved race discrimination, but he ruled the law "an instrument of compulsion peculiarly effective as against the poor and the ignorant, its most likely victims." He saw the statute as an unconstitutional antilabor law, giving employers the chance to criminalize refractory employees who had merely fallen into debt.[25]

Holmes dissented, with only Justice Horace H. Lurton, a Tennessee Democrat, joining him. He seized on Hughes's admission that the race question was not involved, taking that as his starting point. Bailey had simply broken his contract, and "the Thirteenth Amendment does not outlaw contracts for labor." Nor was Bailey a peon. "Peonage is service to a private master at which a man is kept by bodily compulsion against his will." Punishing a man for breaking a contract by means of a fine, imprisonment, or labor "does not make the laborer a slave." Furthermore, if the law were an effective deterrent to contract-breaking, all the better. "I think that obtaining money by fraud may be made a crime as well as murder or theft," Holmes concluded.[26]

Once again, the wider social reality disappeared in the face of Holmes's cold legal logic. Thanks to Booker Washington's careful secret work, the case was publicized in the Progressive press. The *Independent*, *World's Work*, and other journals hailed the outcome. Washington wrote to President William Howard Taft's secretary, calling the ruling "the most important decision in justice to the colored people . . . in many years, and the fact that almost the first decision rendered after a Southern Democrat [Edward Douglas White] was made Chief Justice [is] in favor of the Negro is most encouraging." Taft concurred. Holmes, a darling of such Progressives as Louis Brandeis, ruled to uphold a *status quo* that even Taft would overturn.[27]

In a later, related case, Holmes reluctantly sided with a majority (there were no dissenters, but one justice recused himself) by writing a terse concurring opinion. *U.S. v. Reynolds* and *U.S. v. Broughton*, decided together, were Justice Department challenges to the criminal-surety system of Alabama and Georgia. Under this scheme, a convicted offender could have his fine paid by a third party and work off the debt to the payor. White farmers thus secured cheap black labor and developed a vested interest in maintaining a steady supply of debt peons. Reynolds and Broughton were white Alabama farmers sympathetic to civil rights who agreed to arrange a test case. Justice William R. Day wrote a lengthy opinion finding the surety system in violation of the Thirteenth Amendment. Holmes's one-paragraph concurrence omits the Thirteenth Amendment grounds for overturning the laws, thus suggesting that a state might craft some more limited instrument to similar effect.[28]

Holmes had little sympathy for legal challenges to social segregation. He accepted the notion that state legislatures could mandate segregation without federal interference, even if the separate facilities were unequal, in *McCabe v. Atchison, Topeka and Santa Fe*. In *Buchanan v. Warley*, he was almost a lone dissenter against a decision striking down a Louisville, Kentucky, residential segregation ordinance. Both cases he regarded skeptically as contrived efforts to overturn laws that reflected the general sense of the community.

A 1907 Separate Coach Law in Oklahoma contained a section allowing railroads to provide no sleeping-car or first-class service for black people. In *McCabe*, five black Oklahomans challenged the law. Hughes, writing for a majority, agreed that the law did not live up to the "separate but equal" concept of the *Plessy* formula. Nevertheless the Court ruled on behalf of the railroads because the plaintiffs themselves had not been turned away. The majority essentially asked the plaintiffs to try again, after arranging a direct confrontation with the railroads. Holmes concurred with the outcome, but separated himself from the reasoning, suggesting that for him the case was permanently closed.[29]

Holmes played a similar foot-dragging role in *Buchanan v. Warley*, a challenge to the Louisville, Kentucky, residential segregation ordinance. The case was arranged by the local National Association for the Advancement of Colored People so that a sympathetic white realtor sued the leader of the NAACP for breach of contract to purchase real property, citing the segregation ordinance. The realtor, Buchanan, represented by Moorfield Storey of the NAACP, sought to complete the sale by striking at the ordinance. This the Court did, overturning the law on Fourteenth Amendment grounds. Holmes ultimately joined a unanimous Court, but not before drafting a dissent that he withdrew at the last minute. Complaining that the case was "manufactured," Holmes further decided that it was manufactured poorly. A white plaintiff could not "avail himself of this collateral mode of attack, on the ground of a wrong to someone else." Finding himself in a minority of one, Holmes dropped the dissent for obscure reasons.[30]

Holmes wrote two more opinions on voting rights that showed an advance over his earlier ruling in *Giles*. Additionally, he joined a majority decision written by Chief Justice White that overturned Oklahoma's "grandfather" clause. *U.S. v. Mosley* (1915) ordered that all votes in an Oklahoma election must be counted; and *Nixon v. Herndon* (1927) threw out a Texas white primary law.

Mosley overturned a district court decision that a 1909 federal law did not apply to a conspiracy to ignore votes. There was little doubt that two Blaine County, Oklahoma, election officials had met without the knowledge of the third member to plan the fraudulent counting of votes in eleven precincts during a congressional election. The federal law was drawn from an 1870 anti–Ku Klux Klan statute, and the defendants held that it was not applicable to their actions. Holmes found that the appropriate section "had a general scope and used general words that have become the most important now that the Ku Klux Klan have passed away." Here was Holmes's dynamic conception of the law utilized to put a broad construction upon congressional intent; the spirit of the interpretation is at loggerheads with its author's legalistic finding in *Giles* twelve years earlier.[31]

Holmes authored *Nixon v. Herndon* for a unanimous Court in 1927. This decision, easily arrived at, invalidated a 1923 Texas law that barred Negroes from participating in the Democratic primary. There was no indirection in the law's language. Since Texas was effectively a one-party state, this deprived African-Americans of a meaningful vote. The Court overturned the law on the basis of the Fourteenth Amendment.[32]

Holmes's rulings affecting the fate of African-Americans are uneven. In no sense did he resurrect Boston's tradition of leading the nation in the struggle for civil rights. During Holmes's tenure on the Court, that distinction belonged first to the Kentuckian Harlan and later to the New Yorker Hughes. Holmes was generally willing to support the political rights of African-Americans, as his rulings in *Rogers*, *Mosley*, and *Nixon v. Herndon* show. He steadfastly upheld the rule of law in opposition to mob violence in *Shipp*, the Frank case, and *Moore v. Dempsey*. In *Giles*, where he refused to grant relief in a clear disfranchisement case, and *Brownfield*, where he accepted the indictment of an all-white grand jury in a majority black county, he showed an unwillingness to look forward to civil equality. On desegregation and peonage cases, Holmes's judicial conservatism rendered him deaf to African-American pleas for justice. Had he kept the antislavery tradition alive, together with Harlan or Hughes he might have exerted a powerful influence, and signaled civil rights forces that in the Court they had an ally. He did not, and his record reflects the atrophy of the Brahmin conscience.

WILLIAM HENRY LEWIS AND THE AFRICAN-AMERICAN DILEMMA

During Reconstruction and its aftermath, a small group of notable African-American attorneys practiced in Boston. These men were products of the antislavery crusade and the Radical Republican period. As lawyers, they played a special role within the emerging black upper class, in that they necessarily interacted more with white society than other professionals. Some black lawyers had white patrons who advanced their careers; some were especially influenced by African-American leaders; some enjoyed both advantages. These Bostonians were among the first generation of black lawyers in America.

Robert Morris, Boston's first African-American lawyer, trained in the office of Ellis Gray Loring and assisted Charles Sumner during the school desegregation case (*Roberts v. Boston*) of 1849. John Swett Rock had a remarkably varied career, and was the first black attorney to argue in the Supreme Court. Edwin G. Walker was the son of David Walker, the abolitionist pamphleteer. Governor Benjamin Butler nominated him for the municipal court judgeship in Charlestown, but he was not confirmed. In his place Butler successfully appointed George L. Ruffin. Ruffin was a friend of Frederick Douglass; he wrote a preface for one of Douglass's autobiographies. Ruffin and Walker served in the state legislature. Walker and Morris participated in the freeing of Shadrach, the fugitive slave. Taken as a group, these were distinguished men unalterably committed to the antislavery tradition, who rose with their race.[33]

These men inspired a second generation of African-American attorneys in Boston. Some of them had direct links to their professional predecessors, and many of them had patrons or clients among whites. Born around the time of the Civil War, they came to maturity in the 1890s. This second generation, however, faced more complex problems than the men who preceded them. The earlier generation rose professionally with an ascending antiracist sentiment fostered by the Civil War, emancipation, and Reconstruction. The second generation faced a new rise of racism that generated an alliance between white philanthropists and black accommodationists. Lawyers, more than other black professionals, found that the new national arrangement affected their career path, especially if they aspired to elective or appointive office.

In Boston, attorneys Emery T. Morris, Edgar P. Benjamin, Butler Wilson, Archibald Grimké, and Clement Morgan generally followed the trail blazed by the earlier generation. Emery T. Morris, a nephew of Robert Morris, held a minor post in Cambridge. Edgar P. Benjamin was a community leader in Boston's South End; both he and Morris assisted the protest movement led by Monroe Trotter. Morgan, Harvard's Class Day orator in 1890, was a friend of W. E. B. Du Bois and the leader of the Massachusetts Niagara movement. Butler Wilson was a law partner of Ruffin's son and became a central leader of the local NAACP. Archibald Grimké practiced law only briefly before being appointed consul to Santo Domingo in 1894. His career was by far the most distinguished of this group, but not in the field of law. He won greater fame as a writer and activist, and lived much of his life in Washington, D.C. There he was a community leader and, like his friend Butler Wilson, president of the NAACP. This summary description of the careers of these civil rights–oriented attorneys shows a distinct falling-off from the achievements of the earlier group. None served in the state legislature; none served as a judge; none argued in the Supreme Court. Compared to Robert Morris, Rock, Walker, and Ruffin, their legal careers were more marginal.[34]

However, other second-generation black Boston attorneys did enjoy more elevated positions. These men looked to Booker T. Washington as their leader and thus found more favor with powerful white men. Law partners James H. Wolff and Edward Everett Brown were prominent supporters of Washington. Wolff, a Civil War Navy veteran, was a leader of the Massachusetts Grand Army of the Republic, which included white and black veterans. He delivered Boston's Fourth of July oration in 1910. In the aftermath of Monroe Trotter's confrontation with Booker Washington in Boston, Edward Everett Brown was quoted in several Boston newspapers defending the Tuskegean. A few years later, Mayor John F. Fitzgerald appointed Brown an assistant commissioner of public health, the highest appointive municipal office held by a Boston African-American to that date.[35] These, however, were minor achievements compared to the prominence gained by William Henry Lewis, who was probably the most famous black attorney of his day. Lewis began as a militant, but went over to the opposing camp when he realized that Washington had the inside track with power. His career reveals much about black politics and the law during the era of Booker T. Washington.

Lewis "repeatedly and flagrantly sold his honor and sold out his race in order to get a political position with a salary he has seemed unable to earn at the law," Monroe Trotter charged in 1907. Yet, by 1915 the two worked toward the same goal in a campaign to ban *The Birth of a Nation* in Boston, and worked together to elect David I. Walsh, Democrat, governor of the state. Of all the race leaders in Boston in this period, Lewis is marked most clearly by his ambition, and Trotter by his principles. The collapse of the possibility for advancement of African-Americans in politics during the Woodrow Wilson administration brought a reconciliation between the two antagonists, who had started in the same camp.

Like Butler Wilson, Morgan, Ruffin, and other black attorneys, Lewis migrated to Boston from the South. Born in Virginia in 1868, the child of freedpeople, he arrived at Amherst College at the age of twenty, where college president Julius H. Seelye encouraged him. Academic excellence and outstanding football playing carried him to Harvard Law School, where he became the first African-American named to the All-America team. Theodore Roosevelt's interest in sports brought Lewis to his attention; as governor of New York he entertained Lewis at the Executive Mansion.[36]

Denied service at a Cambridge barbershop in 1893, Lewis, with the aid of Butler Wilson, persuaded a state legislator to present a bill broadening the scope of an 1885 civil rights act. The bill passed, banning discrimination in all public places. When Booker T. Washington came to Boston in 1898 to mend fences with the local elite at a Young's Hotel dinner, Lewis spoke against accommodationism. He won election to the Cambridge Common Council the following year, and served three one-year terms. Lewis was the last African-American to serve in the state house of representatives for many years, winning a seat in 1902 but failing in a reelection bid. His early career was that of a civil rights activist in the mold of Morris, Rock, Walker, or Ruffin.[37]

Oddly enough, it was W. E. B. Du Bois who reconciled Lewis and Washington, and by 1901, the two were corresponding. "I should like very much to have the place of First assistant District Attorney," the Bostonian implored, and by the next year, Lewis had the job. Washington was at first reluctant to approve President Roosevelt's decision to appoint him, but by assenting to it, won Lewis as a key ally in his dispute with Monroe Trotter.[38]

Lewis became a tough factional fighter for his new friend. He accompanied Washington to the 1903 Louisville meeting of the Afro-American Council, at which the radicals were steamrolled. At the July 1903 Boston Riot, Lewis was in the chair to handle any disrupters. He testified against Trotter, and advised Washington in a libel case the Tuskegean loosed upon the *Guardian*, Trotter's newspaper. Lewis foiled a second Trotter scheme to heckle a Washington meeting, and connived with Washington to seize financial control of the *Guardian* when Trotter ally George W. Forbes sold his stock in the paper. The former militant became a key player in the campaign of dirty tricks against Trotter.[39]

Lewis maintained his appointed position until 1906, when he was promoted to assistant United States District Attorney for the New England States (1907–11), handling naturalization cases especially. The timing of this promotion suggests that Lewis's silence on the Brownsville case won him further favor in the president's eyes. "He [Roosevelt] appointed me assistant United States Attorney in Massachusetts," Lewis said of Roosevelt in 1912, "and in return I defended the discharge of the Brownsville soldiers, a thing which no other colored Federal office-holder did."[40]

When some African-Americans flirted with Democratic presidential candidate William Jennings Bryan in 1908, or endorsed him, Lewis remained a steadfast Taft man. The Republican victory set off a flurry of mail between the ambitious Lewis and his patron. "I cannot afford to remain longer in the Federal service unless there is some chance for promotion," Lewis complained. "If I could get a chance in Washington in the Department of Justice, I feel certain that I could 'make good' and put race prejudice to flight in that department." Booker Washington worked behind the scenes with Taft and on 14 June 1911, Lewis sent Washington his thanks upon being confirmed assistant attorney general. Lewis arranged a testimonial in Washington, D.C., for his benefactor.[41]

After Lewis's confirmation, he was accepted as a member of the all-white American Bar Association, along with Boston's Butler Wilson and William Morris, a Minnesota African-American. When racists challenged their admission, the ABA leadership demanded that the men resign, claiming it was unaware of their race. At the 1912 Milwaukee convention of the ABA, Attorney General George W. Wickersham, Lewis's boss, threatened to resign if Lewis was expelled, and none of the black attorneys were kicked out. Wickersham, however, did not oppose the introduction of the color line into the association, suggesting that in the future, applicants should state their race. This policy was adopted with a view toward keeping the organization all-white.[42]

The NAACP later waged a campaign against racial exclusivity in the ABA, but Lewis himself was silent throughout the controversy. He was in the uncomfortable position of being both an apologist for segregation and a victim of it. The entire experience could only have been humiliating for him. Soon afterward he was speedily ousted from office with the coming of the Woodrow Wilson administration. This marked the end of Lewis's political ambition. At first he asked Booker Washington to secure an appointment for him with John D. Rockefeller or Andrew Carnegie, but later decided to honor his wife's request and returned to Boston and private practice.[43]

While in public office, Lewis several times showed a reluctance to break all ties to civil rights activists. He may have sensed that Booker Washington's star was going into eclipse, and that his own career might later depend on the support of his current opponents. When Trotter and Du Bois quarreled in 1907 within the Niagara movement, Lewis organized a banquet for Du Bois. Later Trotter campaigned for Bryan in 1908, and Massachusetts blacks voted overwhelmingly for Taft. Washington wrote to Lewis immediately, urging him to take the leadership of Boston's black community. Lewis was more interested in the appointive office he ultimately secured. Four years later, he consulted Washington about joining the NAACP, although there is no evidence that he did join. Gradually, he rebuilt his ties to his earlier positions.[44]

William H. Ferris described Lewis as "a second Daniel Webster" as an orator, "a man whose eloquence is irresistible." He testified to Lewis's magnificent voice, and claimed to have seen and heard him "sweep the membership of the Twentieth Century Club of Boston off their feet."[45] The state legislature chose him as Lincoln Day speaker on the fiftieth anniversary of the Emancipation Proclamation. There he attacked antimiscegenation laws, then being floated in Congress, as incapable of accomplishing their laudable purpose. Only by granting justice to the Negro would he end his desire to escape blackness by merging with the white. Sounding a Tuskegee theme, he called for economic opportunity and state support for public education as the touchstones of Negro progress. He extolled Massachusetts's abolitionist past and offered its antidiscriminatory legislation as a model for the nation. He challenged the state to live up to its noble traditions. This skillful blending of accommodationist and civil rights themes foreshadowed a new course for the Lewis who was through with office-seeking. In 1915 he participated in the campaign against *The Birth of a Nation* and spoke at a testimonial for the *Guardian*.[46]

In one sense, William Henry Lewis can be seen as a careerist who simply did whatever was necessary to get ahead. He provided a fig-leaf cover for the Republican betrayal of the promise of Reconstruction. He defended President Theodore Roosevelt after the Brownsville incident, and worse than that, failed to speak out against the panoply of abuse in the South. He was a product of the Tuskegee Machine, and the dilemma of accommodation was that its advocates rose as the race declined. Lewis's career followed exactly that path. Despite the high position he reached, he was never able to strike a blow for freedom within the corridors of power, or by representing a civil rights litigant. On the national stage, it would not be until the 1930s that African-American attorneys, operating out of the NAACP's legal department, would begin the long march to freedom through the courts.

MOORFIELD STOREY: CHARLES SUMNER'S HEIR

More than any other white person in the history of Boston, Moorfield Storey represents the rebirth of the abolitionist spirit. As a young man he served briefly as Senator Charles Sumner's secretary during Reconstruction; in midcareer he was an economically conservative corporation counsel and president of the American Bar Association; and as an older man he became the first president of the National Association for the Advancement of Colored People. The spur to Storey's renewed commitment was his outrage over America's imperial policy in the Philippines. In this he followed Sumner's opposition to U.S. designs upon the Dominican Republic. Through this process he rediscovered for himself and the nation the defining impulse of Sumner's life: to establish equality before the law for all Americans.

Storey served as president of the NAACP, a symbolic post, from 1909 until his death in 1929. Sixty-four years old at the time of the association's birth, and resident in Boston while the movement's headquarters was in New York, he provided the new organization an aura of respectability as a corporation lawyer, and of principle, as the former leader of American anti-imperialism. While he did not participate in the squabbles of the NAACP's New York office, or in the activities of the Boston branch, he was no mere figurehead. Storey was the leading legal strategist for an organization that relied in part upon the courts to win justice. In addition, he thoroughly understood the need to mobilize public opinion for civil rights and helped the NAACP to do that in the most effective manner. The combination of his prominence in Boston (which was probably greater than that of any other NAACP leader in his respective city), his connection to Sumner, and his dignified character, made him the perfect symbol of the association in its earliest days.

The course of Storey's career, especially when viewed in relation to that of Henry Cabot Lodge, reveals a paradox regarding the course of the civil rights impulse among the Brahmins. Lodge was influenced by Sumner too, albeit not so directly as Storey. Like Sumner, Lodge and Storey opposed government corruption during the Ulysses S. Grant administration. Lodge stayed with the Republican Party, however, through the unsuccessful presidential campaign of James G. Blaine in 1884, and as a party loyalist authored the election bill of 1890, which would have protected African-American voters had it passed. Storey broke with the party in 1884, because of his opposition to the perceived opportunism of Blaine. He opposed the Federal Elections bill as a partisan scheme. Lodge and Storey subsequently moved in opposite directions on civil rights matters, with the former becoming increasingly indifferent and the latter increasingly outspoken. The abolitionist impulse thus went underground within Storey, for about twenty-five years.

When the spirit reemerged within him, it came out full-blown. He was as deeply rooted in the New England tradition as Holmes or Lodge. He was a Harvard man and Brahmin corporation lawyer, but the values of the preindustrial New England town seemed forever his polestar. In various parts Puritan Reformer, Transcendentalist, and Conscience Whig, he had the vision of John Winthrop, the optimism of Ralph Waldo Emerson, and the militancy of Charles Sumner. His career exemplifies the endurance of the abolitionist tradition into the twentieth century.[47]

A Brahmin descendant of Puritan forebears, Storey's own father failed at the law. Charles Storey anticipated receiving an inheritance that never materialized, and consequently abjured the virtue of industry for the pleasures of conviviality. He numbered among his friends Judge Ebenezer Rockwood Hoar, the antislavery poet James Russell Lowell, and John Holmes, brother of the famous doctor. To the extent that he was politically inclined, Charles Storey was a Conscience Whig, and his connections facilitated the appointment of his son, then a student at the Harvard Law School, as an aide to Senator Sumner.[48]

This position was a powerful influence upon the career of an impressionable young man, even though he served only from November 1867 until the spring of 1869. Storey was more than an employee, and for part of the time he shared living quarters with the senator. In his capacity as amanuensis Storey entertained the luminaries of Washington society. During this service he saw the lonely Sumner through the impeachment of Andrew Johnson and the early days of Reconstruction. His later efforts against imperialism and for civil rights paralleled those of his mentor.[49]

There is an air of the amused young bon vivant in Storey's letters of this period. He displayed none of Sumner's moral intensity. Storey saw this quality in Sumner as an admirable trait born of the direct confrontation with the slavocracy that the senator had endured.[50] Storey himself was too young to have experienced the fervor of the antislavery crusade, and, a crucial five years younger than Holmes, did not serve in the Union Army. Storey defended Sumner's ideas when they were at ebb tide, but because he was diplomatic, he never experienced the personal isolation that Sumner suffered during his career.

As a young man, Storey's racial attitudes hardly matched those of the abolitionists. He met black people for the first time in Washington. "Nothing amuses me so much here as the Negroes," he wrote to his sister. "The older they grow the less attractive they become and the less laudable their pursuits." These offending activities included selling oysters and the Sunday newspapers, and others of the race, Storey noted, served as waiters, one of whom he described as a "gorilla." Another performed buffoonlike antics, yet, "something kindred in our nature makes me love him." Storey was no zealot, but a young man of the times whose vision grew with age.[51]

Returning to Massachusetts to begin his professional career, Storey established himself as a successful and conservative corporation lawyer. He represented railroad interests, and maintained a friendship with Charles Francis Adams II, who served as the state's railroad commissioner. He developed a reputation as a skilled trial lawyer, and was elected president of the American Bar Association in 1895. Throughout his life, Storey remained an economic conservative. He opposed strikes and regarded labor unions with suspicion. He was never drawn toward the anticorporate style of Progressivism and he testified in Washington against the Supreme Court nomination of fellow Bostonian Louis Brandeis.[52]

In local Boston politics, he lined up with reforming Brahmin Republicans who opposed what they perceived as corrupt practices by Irish politicians. In 1910 he backed James J. Storrow for mayor against John F. Fitzgerald. When Fitzgerald ran advertisements alleging that Storey had earlier criticized Storrow's business practices, Storey hotly denied the allegation. He spoke on Storrow's behalf at a meeting of African-American supporters at a Baptist church. He opposed building a memorial to Irish favorite Benjamin F. Butler, and in 1920 he spoke at a meeting of the Loyal League, which opposed Irish independence.[53]

Thus, Storey's anti-imperialism and civil rights advocacy were not grounded in a generally radical outlook. Rather, they were rooted in a backward-looking defense of the early principles of the Republic. There is a certain antimodernity about Storey, exemplified in his sponsorship of a tiny organization decrying the excesses of automobile drivers.[54]

Storey's biographer, William B. Hixson Jr., argues convincingly that "the decisive event in Moorfield Storey's public career was the Spanish-American War." He opposed the declaration of war, spoke out during the war, and especially criticized the imposition of American rule over the Philippines. Supporters of imperialism argued that the Filipinos were incapable of governing themselves. When Storey joined the anti-imperialist camp, the movement took an agnostic position on this question; some among the anti-imperialists opposed American rule over the islands precisely because they believed in the inferiority of Filipinos. Storey argued for the right of the islanders to self-determination. Writing to Emerson's daughter he declared, "Here I am brought up under Lincoln, Sumner, Andrew, and last and best, your father," and he then asserted the applicability of the Declaration of Independence to a variety of nationalist struggles. In a public speech he stressed the educational level of the Filipino leadership, and the Christian beliefs they shared with Americans. The process of declaring solidarity with a colored people fighting for independence soon alerted Storey to the plight of African-Americans, and reconnected him with his early experiences during the Civil War and Reconstruction.[55]

Storey lost an independent campaign for Congress in 1900, during which he argued against colonialism and for civil rights, joining the two issues. A speech on behalf of voting rights in March 1903, responded to Secretary of State Elihu Root's contention that Negro suffrage had been a failure. Quoting Emerson and Sumner, Storey insisted that the real failure was that of the founders of the Republic, who should have abolished slavery at the birth of the new nation. He traced the development of race prejudice to slavery, not to inborn human traits. At the end of the Civil War, "the conditions which confronted Congress were the legitimate fruits of slavery, and it was the clear duty of the nation to make an end of the evil, root and branch, to lay the foundation of a free society deep and sound." This was, by 1903, a bold assertion of the goals of Reconstruction. Recalling the loyalty of the slaves both to their masters and to the nation, he placed the corruption of Reconstruction governments in the context of their times. The Negro politicians, he declared, were no worse than the white ones.[56]

Storey's new outspokenness brought him to the attention of William Monroe Trotter, leader of the militant faction of Boston's black community. As early as May 1902, Storey appeared at a Trotter-sponsored meeting calling for passage of the Crumpacker Amendment, which would reduce the congressional representation of states that denied equal ballot access, in accordance with the Fourteenth Amendment. Unlike most other future Boston NAACP leaders, Storey continued to speak at Trotter's meetings throughout his career. Storey respected Trotter's authority in the African-American community and engaged him in dialogue, trying to mitigate the editor's sectarianism. Trotter repaid Storey with flattering accolades in his newspaper and in 1918 arranged a testimonial dinner for him.[57]

Several factors explain this unique relationship. First of all, Storey had no prior connection with Booker Washington, whose policies had called Trotter's newspaper into being. Other future Boston NAACP leaders, like branch president Francis Jackson Garrison, had been confidants of Washington and despised Trotter. Second, Storey was, like Trotter, a political independent, and as often as not voted Democrat in the presidential elections. Finally, Storey's racial attitudes had changed enough so that he recognized in Trotter a man of intelligence, character, and uncompromising self-sacrifice, the very qualities he attributed to the Filipino insurgents.

More than anyone else during the NAACP's early years, Storey guided the association's legal strategy. No prominent leader in the New York office, with the exception of Arthur B. Spingarn, was a lawyer, and so Mary White Ovington, John Shillady, Joel Spingarn, W. E. B. Du Bois and Oswald Garrison Villard looked to Storey for advice on how best to approach the courts. He contributed to three important Supreme Court cases—on voting rights, residential segregation, and jury selection—and he helped to conceptualize the NAACP's attack on lynching.

This remarkable legal accomplishment was achieved by a man in his late sixties and seventies, who was engaged in many other professional and reform activities at the same time. Storey's legal work for the NAACP was episodic, for the association had no directing legal center in New York. This haphazard arrangement meant that the association's legal agenda was reactive rather than proactive. The organization struck a promising blow for voting rights in 1915, but was unable to follow through on this front. As lynching and mob violence against African-Americans grew in intensity (the number of lynchings declined, but they became increasingly public and barbaric spectacles), the association launched an antilynching campaign and dropped its voting rights work. Storey and the NAACP accomplished what they did despite the lack of a central legal team.

Underlying all legal problems confronting civil rights activists was, as it had ever been, the federal system. Surprisingly, Storey defended states' rights. Speaking at the Jamestown, Virginia, Exhibition in 1907 (before the birth of the NAACP), he opposed any attempt to shift the balance of power between the federal government and the states in Washington's direction. He saw this as tampering with the Constitution, and suggested that President Theodore Roosevelt was inclined to do just that. Similarly, he feared the expansion of executive power at the expense of judicial authority. These notions, linked in Storey's mind, bespoke a legal conservatism that was at odds with his civil rights activism.[58]

The NAACP's first victory before the Supreme Court came in *Guinn v. Oklahoma*, in which Storey wrote an amicus curiae brief on behalf of a federal case against Oklahoma registrars filed by the Taft administration. The registrars enforced a 1910 Oklahoma constitutional amendment that provided a grandfather-clause exemption from literacy requirements. The government argued that the registrars had violated the Fifteenth Amendment and won a conviction; the defendants appealed to the high court. Two years later Chief Justice Edward White, a former Confederate officer, upheld the convictions for a unanimous bench. After the victory, which Storey attributed to the "very able brief" prepared by the solicitor general, the NAACP was faced with the question of how to proceed. The grandfather clause was dead, but how to deal with literacy or property requirements without the grandfather clause?[59]

Storey feared that the Fifteenth Amendment would have no bearing upon such restrictions, for the southern laws were "so drawn that it would be impossible for the court to say that they restricted suffrage only of colored men" once the grandfather clause was omitted. This left the second clause of the Fourteenth Amendment as an avenue of redress. However, Storey wrote in an unusually long letter to May Childs Nerney in the national office, it would "be difficult to get any law enforcing the Fourteenth Amendment passed [this refers to the fifth clause], because it would disturb the basis of representation in Massachusetts and other states which impose educational and property requirements." Even if such legislation were passed, the South might simply accept reduced representation as the price of an all-white electorate.[60]

Another problem in raising the issue was the sheer chaos a victory would bring, which made such an outcome unlikely in the Supreme Court. If, for example, a state without voting restrictions asked the Court to compel the Congress to reapportion the legislators, it would probably be constitutionally correct, but "this power the court would be very slow to exercise." The problem was simply too big to be solved judicially. Surprisingly, Storey did not even consider that this strategy had already been tried and failed in the Congress in 1901 when Indiana Congressman Edgar D. Crumpacker introduced an amendment to a reapportionment bill, seeking to reduce the representation of several southern states. One of Storey's first acts on behalf of civil rights was to speak at a meeting on its behalf. The amendment itself was never voted, and the whole bill, in which it was included, failed. Not until the Voting Rights Act of 1965 was the ballot returned to African-Americans in the South.[61]

Storey was still caught on the horns of this dilemma in 1919, when he wrote in almost the same terms to James Weldon Johnson as he had to Nerney four years earlier. The NAACP made little progress on voting rights in Storey's lifetime. The association struck down Texas's white primary law in *Nixon v. Herndon* in 1927. The NAACP essentially had a triage problem: too few doctors in the civil rights war zone. When a wealthy donor contributed funds for an antilynching campaign in 1916, the association turned to that problem. As Storey woefully concluded in his 1915 letter on voting rights, "It is after all a question of power." In that year the former Woodrow Wilson supporter hoped for a Republican presidential victory, but did not "expect much from the leaders of either party."[62]

The limits of judicial remedies against discrimination were manifest in two cases Storey helped present to the Supreme Court regarding residential segregation. *Buchanan v. Warley* struck down a Louisville residential segregation law and was an important victory against de jure segregation. However, when Storey aided Louis Marshall in *Corrigan v. Buckley*, the association was unable to halt residential segregation by means of the private restrictive covenant.

In *Buchanan v. Warley* (discussed earlier in this chapter) Storey contrived a case in which a white property owner sued an African-American purchaser who breached his contract to buy property for fear of violating the Louisville residential segregation ordinance. Storey argued that the law violated the property owner's rights under the Fourteenth Amendment. Moreover, he contended, the *Plessy* decision was not relevant in matters of housing. Although the argument was cast in conservative legal terms, Storey attacked the underlying assumption of segregation, that the purity of the races must be preserved.[63]

Storey argued the case in April 1916 along with a Louisville attorney, and hoped for a split decision at best. He suspected that two southern justices were unconvinced, and if he reckoned that Holmes might dissent there is no record of it. When the unanimous verdict was announced, he regarded it as "one of the most important decisions on the colored question that has ever been made," likening it to the Dred Scott decision in reverse.[64]

This was surely an exaggeration. As with the *Guinn* case, southern racists defeated civil rights anyway. In the housing matter, the restrictive covenant, by which white property purchasers agreed to sell their homes only to whites, became the new method of ensuring residential segregation. The elderly Storey advised the association's Louis Marshall in *Corrigan v. Buckley*, which challenged the restrictive covenant. Storey and Marshall tried to build upon the success of *Buchanan*, but the Court decided that it lacked jurisdiction.[65]

One of Storey's greatest strengths as a legal strategist was that he saw the evolution of the law in its social and political context. Where Holmes argued this point in *The Common Law*, Storey simply assumed it. He never considered that law might be "discovered" by dispassionate legal scientists. Unlike Holmes, Storey was an activist who believed that social reality could be changed in the court of public opinion. He put this precept to good use during the NAACP's campaign against lynching, the first round of which began in 1916 and ended with the failure of the Dyer antilynching bill in the Senate in 1922.

Although the number of lynchings annually was declining by 1916, the practice was becoming increasingly brutal and public. When Boston philanthropist Philip G. Peabody offered the association $10,000 to attack lynching, the group assigned a small committee, headed by Storey, to work up a strategy. The philanthropist's offer constituted a huge sum in relation to the association's operating budget and could not be ignored. Peabody soon changed the offer to $1,000, with another $1,000 if the association could raise $9,000 on its own. If that was a less generous offer, matching funds do generate a political imperative to broaden one's appeal, and the Peabody fund accomplished that for the association. Storey volunteered $1,000 of his own money, and the fund drive began. A special *Crisis* supplement on the "Waco Horror" after a brutal lynching there in July 1916 helped put the fund over the top. To dramatize the proportions of this campaign, we may note that the next largest special account contained only $300 at the time. Bostonians contributed significantly to the fund, which for six years was at the center of the association's agenda.[66]

One possible strategy was to press for national legislation making lynching a federal crime. At first, Storey discouraged this idea. He was still a careful constitutional lawyer, and he would not advocate a law whose constitutionality was suspect. After the Waco lynching, Storey raised the idea of a national conference, including southerners, to suggest appropriate remedies. He did not want a meeting composed of northerners intent upon morally chastising the South. This would only cause a "backlash," he advised the national office, "which is what happened in the [Leo] Frank case." Without a change in public opinion, "the grand jury would not indict, juries would not convict, witnesses would not testify." He was convinced that only when southerners themselves were moved to action could the practice be stopped.[67]

Little progress was made on the conference for several years. In the meantime, Congressman Leonidas C. Dyer of Missouri began to prepare an anti-lynching bill in the wake of the 1917 East St. Louis race riot. This was a strong measure that would allow U.S. attorneys to prosecute perpetrators of mob violence, local law enforcement officers who allowed mobs to go unchecked, and the counties where the crimes occurred. The association's Joel Spingarn, then a military intelligence officer, initiated a more limited bill. This would make the lynching of servicemen a federal crime; Spingarn probably hoped it might serve as a precedent for a more comprehensive measure.[68]

Storey regretfully concluded that the Dyer bill would not stand the test of constitutionality. The Fourteenth Amendment protected citizens against states, but not against private citizens, and even if such a bill passed it would fail in the courts. He was more sanguine about Spingarn's proposal, but even this he thought could pass only if advanced in a color-blind fashion. "If the House believes that under the guise of trying to protect the soldiers we are really undertaking to commit the government against lynching of negroes I think the bill will never pass," he advised the national office. The bill would do better without the association's public support. Storey still believed that the association's key task was to "start a movement over the South" to change public opinion and state law. As the army was demobilized after the war Spingarn's bill was abandoned. Congressman Dyer waited to introduce his bill.[69]

Storey pressed again for the national conference idea in 1919. He wanted "a non-partisan and non-sectional atmosphere," urging national officer John Shillady to secure such speakers as former Republican presidential nominee Charles Evans Hughes, Attorney General A. Mitchell Palmer, Alabama Governor Emmet O'Neal, and others. Twenty-five hundred people attended the Carnegie Hall conference on 5 and 6 May. Storey delivered the welcoming address and called for a publicity campaign on lynching to rival that for women's suffrage and the League of Nations. Hughes's keynote address declared that the Negro's participation in the world war demanded an end to lynching, and proposed that the Covenant of the League of Nations begin at home.[70]

The conference did not demand federal legislation. Its "suggested objectives" called only for discussion of that idea, along with the possibility of passing state laws, strengthening existing law enforcement, and generating more publicity. At its conclusion, the assembly adopted an address to the nation urging governors and law officers to take forceful action, but urging upon Congress only "a nation-wide investigation of lynching and mob murder to the end that means may be found to end this scourge." Hughes, Palmer, former president Taft, former secretary of state Elihu Root, and eleven governors, including two southerners, signed the call.[71]

This meeting was undoubtedly an impressive achievement, and Storey, as the Boston black community newspaper the *Chronicle* pointed out, was "the single driving force who made the conference possible." The organizer, however, was disappointed by the aftermath. Many of the prominent signers of the original call failed to attend, and of those who did, many declined to work with the NAACP later. Meanwhile, the tide of violence continued to rise; 1919 was the year of the Chicago, Washington, D.C., and Elaine, Arkansas, attacks against black Americans. Storey began to rethink his original hesitation regarding the Dyer bill.[72]

James Weldon Johnson and Joel Spingarn led the association's campaign for the bill in the House during 1920 and 1921. A few weeks before the bill passed in a dramatic 230–119 vote in January 1922, Storey submitted a letter that was read into the record by a West Virginia congressman. Storey had now concluded that "the inaction of the states makes action by the United States imperative." This argument he based on the Fifth Amendment, which simply states that "no person shall be . . . deprived of life, liberty or property without due process of law." Unlike the Fourteenth Amendment, there is no reference to relations between states and individuals, merely a statement of the individual's rights. If an American was lynched abroad, we would hold the foreign government responsible, he argued. "It seems absurd to suppose that the Government of the United States can not protect its citizens against attacks made by men who are subject to its jurisdiction and control."[73]

A few months after the victory in the House, Storey addressed the Twentieth Century Club in Boston on the subject, making an eloquent appeal for the bill, now in the Senate. Congressman Dyer and James Weldon Johnson spoke the following day at Unity House in Park Square, urging the public to pressure Senator Henry Cabot Lodge to vote aye. Storey and Lodge had come full circle in thirty years, each reversing his civil rights stance of a generation ago. Storey wrote a brief on the bill's behalf for the Senate Judiciary Committee, which reported the bill favorably. The Dyer antilynching bill, however, succumbed to southern obstructionism and parliamentary maneuvering, and, like the Federal Elections bill of 1890, died in November 1922 without coming to the floor.[74]

Storey made one last plea before the Supreme Court in 1923; ironically enough, the occasion found him and Holmes in earnest agreement. In *Moore v. Dempsey* Storey represented six black Arkansas prisoners condemned to death for their part in an exchange of gunfire outside a meeting of sharecroppers in 1919. Afterward scores of blacks were killed by vigilantes, sixty-seven were sentenced to prison terms ranging from twenty years to life, and twelve were sentenced to death. Storey argued that during the original trial the defendants had been tortured, and that a mob atmosphere pervaded the proceedings. The original defense attorney had been terrified into resigning. Oliver Wendell Holmes wrote the decision in the case, which followed the same line of argument he and Justice Hughes had employed in the Leo Frank decision. The Court freed the six men, pending a hearing in the local federal court. This validation of the principles of the Fourteenth Amendment placed Storey squarely in the tradition of Sumner, who had contributed mightily to the amendment. The defendants were ultimately freed, and Fourteenth Amendment doctrines significantly strengthened. The elderly Moorfield Storey had recovered for himself and the nation the inheritance of his city and his youth.[75]

Notes

PREFACE

1. W. E. B. Du Bois, *The Souls of Black Folk* (1903), in *Three Negro Classics* (New York: Avon Books, 1965), 209.

2. For comparisons to other northern cities, see Ray Stannard Baker, *Following the Color Line: American Negro Citizenship in the Progressive Era* (1908; New York: Harper Torchbooks, 1964); Abraham Epstein, *The Negro Migrant in Pittsburgh* (1918; New York: Arno and New York Times, 1969); Florette Henri, *Black Migration: Movement North, 1900–1920* (Garden City, N.Y.: Anchor Books, 1976); Gilbert Osofsky, *Harlem: The Making of a Ghetto: Negro New York, 1890–1930* (New York: Harper and Row, 1966); Allan H. Spear, *Black Chicago: The Making of a Negro Ghetto, 1890–1920* (Chicago: University of Chicago Press, 1967); Joe William Trotter Jr., ed., *The Great Migration in Historical Perspective* (Bloomington: Indiana University Press, 1991); Kenneth L. Kusmer, *A Ghetto Takes Shape: Black Cleveland, 1870–1930* (Urbana: University of Illinois Press, 1976).

3. James M. McPherson, *The Struggle for Equality: Abolitionists and the Negro in the Civil War and Reconstruction* (Princeton: Princeton University Press, 1964), and esp. *The Abolitionist Legacy: From Reconstruction to the NAACP* (Princeton: Princeton University Press, 1975).

4. An extensive historiography discusses Boston and abolition. An excellent recent addition is Donald M. Jacobs, ed., *Courage and Conscience: Black and White Abolitionists in Boston* (published for the Boston Atheneum; Bloomington: Indiana University Press, 1993).

5. Arthur Mann, *Yankee Reformers in the Urban Age* (Cambridge: The Belknap Press of Harvard University Press, 1954).

6. George M. Fredrickson, *The Black Image in the White Mind: The Debate on Afro-American Character and Destiny, 1817–1914* (1971; Hanover, N.H.: Wesleyan University Press, 1987), xiii.

7. See McPherson, *The Struggle for Equality*, or Aileen Kraditor, *Means and*

Ends in American Abolitionism: Garrison and His Critics on Strategy and Tactics, 1834–1850 (New York: Pantheon, 1969).

INTRODUCTION: WHAT KEPT ABOLITION ALIVE IN BOSTON?

1. Comparisons of northern African-American communities may be found in August Meier, *Negro Thought in America, 1880–1915: Racial Ideologies in the Age of Booker T. Washington* (1963; Ann Arbor: University of Michigan Press, 1968); Willard B. Gatewood, *Aristocrats of Color: The Black Elite, 1880–1920* (Bloomington: Indiana University Press, 1990); and Louis R. Harlan, *Booker T. Washington: The Wizard of Tuskegee, 1901–1915* (New York: Oxford University Press, 1986), 94–106.

2. *Fourteenth Census of the United States, 1920* (hereafter *Census*) 3:77, Table 19.

3. *Census*, 3:27, Table 1; 3:35, Table 9.

4. *Census*, 1:76, Table 33; 3:47, Table 13.

5. *Census*, 3:457–58, Table 13; Richard A. Ballou, "Even in 'Freedom's Birthplace'! The Development of Boston's Black Ghetto, 1900–1940" (Ph.D. diss., University of Michigan, 1984); James Oliver Horton and Lois E. Horton, *Black Bostonians: Family Life and Community Struggle in the Ante-bellum North* (New York: Holmes and Meier, 1979), 1–14.

6. Ballou, "Boston's Black Ghetto," 56, Table 2.15; Robert A. Woods, ed., *The City Wilderness: A Settlement Study* (1898; New York: Garrett, 1970), 232.

7. On job rivalry, James Green and Hugh Carter Donahue, *Boston's Workers: A Labor History* (Boston: Trustees of the Public Library of the City of Boston, 1979), 55–71; William Foote Whyte, "Race Conflicts in the North End," *New England Quarterly* 5 (1939).

8. Florette Henri, *Black Migration*; John Hope Franklin, *From Slavery to Freedom: A History of Negro Americans*, 3d ed. (New York: Knopf, 1967), 443–46.

9. Al-Tony Gilmore, *Bad Nigger! The National Impact of Jack Johnson* (Port Washington, N.Y.: National University Publications, n.d.); *Boston Globe*, 4 July 1910 (evening ed.), 3, and 5 July 1910, 4.

10. See chapters 5 and 6.

11. *Woman's Era* (May 1895); Susie King Taylor, *Reminiscences of My Life in Camp* (New York: Arno Press and the New York Times, 1968), 62; *Colored American Magazine* 5, no. 5 (May 1904): 310–17; *Boston Guardian*, 12 August 1911, 1.

12. *Boston Globe*, 7 May 1902, 1.

13. Ray Stannard Baker, *Following the Color Line*; John Daniels, *In Freedom's Birthplace: A Study of the Boston Negroes* (1914; New York: Negro Universities Press, 1968); Adelaide Cromwell Hill, "The Negro Upper Class in Boston: Its Development and Present Social Structure" (Ph.D. diss., Radcliffe College, 1952). This last work was recently published as Adelaide M. Cromwell, *The Other Brahmins: Boston's Black Upper Class, 1750–1950* (Fayetteville: University of Arkansas Press, 1994); Ballou, "Boston's Black Ghetto," 348–56.

14. Gatewood, *Aristocrats*, 109–13; quotation on 111.

15. See chapter 2.

16. Stephan Thernstrom, *The Other Bostonians: Poverty and Progress in the American Metropolis, 1880–1970* (Cambridge: Harvard University Press, 1973), 192–93.

17. Elizabeth Hafkin Pleck, *Black Migration and Poverty: Boston, 1865–1900* (New York: Academic Press, 1979), 122–51.

18. Ibid., 151–57.

19. Daniels, *In Freedom's Birthplace*, 113–15; Thernstrom, *Other Bostonians*, 181.

20. Pleck, *Black Migration and Poverty*, 44–90.

21. Violet Mary-Ann Johnson, "The Migration Experience: Social and Economic Adjustment of British West Indian Immigrants in Boston, 1915–1950" (Ph.D. diss., Boston College, 1992); Edmund David Cronon, *Black Moses: The Story of Marcus Garvey and the Universal Negro Improvement Association* (Madison: University of Wisconsin Press, 1968), 206.

22. Daniels, *In Freedom's Birthplace*, 133–35, 185–89, 213–22, 308–97; Frederic Bushee, "Ethnic Factors in the Population of Boston" (Publications of the American Economic Association 4, 2 May 1903; microfiche ed.), 22, 31–37, 45–50, 101–20; *Census*, 3:1183, Table 15 and 4:367, Table 12; Peter C. Holloran, *Boston's Wayward Children, Social Services for Homeless Children, 1830–1930* (Boston: Northeastern University Press, 1994), 137–57.

23. Hortons, *Black Bostonians*, 27–66; Robert C. Hayden, "Faith, Culture and Leadership: A History of the Black Church in Boston" (Boston Branch, National Association for the Advancement of Colored People and Robert C. Hayden, 1983); Hill, "Negro Upper Class."

24. Donald Martin Jacobs, "A History of the Boston Negro from the Revolution to the Civil War" (Ph.D. diss., Boston University, 1968), 22–29.

25. Ibid., 55–79.

26. Louis Ruchames, "Jim Crow Railroads in Massachusetts," *American Quarterly* 8 (1956): 61–75; Ruchames, "Race, Marriage and Abolition in Massachusetts," *Journal of American Negro History* 40 (1955): 250–73; William S. McFeely, *Frederick Douglass* (New York: Norton, 1991), 91–103.

27. Robert P. Smith, "William Cooper Nell: Crusading Black Abolitionist," *Journal of Negro History* 55 (1970): 182–99; Carleton Mabee, "A Negro Boycott to Integrate Boston Schools," *New England Quarterly* 41 (September 1968).

28. I am grateful to Lance Carden, whose unpublished and untitled manuscript argues that Garrisonian abolition, with its insistence on interracial organization, restricted the growth of African-American community institutions. While I do not share this view, his manuscript at least called my attention to this possibility. The Hortons present a more holistic picture of antebellum black Bostonians: they see a range of different leaders among whom the Garrisonians were one group. Jacobs shows how Garrisonian abolition encouraged community development.

29. Stanley J. Robboy and Anita W. Robboy, "Lewis Hayden: From Fugitive Slave to Statesman," *New England Quarterly* 46 (December 1973): 591–613; Hortons, *Black Bostonians*, 97–114; Jacobs, "Boston Negroes," 265–91.

30. Luis F. Emilio, *A Brave Black Regiment: History of the Fifty-Fourth Regiment of Massachusetts Volunteer Infantry, 1863–1865* (1894; rev. ed., New York: Bantam Books, 1992).

31. Daniels, *In Freedom's Birthplace*, 81–105.

32. The following notes in this chapter refer to very general points, all of which have been widely discussed. The references are selective and only to those sources I have used. Perry Miller, *Errand Into the Wilderness* (Cambridge: The Belknap Press of Harvard University Press, 1978); Edmund Morgan, *Visible Saints: The History of a Puritan Idea* (New York: New York University Press, 1963); Darret Rutman, *Winthrop's Boston: Portrait of a Puritan Town* (Chapel Hill: University of North Carolina Press, 1965).

33. Gordon S. Wood, *The Radicalism of the American Revolution* (New York: Knopf, 1992), 172–73, 186–87; Thomas H. O'Connor and Alan Rogers, *This Momentous Affair: Massachusetts and the Ratification of the Constitution of the United States* (Boston: Boston Public Library, 1987), 49–50.

34. Gilbert Hobbs Barnes, *The Anti-Slavery Impulse, 1830–1844* (1933; New York: Harcourt, Brace and World, 1964); Louis Filler, *The Crusade Against Slavery, 1830–1860* (New York: Harper Torchbooks, 1960).

35. Lawrence Lader, *The Bold Brahmins: New England's War Against Slavery 1831–1863* (1961; Westport, Conn.: Greenwood, 1973), 87–111, 255–67; David Herbert Donald, *Charles Sumner and the Coming of the Civil War* (1960; New York: Fawcett Columbine, 1989), 106–12; Eric Foner, *Free Soil, Free Labor, Free Men: The Ideology of the Republican Party Before the Civil War* (London: Oxford University Press, 1973); William Lee Miller, *Arguing About Slavery: The Great Battle in the United States Congress* (New York: Knopf, 1996).

36. Thomas H. O'Connor, *Lords of the Loom: The Cotton Whigs and the Coming of the Civil War* (New York: Scribner's, 1968).

37. Louis Ruchames, *The Abolitionists: A Collection of Their Writings* (New York: Capricorn Books, 1963), 13–24.

38. In addition to works already cited, Aileen S. Kraditor, *Means and Ends*; Gerda Lerner, *The Grimké Sisters From South Carolina: Rebels Against Slavery* (Boston: Houghton Mifflin, 1967); Irving H. Bartlett, *Wendell Phillips: Brahmin Radical* (Westport, Conn.: Greenwood, 1961); Archibald H. Grimké, *William Lloyd Garrison: The Abolitionist* (1891; New York: Negro Universities Press, 1969).

39. Constance K. Burns, "The Irony of Progressive Reform: Boston 1898–1910," in *Boston, 1700–1980: The Evolution of Urban Politics*, ed. Ronald P. Formisano and Constance K. Burns (Westport, Conn.: Greenwood, 1984), 133–64.

40. See chapter 6.

41. Cleveland Amory, *The Proper Bostonians* (New York: Dutton, 1947), 187–207.

42. John Higham, *Strangers in the Land: Patterns of American Nativism, 1860–1925* (New York: Atheneum, 1963); Barbara Miller Solomon, *Ancestors and Immigrants: A Changing New England Tradition* (New York: John Wiley and Sons, 1965).

43. See chapter 3. Also Thomas Wentworth Higginson, *Army Life in a Black Regiment* (1869; Boston: Beacon, 1970).

44. Arthur Mann, *Yankee Reformers*, 1–23; Green and Donahue, *Boston's Workers*, 55–93.

45. Robert L. Beisner, *Twelve Against Empire: The Anti-Imperialists, 1898–1900* (1968; New York: McGraw Hill, 1971); Daniel B. Schirmer, *Republic or Empire: American Resistance to the Philippine War* (Rochester, Vt.: Schenkman Books, n.d.).

46. George E. Mowry, *The Era of Theodore Roosevelt and the Birth of Modern America, 1900–1912* (New York: Harper Torchbooks, 1962); Arthur S. Link, *Woodrow Wilson and the Progressive Era, 1910–1917* (1954; New York: Harper and Row, 1963).

47. Richard Hofstadter, *The Age of Reform: From Bryan to F.D.R.* (New York: Vintage Books, 1955); Richard M. Abrams, *Conservatism in a Progressive Era: Massachusetts Politics, 1900–1912* (Cambridge: Harvard University Press, 1985); C. Vann Woodward, *Origins of the New South, 1877–1913* (Baton Rouge: Louisiana State University Press, 1951), 369–95.

48. Florette Henri, *Black Migration*.

49. Woodward, *Origins*, 235–63; 321–49.

50. George Brown Tindall, *The Emergence of the New South, 1913–1945* (Baton Rouge: Louisiana State University Press, 1967), 143–83.

51. Ibid., 170–86; W. Fitzhugh Brundage, *Lynching in the New South: Georgia and Virginia, 1880–1930* (Urbana: University of Illinois Press, 1993).

CHAPTER ONE: THE FEDERAL ELECTIONS BILL OF 1890

1. Amory, *The Proper Bostonians*, 17.

2. Stanley P. Hirshson, *Farewell to the Bloody Shirt: Northern Republicans and the Southern Negro, 1877–1893* (1962; Chicago: Quadrangle Paperbacks, 1968), 170–259.

3. C. Vann Woodward, *Reunion and Reaction: The Compromise of 1877 and the End of Reconstruction* (1951; Boston: Little, Brown, 1966); Woodward, *Origins of the New South*.

4. Petition of Ezra Nat. Hill, Misc. Doc. 244, Pamphlets Box 11, George Frisbie Hoar Papers (hereafter GFH), Massachusetts Historical Society (hereafter MHS), Boston.

5. Hirshson, *Farewell*, 202.

6. John A. Garraty, *Henry Cabot Lodge: A Biography* (New York: Knopf, 1953),

3–87; Karl Schriftgiesser, *The Gentleman from Massachusetts: Henry Cabot Lodge* (Boston: Little, Brown, 1944), 1–92.

7. Garraty, *Lodge*, 88–107; Schriftgeisser, *Gentleman*, 93–109; Hirshson, *Farewell*, 168–89.

8. Hirshson, *Farewell*, 190–204.

9. Ibid., 200–205; Garraty, *Lodge*, 117–18.

10. Sigourney Butler to Henry Cabot Lodge (hereafter HCL), 21 March 1890, Box 7, HCL Papers; *Frank Leslie's Illustrated Newspaper*, 3 May 1890, in Lodge Scrapbook, HCL Papers, MHS.

11. G. G. Alexander to HCL, 6 May 1890; Henry F. Downing to HCL, undated; R. Scott Parks to HCL, 30 June 1890; Albion Tourgee to HCL, 31 March 1890, 9 and 30 April 1890; Box 7, HCL Papers, MHS. All subsequent dates are 1890 unless otherwise noted.

12. Hirshson, *Farewell*, 204–5.

13. *Boston Globe*, 27 June, 3.

14. Curtis Guild Jr. to HCL, 11 July; Curtis Guild Sr., to HCL 28 June; Albert Bushnell Hart to HCL, 13 August; Benjamin R. Curtis to HCL 11 October, HCL Papers.

15. *Boston Advertiser*, 27 June, 1 and 4; 28 June, 4; 30 June, 1.

16. Garraty, *Lodge*, 90; Richard E. Welch Jr., *George Frisbie Hoar and the Half-Breed Republicans* (Cambridge: Harvard University Press, 1971), 106 n. 20; *Boston Journal*, 17 March.

17. Hirshson, *Farewell*, 211–14.

18. Meier, *Negro Thought*, 26–41.

19. *New York Age*, 25 January 1890, 1; Emma Lou Thornbrough, "The National Afro-American League, 1887–1908," *Journal of Southern History* (November 1961): 494–512.

20. *New York Age*, 8 February, 4; 15 February, 1; Meier, *Negro Thought*, 70–71.

21. *New York Age*, 21 December 1889, 4; 28 December 1889, 1 and 2; 18 January 1890, 1.

22. *New York Age*, 14 December 1889, 1.

23. *New York Age*, July 1890, 6.

24. *New York Age*, 9 August; unidentified newspaper article 1890 scrapbook, HCL Papers, MHS; Richard P. Hallowell to GFH, 5 August, Correspondence Box 122, MHS.

25. Pleck, *Black Migration and Poverty*, 84; John Daniels, *In Freedom's Birthplace*, 101, 103.

26. Clarence G. Contee, "Edwin Garrison Walker," *Dictionary of American Negro Biography*, 623.

27. *New York Age*, 23 and 30 August.

28. *New York Age*, 27 September, 2; 4 October, 1; 18 October, 1.

29. Welch, *Hoar*, 1–27.

30. Ibid., 28–144.

31. GFH to D. W. Farquhar, 12 August, Correspondence Box 122, GFH Papers, MHS.

32. Hirshson, *Farewell*, 215–35.

33. Albert Clarke to GFH, 21 August, Correspondence Box 123, GFH Papers, MHS.

34. White Citizens of Anniston, Ala. to GFH, 21 August; George M. Robbins to GFH, 2 August; J. H. Crane to GFH, 4 August; Box 122, GFH Papers, MHS.

35. Welch, *Hoar*, 151–62; Hirshson, *Farewell*, 215–35.

36. Garraty, *Lodge*, 119–21.

37. Welch, *Hoar*, 162.

38. *Boston Journal*, 13 December 1889, 1 and 2; *Boston Post*, 13 December 1889, 1.

39. *Boston Journal*, 24 December 1889, 1 and 2; *Boston Post*, 13 December 1889, 1.

40. Geoffrey Blodgett, *The Gentle Reformers: Massachusetts Democrats in the Cleveland Era* (Cambridge: Harvard University Press, 1966), 86–94.

41. *Boston Post*, 14 February, 1; J. G. Oglesby to William E. Russell, 28 December 1889, Box 1, File 17, William E. Russell Papers, MHS; Blodgett, *Gentle Reformers*, 174–75.

42. Robert Lincoln O'Brien, "Journalism," in *Fifty Years of Boston: A Memorial Volume*, by Elizabeth M. Herlihy (Boston: Boston Tercentenary Committee, 1932), 508–10.

43. *Boston Globe*, 19 December 1889, 4.

44. *Boston Globe*, 11 June, 5.

45. *Boston Globe*, 12 June, 1.

46. *Boston Globe*, 13 June, 1.

47. *Boston Globe*, 3 July, 4.

48. Geoffrey Blodgett, "The Mind of the Boston Mugwump," *Mississippi Historical Review* 48, no. 4 (March 1962): 614–34; Gordon S. Wood, "The Massachusetts Mugwumps," *New England Quarterly* (December 1960): 435–51.

49. Tilden G. Edelstein, *Strange Enthusiasm: A Life of Thomas Wentworth Higginson* (New Haven: Yale University Press, 1968); Thomas Wentworth Higginson, *Army Life*; Edward J. Renehan, *The Secret Six: The True Tale of the Men Who Conspired with John Brown* (New York: Crown, 1995).

50. Joseph Edgar Chamberlain, *The Boston Transcript: A History of Its First Hundred Years* (Boston: Houghton Mifflin, 1930), 1–123.

51. Ibid., 160–70.

52. *Boston Evening Transcript* (hereafter *BET*), 2 December 1889, 4; 3 and 4 December; 4 and 6 December.

53. *BET*, 26 December 1889, 4; 20 March 1890, 4.

54. *BET*, 28 June, 4.

55. *BET*, 3 July, 4; 15 August, 4; 27 January 1891, 4.

56. Richard Peter Harmond, "Tradition and Change in the Gilded Age: A Political History of Massachusetts, 1878–1893" (Ph.D. diss., Columbia University, 1966), 319–20; Blodgett, "Mugwump."

57. *Lynn City Item*, 12 September, 4; 10 October, 4.

58. *Lynn City Item*, 3 October, 2.

59. *Lynn City Item*, 24 October, 3; 31 October, 2; *Boston Globe*, 3 November, 1; 4 November, 4.

60. *Lynn City Item*, 7 November, 2; Harmond, "Tradition," 319–20.

61. *Lynn City Item*, 7 November, 3.

62. Unidentified news article by George Frisbie Hoar, Correspondence Box 124, GFH Papers; Undated Typescript, Correspondence Box 125, in "Jan. 1891" File, GFH Papers, MHS.

63. *New York Age*, 15, 22, and 29 November.

64. *New York Age*, 7 February and 13 June 1891.

65. Harmond, "Tradition," 320–27; *Boston Globe*, 5 November, 4; *Lynn City Item*, 7 November, 4.

66. Barbara Miller Solomon, *Ancestors and Immigrants*, 111–19.

67. Quoted in Daniel B. Schirmer, *Republic or Empire: American Resistance to the Philippine War* (Rochester, Vt.: Schenkman Books, n.d.), 240; Garraty, *Lodge*, 208–10.

68. Ann J. Lane, *The Brownsville Affair: National Crisis and Black Reaction* (Port Washington, N.Y.: National University Publications, Kennikat Press, 1971); Curtis Guild Jr. to Theodore Roosevelt, 7 and 8 November 1906, Theodore Roosevelt to Curtis Guild, 7 November 1906, Box 24, HCL Papers, MHS; *Boston Guardian*, 30 November 1907, 1; see, for example, *Boston Guardian*, 28 January 1911, in which the *Guardian* recounted alleged financial improprieties of Lodge; HCL to Theodore Roosevelt, 20 June 1907, Box 88, HCL Papers, MHS; *Boston Guardian*, 21 March 1908, 1.

69. John E. Bruce to GFH, 20 February 1895; GFH to John E. Bruce, 25 February 1895, Box 152, GFH Papers, MHS.

70. Blodgett, *Gentle Reformers*, 206–15.

71. Edelstein, *Higginson*.

72. *New York Age*, 15 and 29 August; 12, 19, and 26 September.

73. Chamberlain, *Transcript*, 165; Edward Henry Clement to Booker T. Washington, 2 January 1899, 5:5; Timothy Thomas Fortune to Booker T. Washington, 25 September 1899, 5:220, in Louis R. Harlan, ed., *Papers of Booker T. Washington* (Urbana: University of Illinois Press, 1972; hereafter cited as *BTW Papers*); *BET*, 18 September, 1 and 4; 19 September 1895, 4; *Boston Globe*, 19 September 1895, 1; 20 September 1895, 6. *BET*, 10 November 1898, 8; *Boston Globe*, 10 November 1898, 1; 11 November 1898, 1; *BET*, 11 November 1895, 4.

74. *Boston Globe*, 10 November 1895, 4; 11 November 1895, 4; 24 September 1906, 1; 25 September 1906, 6; 26 September 1906, 10.

CHAPTER TWO: BOOKER T. WASHINGTON

1. Louis R. Harlan, *Booker T. Washington: The Making of a Black Leader, 1856–1901* (London: Oxford University Press, 1975); Harlan, *Wizard*; *BTW Papers*; August Meier, *Negro Thought.*

2. Louis R. Harlan, "The Secret Life of Booker T. Washington," in *Booker T. Washington in Perspective*, ed. Raymond W. Smock, (Jackson: University Press of Mississippi, 1988), 110–32.

3. Harlan, *Making of a Black Leader*, 218.

4. Harlan, *Making of a Black Leader*, 42–43 (Ruffner), 52–77 (Armstrong), 126–27 (Olivia Davidson and Hemenway), 151–52 (Stearns), 238 (Higginson); Henry Clay Alvord to Booker T. Washington (hereafter BTW), 4 June 1902, in *BTW Papers* 6:477.

5. Harlan, *Making of a Black Leader*, 235–36; Booker T. Washington, *Up From Slavery*, in *Three Negro Classics* (New York: Avon Books, 1965), 128; Max Bennett Thrasher contract, in *BTW Papers*, 5:59; Harlan, *Wizard*, 290–91 for Park.

6. Adelaide Cromwell Hill, "The Negro Upper Class," 101; Willard B. Gatewood, *Aristocrats*, 110.

7. Dorothy West, *The Living Is Easy* (Old Westbury, N.Y.: Feminist Press, 1982); Walter J. Stevens, *Chip On My Shoulder* (Boston: Meador, 1946).

8. David Levering Lewis, *W. E. B. Du Bois: Biography of a Race 1868–1919* (New York: Henry Holt, 1993), 229.

9. Samuel E. Courtney to BTW, 27 October 1901, *BTW Papers*, 6:280–81. Unfortunately, the African-American community newspaper for the 1890s, the *Courant*, has not survived, except in very isolated numbers for one year.

10. *Boston Evening Transcript*, 25 April 1899, 7; *Boston Evening Transcript*, 10 May 1899, 4; Dickson D. Bruce Jr., *Archibald Grimké: Portrait of a Black Independent* (Baton Rouge: Louisiana State University Press, 1993), 82–85.

11. *Colored American Magazine* (hereafter *CAM*; May 1900).

12. *CAM* (May 1901).

13. Ann Allen Schockley, "Pauline Elizabeth Hopkins: A Biographical Excursion Into Obscurity," *Phylon* 33, no. 1 (Spring 1972): 22–26; Jane Campbell, "Pauline Elizabeth Hopkins," in *Dictionary of Literary Biography* 50, ed. Trudier Harris and Thadious M. Davis, (Detroit: Gale Research, 1986).

14. Pauline Elizabeth Hopkins, *Contending Forces: A Romance Illustrative of Negro Life North and South* (Boston: Colored Co-operative Publishing, 1900); "Hagar's Daughter, A Story of Southern Caste Prejudice," under pseudonym Sarah A. Allen, serialized in *CAM* (March 1901–March 1902); "A Dash for Liberty," *CAM* (August 1901); "Winona: A Tale of Negro Life in the South and Southwest," *CAM* (May 1902–October 1902).

15. BTW to Francis Jackson Garrison (hereafter FJG), 17 May 1905, *BTW Papers*, 6:184; August Meier, "Booker T. Washington and the Negro Press, With Special Reference to the *Colored American Magazine*," *Journal of Negro History* 38

(January 1953): 67–90; Walter N. Wallace to BTW, 6 August 1901, *BTW Papers*, 6:184.

16. *CAM* (January 1901); Lt. F. H. Wheaton, "A Feast With the Filipinos," *CAM* (June 1901); Capt. W. H. Jackson, "From Our Friends in the Far East," *CAM* (August 1901); Rienzi B. Lemus, "The Embattled Man in Action or the Colored American Soldier," *CAM* (May 1902); *CAM* viewed the African-American soldier as part of America's civilizing mission in the Philippines. Augustus M. Hodges, "The Solution to the Negro Problem," *CAM* (June 1901).

17. "Editorial and Publishers' Announcements," *CAM* (May 1900).

18. Harlan, *Making of a Negro Leader*, 262–64; Meier, *Negro Thought*, 108–9.

19. Charles H. Williams, "The Race Problem," *CAM* (September 1901); "In Columbia's Fair Land: A Lesson of Barbarism and Injustice," *CAM* (November 1901); James Parker, "Our Uncrowned Hero"; Robert W. Carter, "Our Late President," *CAM* (October 1901); Quincy Ewing, "The Beginning of the End," *CAM* (November 1901); "The Wilmington Lynching" *CAM* (August 1903); and "Jew-Hating and Negro-Hating," from the *Boston Herald*, in *CAM* (September 1903).

20. Harlan, *Making of a Black Leader*, 289–302; Meier, *Negro Thought*, 109–11.

21. Richard P. Hallowell, "Why the Negro Was Enfranchised," *CAM* (September 1903): 657–61; Hallowell, "Negro Suffrage Justified," *CAM* (October 1903); Moorfield Storey, "Negro Suffrage Not a Failure," *CAM* (December 1903): 909–11.

22. Harlan, *Making of a Black Leader*, 292–96; Murphy is described as a "white Washingtonian" and "accommodationist racist" in Frederickson, *Black Image;* M. F. Hunter, "The Alabama Conference," *CAM* (June 1900); Robert W. Carter, "Shall the Fourteenth Amendment Be Repealed?" *CAM* (August 1900).

23. "Fair Play," pseudonym for Kelly Miller, "Washington's Policy," *CAM* (November 1903). The article originally appeared in the *Boston Evening Transcript*, 18 and 19 September 1903. A 24 September 1903 letter from Miller to Emmet J. Scott in *BTW Papers*, 6:292, shows that Washington knew the author's identity. A. Kirland Soga, "Call the Black Man to Conference," *CAM* (December 1903 and January 1904).

24. Harlan, *Wizard*, 58–61; Meier, "Booker T. Washington and the Negro Press"; FJG to Oswald Garrison Villard (hereafter OGV), 22 June 1909 in OGV Papers, File 1446, Houghton Library, Special Collections, Harvard University.

25. Harlan, *Wizard*, 59–60.

26. All entries from *Alexander's Magazine* (hereafter *AM*): "Missionary Work and African Education" (May 1905); "Storer College and its Achievement for the Negro" (October 1905); "Tuskegee Celebration" (May 1906); "Dr. Washington a Mason" (December 1907).

27. All entries from *AM:* "Negro Journalism" (March 1906); unsigned editorial (July 1906): 10–11; John Daniels, "Book Notes and Comments" (September 1905); unsigned editorial, "Dr. Du Bois and 'The Moon' " (February 1906): 26; unsigned editorial, "The Niagara Movement" (September 1906): 18.

28. All entries from *AM:* unsigned editorials (September 1905): 40; "The Political Situation in Massachusetts" (October 1905): 18; "A Manly Protest" (March 1906); "Voting Time" (November 1906): 11–12.

29. Harlan, *Wizard*, 333–34; James S. Stemons, "Mr. Taft and Negro Suffrage," *AM* (January 1909).

30. Unsigned editorial, "What of the Future?" *AM* (June 1906).

31. Harlan, *Wizard*, 295–304; Ray Stannard Baker, *Following the Color Line*, 3–25.

32. All entries from *AM:* unsigned editorials, "The Atlanta Mob Spirit" (October 1906): 15; "The Negro Massacre at Atlanta" (November 1906): 15; "Good Advice" (December 1906); "The Lessons of the Atlanta Riot" (December 1906).

33. Harlan, *Wizard*, 309–13; Franklin, *From Slavery to Freedom*, 441–42; Lane, *Brownsville Affair*.

34. Joseph Smith, "The True Story of the Brownsville Affair," (from *Boston Herald*), *AM* (January 1907): 158–62; Archibald Grimké, "The Honorable Joseph Benson Foraker or the Man and the Hour," *AM* (May 1907): 31–43.

35. Unsigned editorial, "Co-operation vs. Antagonism," *AM* (October 1906): 12–13.

36. Bruce, *Grimké*, 1–77.

37. Bruce, *Grimké*, 78–92.

38. Bruce, *Grimké*, 93–146.

39. Bruce, *Grimké*, 160–71.

40. Unsigned editorial, *AM* (September 1907); Archibald Grimké, "The Third Term Spectre," *AM* (November 1907).

41. Unsigned editorial, "The Negro Vote," *AM* (July 1908); Horace Bumstead, "The Ballot as a Whip," *AM* (July 1908); unsigned editorial, "The Negro Vote and the Presidential Campaign," *AM* (August 1908); unsigned editorial, "The Negro Shall Be Loyal," *AM* (September 1908); unsigned editorial, "The Taft Seance—A Hallucination," *AM* (October 1908). Harlan, *Wizard*, 333; Charles W. Anderson to BTW, 10 September 1908, *BTW Papers*, 9:621–22. James S. Stemons, "Mr. Taft and Negro Suffrage," *AM* (January 1909); *AM* (March–April 1909).

42. Louis R. Harlan, "Booker T. Washington and the National Negro Business League," in *Booker T. Washington in Perspective*, 98–109; Meier, *Negro Thought*, 124–27.

43. BTW interview in *Boston Journal*, 11 August 1900, in *BTW Papers*, 5:594. *Boston Daily Advertiser*, 17 August 1900, 5.

44. John Howard Burrows, "The Necessity of Myth: A History of the National Negro Business League, 1900–1945" (Ph.D. diss., Auburn University, 1977).

45. Daniels, *Freedom's Birthplace*, 351–72.

46. *Proceedings*, National Negro Business League (hereafter NNBL), 23–24 August 1900. BTW to Emmet J. Scott, 8 July 1900, *BTW Papers*, 5:572 and n. 573; "Joseph Lee and His Bread Machine," *CAM* (May 1902).

47. Daniels, *Freedom's Birthplace*, 368–70; Baker, *Following the Color Line*, 226; *Proceedings*, NNBL, 23–24 August 1900; Souvenir Poster 1915 NNBL Convention, Department of African-American Studies, Boston College.

48. *Boston Globe*, 19 August 1915, 4; *Boston Evening Transcript*, 18 August 1900, 6.

49. Harlan, "Booker T. Washington and the National Negro Business League," 106–9.

50. James M. McPherson, *Abolitionist Legacy*.

51. BTW, *Up From Slavery*, 164–67.

52. For Eliot, 4:174, *Boston Globe*, 4 October 1904, 8:79 in *BTW Papers*; see, for example, William James to BTW, 5 June 1897, 4:292–93; Albert Bushnell Hart to BTW, 3 January 1896, 4:98, 99, in *BTW Papers*.

53. William Lloyd Garrison Jr., letter published in *Boston Transcript*, 11 January 1908, in *BTW Papers*, 9:438; FJG to OGV, 9 January 1908, File 1445.

54. *BTW Papers*, 3:44 n.; Edwin Doak Mead to BTW, 2 January 1908, 9:429–30; *Boston Transcript*, 13 January 1908, in *BTW Papers*, 9:438–40.

55. FJG to BTW, 13 July 1903, *BTW Papers*, 7:205; BTW to FJG, 24 November 1899, 5:271.

56. BTW to FJG, 23 September 1899, *BTW Papers*, 5:211 n. 212; BTW to FJG, 24 and 29 November 1899; FJG to BTW, 17 October and 18 November 1899.

57. Harlan, *Making of a Black Leader*, 294.

58. Ibid., 297–98; *BTW Papers*, Albert E. Pillsbury to BTW, 25 February 1900, 5:449; BTW to FJG, 27 February 1900, 5:450–51; Richard Price Hallowell to BTW, 2 March 1900, 5:451.

59. FJG to OGV, 19 April 1905, File 1442, OGV Papers. Hereafter FJG-OGV Correspondence from this collection, unless otherwise noted.

60. FJG to OGV, 7 April 1905, File 1442.

61. FJG to BTW, 8 May 1905, FJG Papers, Schomburg Collection, New York Public Library.

62. BTW to FJG, 17 May 1905, FJG Papers, Schomburg Collection, New York Public Library.

63. Harlan, *Wizard*, 359–79; FJG to OGV, 8 June 1909, File 1446.

64. FJG to OGV, 5 December 1909, File 1446.

65. FJG to OGV, 17 March 1911, File 1449.

CHAPTER THREE: THE LEGACY OF LUCY STONE

1. Alice Stone Blackwell, *Lucy Stone* (Boston: Little, Brown, 1930; Kraus Reprint, 1971), 3–102; Eleanor Flexner, *Century of Struggle: The Woman's Rights Movement in the United States* (1959; Cambridge: The Belknap Press of Harvard University Press, 1975), 68–70, 80–85.

2. Blackwell, *Stone*, 136–78.

3. Blackwell, *Stone*, 206–31; Flexner, *Century*, 144–58.

4. Blackwell, *Stone*, 256–72; Flexner, *Century*, 150–54; Mann, *Yankee Reformers*, 200–16.

5. Blackwell, *Stone*, 228–31; Flexner, *Century*, 222–30.

6. Aileen S. Kraditor, *The Ideas of the Woman Suffrage Movement, 1890–1920* (1965; New York: Norton, 1981), xiv–xv.

7. Ibid., 43–45, 162.

8. Ibid., 168–69.

9. *Woman's Journal* (27 September 1890): 305.

10. *Woman's Journal* (1 September 1894): 276; (27 October 1894): 340.

11. *Woman's Journal* (3 November 1894): 348.

12. *Woman's Journal* (10 and 17 November, 1 and 8 December 1894).

13. Blackwell, *Stone*, 232–36 for home life. A very large portion of Henry Brown Blackwell's correspondence concerns his real estate ventures; see Boxes 9 and 10, Blackwell Family Papers (hereafter BF Papers), Schlesinger Library, Radcliffe College.

14. Election Ticket, BF Papers, Box 9, File 127; Henry Brown Blackwell to Howard Blackwell, 4 April 1898; unidentified clipping dated 4 May 1895, Box 10, File 145, BF Papers.

15. Susan B. Anthony and Ida Husted Harper, eds. *History of Woman's Suffrage, 1883–1900*, (reprint, Salem, N.H.: Ayer, 1985), 4:735–39; Flexner, *Century*, 230.

16. *Woman's Journal* (27 October 1894): 340.

17. *Woman's Journal* (16 August 1890): 260; (8 July 1893); (12 May 1894); (3 August 1895): 244; (4 January 1890): 418; (27 October 1894): 340.

18. Alice Stone Blackwell to Emma Blackwell, 7 April 1893, Box 54, File 689, BF Papers.

19. Alice Stone Blackwell to Emma Blackwell, 23 October 1901, Box 51, File 667, BF Papers.

20. *Woman's Journal* (27 September 1890): 308; (9 June 1895); (23 June 1895).

21. *Woman's Journal* (28 March 1903); Anthony and Harper, *History*, 4:343; Kraditor, *Ideas*, 169–72.

22. *Woman's Journal* (4 April 1903): 106.

23. *Woman's Journal* (7 and 28 March 1903).

24. *Woman's Journal* (11 April 1903): 116.

25. *Woman's Journal* (2 May 1903).

26. Ibid.

27. *Woman's Journal* (7 March 1903): 106; (4 and 25 April 1903).

28. *Boston Globe*, 3 November 1915, 1; Flexner, *Century*, 280.

29. Geoffrey Blodgett, "Blackwell, Alice Stone," in *Notable American Women, 1607–1950: A Biographical Dictionary*, ed. Edward T. James (Cambridge: The Belknap Press of Harvard University Press, 1971), 156–58.

30. John Daniels, *In Freedom's Birthplace*, 212–13; *Census, 1920*, 4:368, Table

13. Daniels's chapter on "Economic Achievement" does use persuasive statistical information on the income levels of black men and women, 333–60.

31. Daniels, *Birthplace*, 211; *Boston Globe*, 26 April 1915, 9; Richard A. Ballou, "Even in 'Freedom's Birthplace'!" 51, Table 2.13, and 56, Table 2.15.

32. Adelaide Cromwell Hill, "Ruffin, Josephine St. Pierre," in *Notable American Women*, 206–7; Hill, "The Negro Upper Class," 137; Clarence G. Contee Sr. "Ruffin, George Lewis" and "Ruffin, Josephine St. Pierre," in *Dictionary of American Negro Biography*, ed. Rayford W. Logan and Michael Winston (New York: Norton, 1982), 535–36.

33. *Woman's Era* (March 1894): 4; Ida B. Wells-Barnett, *Crusade for Justice: The Autobiography of Ida B. Wells*, ed. Alfreda M. Duster (Chicago: University of Chicago Press, 1970), 77–81. Dorothy C. Salem, "To Better Our World: Black Women in Organized Reform, 1890–1920" (Ph.D. diss., Kent State University, 1986), 8–21; Paula Giddings, *When and Where I Enter: The Impact of Black Women on Race and Sex in America* (New York: William Morrow, 1984), 117–30; Rosalyn Marian Terborg-Penn, *Afro-Americans in the Struggle for Woman Suffrage* (Ph.D. diss., Howard University, 1977), 102–36.

34. *Woman's Era* (March 1894): 4.

35. Wells-Barnett, *Crusade for Justice*, 83–223. Wells and Duster discuss the British episode thoroughly, suggesting that they wished to set the record straight on a complicated exchange.

36. *Woman's Era*, (June 1894): 8, 14; (July 1894): 7; (August 1894): 1, 7; (December 1894): 1.

37. *Woman's Era* (May 1895); Salem, "To Better Our World," 36–38.

38. *Woman's Era* (June 1894): 5; (May 1895).

39. *Woman's Era* (August 1895).

40. Gatewood, *Aristocrats of Color*, 96–114; Salem, "To Better Our World," 68–70; Wells-Barnett, *Crusade for Justice*, 258–61; Lewis, *Du Bois*, 235, 246.

41. *Woman's Era* (April 1895): 8; (October–November 1896): 8; (January 1897): 8.

42. *Boston Globe*, 22 July 1894; Lewis, *Du Bois*, 107–8.

43. *Woman's Era* (March 1894): 8; (August 1896): 8.

44. *Woman's Era* (July 1895): 4; (August 1895); Peter Holloran, Boston's Wayward Children, 150.

45. *Woman's Era* (March 1894); (November 1894): 8; (August 1895): 10.

46. *Colored American Magazine* (June 1900): 122; Salem, "To Better Our World," 84.

47. Wells-Barnett, *Crusade for Justice*, 225–32.

48. *Boston Globe*, 5 June, 6; 6 June, 4; 8 June, 6; 9 June, 4; 10 June, 5; *Boston Evening Transcript*, 5 June, 6; 7 June, 7; 11 June, 4 and 6 (all 1900); Rayford W. Logan, *The Negro in American Life and Thought: The Nadir, 1877–1901* (New York: Dial, 1954), 236–38.

49. *Woman's Journal* (23 June 1900): 196.

50. *CAM* (August 1902): 273–77.

51. Clarence G. Contee Sr. "Ruffin, Josephine St. Pierre"; Adelaide Cromwell Hill, "Ruffin, Josephine St. Pierre."

52. Salem, "To Better Our World," 68–72; Kraditor, *Ideas*, 213–17.

53. Dorothy B. Porter, "Baldwin, Maria Louise," in *Notable American Women*, 87–88 and *Dictionary of American Negro Biography*, 21–22; *The Crisis* (April 1922): 248–49.

54. Maria Baldwin, "The Changing Idea of Progress," *Southern Workman* (January 1900): 15–16; *The Crisis* (August 1915): 189.

55. *New York Age*, 14 December 1905, 7; 21 December 1905, 2 and 4; Bruce, *Archibald Grimké*, 143–44.

56. See chapters 4 and 5.

57. Minutes, League of Women for Community Service, 1918–21, microfilm, Schlesinger Library; Women's Service Club Souvenir Program in Cora V. (Reid) MacKerrow Papers, Schlesinger Library.

58. *The Crisis* (August 1915): 189.

59. *Boston Evening Transcript*, 10 January 1922, 5; 12 January 1922, 7.

CHAPTER FOUR: WILLIAM MONROE TROTTER

1. Stephen R. Fox, *The Guardian of Boston: William Monroe Trotter* (New York: Atheneum, 1970), 3–13.

2. Ibid., 14–19.

3. Ibid., 21–30; Hill, "The Negro Upper Class in Boston," 338–40; *Boston Herald*, 20 February 1907; William Monroe Trotter (hereafter WMT) to John A. Fairlie, 10 August 1893, Box 17, File 3, WMT Papers, Mugar Library, Boston University.

4. WMT to John A. Fairlie, 8 September 1895, Box 17, File 3, WMT Papers.

5. Fox, *Trotter*, 27–30.

6. W. E. B. Du Bois, *The Souls of Black Folk*, in *Three Negro Classics*; Du Bois, *The Autobiography of W. E. B. Du Bois* (1968; New York: International Publishers, 1988).

7. *Guardian*, 12 August 1911, 1; 26 August 1911, 1.

8. Wells-Barnett, *Crusade for Justice*, 375–79.

9. Fox, *Trotter*, 98–99, 209–10. Timothy Thomas Fortune also was an editor and protest movement leader, but not for the course of his entire career. In addition, Fortune did outside work as a freelance journalist for the *New York Sun* and other papers to support himself. See Emma Lou Thornbrough, *T. Thomas Fortune: Militant Journalist* (Chicago: University of Chicago Press, 1972).

10. W. E. B. Du Bois to Alexander Walters, 7 April 1908, Reel 3, Papers of W. E. B. Du Bois, microfilm edition, viewed at Boston Public Library.

11. An early expression of Trotter's independence from Republican Party politics appears in the *Guardian*, 12 March 1904, 4.

12. Louis R. Harlan, *Wizard*, 323–37; Charles Flint Kellogg, *NAACP: A History of the National Association for the Advancement of Colored People*, Vol. 1, *1909–1920* (Baltimore: Johns Hopkins University Press, 1967), 155–58; *Guardian*, 21 March 1908, 4.

13. *Guardian*, 21 May 1904, 1; Harlan, *Wizard*, 348–49.

14. *Guardian*, 12 March 1904, 1 and 4.

15. "A Brief Resume of the Massachusetts Trouble in the Niagara Movement," 1907 report by W. E. B. Du Bois, in Du Bois Papers, Reel 2.

16. Ibid.; Fox, *Trotter*, 64–66, for George Forbes.

17. *Guardian*, 27 July 1907, 1; *Boston Globe*, 29 August 1907, 3.

18. Du Bois, "A Brief Resume"; Minutes, Niagara Movement, 27 and 29 August 1907, in Reel 2, Du Bois Papers.

19. *Guardian*, 8 November 1907, 1; *Boston Globe*, 7 November 1907, 7; *Guardian*, 28 March 1908, 1; *Boston Globe*, 26 March 1908, 10.

20. *Guardian*, 11 April 1908, 1 and 4.

21. Alexander Walters to W. E. B. Du Bois, 4 August 1908, 11 August 1908; W. E. B. Du Bois to Walters, 7 August 1908, 16 August 1908, Reel 3, Du Bois Papers. Fox, *Trotter*, 110–14, relying upon pro-Washington newspapers suggests a small and dispirited meeting, including the detail that James Hayes did not attend and that Trotter claimed two hundred at the meetings. The *Guardian* report is vivid, detailed, and reports Hayes's speech to an audience of two thousand. Walters had reason to hope for a failure, but reports success. The white Boston press generally corroborates *Guardian* accounts of Boston meetings, and the detail in the *Guardian* seems persuasive.

22. *Guardian*, 31 December 1910, 1; 7 January 1911, 1; 14 January 1911, 1–6; *Boston Globe*, 6 January 1911 (evening ed.), 20; 7 January 1911, 1.

23. *Guardian*, 21 January 1911, 1, 4, 5; 28 January 1911, 1 and 4; *Boston Globe*, 7 January 1911, 1.

24. Fox, *Trotter*, 126–30; Kellogg, *NAACP*, 81, 93; *Guardian*, 25 March 1911, 4.

25. *Guardian*, 18 March 1911, 1; 25 March 1911, 1 and 4; 1 April 1911, 1 and 4.

26. *Guardian*, 18 April 1911, 1; Fox, *Trotter*, 137–44.

27. *Guardian*, 18 March 1911, 1; 25 March 1911, 1; Kellogg, *NAACP*; and Warren D. St. James, *The National Association for the Advancement of Colored People: A Case Study in Pressure Groups* (New York: Exposition Press, 1958).

28. *Guardian*, 1 April 1911, 6.

29. *Guardian*, 20 May 1911, 1; 5 August 1911, 1.

30. *Guardian*, 19 August 1911, 1; *Boston Globe*, 29 August 1911, 4; 30 August 1911, 5.

31. Fox, *Trotter*, 161–68; Kellogg, *NAACP*, 155–59; Du Bois, *Autobiography*, 263–64.

32. WMT to Woodrow Wilson, 11 March 1913, WMT Papers, Box 17, File 8.

33. Fox, *Trotter*, 168–87; Arthur S. Link, *Woodrow Wilson and the Progressive Era, 1910–1917* (1954; New York: Harper and Row, 1963), 63–66; *Boston Globe*, 13 November 1914, 1; *Guardian*, 15 November 1913, 1.

34. *Boston Globe*, 13 November 1914, 1.

35. Fox, *Trotter*, 185–87.

36. Ibid., 266–72.

37. Ibid., 201–6; Kellogg, *NAACP*, 87–88; Langston Hughes, *Fight for Freedom: The Story of the NAACP* (New York: Norton, 1962), 32–33; B. Joyce Ross, *J. E. Spingarn and the Rise of the NAACP, 1911–1939* (New York: Atheneum, 1972), 46–48. Kellogg and Ross place Trotter at Amenia, based upon his name appearing on the literature, but Fox shows that he did not attend.

38. Theodore Kornweibel Jr., *No Crystal Stair: Black Life and the Messenger, 1917–1928* (Westport, Conn.: Greenwood, 1975), 3–41.

39. Fox, *Trotter*, 214–21; *Guardian*, 28 April 1917, 1, 4.

40. Jervis Anderson, *A. Phillip Randolph: A Biographical Portrait* (1972; Berkeley and Los Angeles: University of California Press, 1986), 108, 247; A. Phillip Randolph to Stephen R. Fox, 16 June 1969, Box 17, File 10, WMT Papers.

41. Fox, *Trotter*, 221–35; *Guardian*, 12 July 1919, 1; 19 July 1919, 1.

42. *Boston Globe*, 19 April 1915, 1; *Guardian*, 14 June 1919, 1; 19 July 1919, 1.

43. Fox, *Trotter*, 251; *Guardian*, 4 February 1911, 4.

44. *Boston Sunday Post*, 8 November 1903, 10.

45. W. E. B. Du Bois to George Foster Peabody, 28 December 1903, Du Bois Papers, Reel 2.

46. *Boston Globe*, 30 July 1903, 2.

47. *Boston Globe*, 31 July 1903, 1.

48. *Boston Herald*, 31 July 1903, 1; *Boston Transcript*, 31 July 1903, 1.

49. See chapter 2.

50. *Guardian*, 9 November 1901, 2; 8 October 1904, 4; 26 February 1910, 1.

51. *Guardian*, 8 October 1904, 4; 27 July 1904, 1; 30 November 1907, 1; 28 March 1908, 1; 27 April 1912, 1.

52. *Guardian*, 16 November 1907, 30; 7 December 1907, 1; 11 January 1908, 1; *Boston Globe*, 4 December 1907, 14.

53. *Guardian*, 17 May 1902, 1 and 4.

54. *Guardian*, 30 April 1904, 1 and 4; *Boston Globe*, 23 April 1904, 2.

55. FJG to OGV, 9 and 18 November 1905, OGV Papers; *Alexander's Magazine* (January 1906); *Guardian*, 16 December 1905, 1–12.

56. Fox, *Trotter*, 132–33; Kellogg, *NAACP*, 55–56.

57. For Alfred P. Russell, see Alfred P. Russell Papers, Mugar Library, Boston University; M. Cravath Simpson appears often in the *Guardian*, for example, a letter demanding that Booker Washington prosecute his attacker Henry Albert Ulrich (16 September 1911), or her speech to a Jewish rally proposing an anti–Jim Crow resolution (23 December 1911).

58. *Guardian*, 12 February 1910, 1 and 4.

59. *Black Biographical Dictionaries*, title 120, 433 (microfiche ed.): William Newton Hartshorn, *An Era of Progress and Promise, 1863–1910*.

60. *Guardian*, 19 July 1919, 1 and 4. *Black Biographical Dictionaries*, title 166, 126 (microfiche ed.): Frank Lincoln Mather, *Who's Who of the Colored Race*.

61. Reverdy Ransom, *The Pilgrimmage of Harriet Ransom's Son* (Nashville, Tenn.: Sunday School Union, n.d.).

62. For Grimké, see Bruce, *Archibald Grimké*; for Forbes, Ransom, *Pilgrimmage*, 145.

63. Fox, *Trotter*, 266–72; *Boston Globe*, 11 April 1934; *Boston Post*, 11 April 1934, 4.

CHAPTER FIVE: BOSTON'S NAACP, 1909–1920

1. Kellogg, *NAACP*, 9–30.

2. OGV, *Fighting Years: Memoirs of a Liberal Editor* (New York: Harcourt, Brace, 1939).

3. Washington, D.C., branch NAACP brochure, in Archibald H. Grimké Papers, Moorland-Spingarn Room, Howard University, Correspondence Box 1915. Correspondence in this collection is boxed annually, hereafter correspondence from this collection will be identified simply by date, AHG.

4. St. James, *National Association for the Advancement of Colored People*, 17–55; Ross, *J. E. Spingarn*, 16–80.

5. Kellogg, *NAACP* 136–37, 155–275.

6. NAACP Branch Bulletin, June–July 1918, NAACP Papers, Library of Congress Manuscript Division, Group I, Microfilm Reel C433. All NAACP Papers for this period are in Group I. Hereafter, those NAACP Papers viewed at the Library of Congress will be designated "LC"; others are from excerpted microfilm edition viewed at Lamont Library, Harvard University.

7. *Boston Globe*, 31 March 1911, 4. The best recent discussion of Boston abolitionists and their relation to Boston is Jacobs, ed., *Courage and Conscience*.

8. Clarence G. Contee, "Butler R. Wilson and the Boston NAACP Branch," *The Crisis* (December 1974): 346–48; Clarence G. Contee, "Wilson, Butler R.," in *Dictionary of American Negro Biography*, ed. Rayford W. Logan and Michael R. Winston (New York: Norton, 1982).

9. Mary Evans Wilson to May Childs Nerney, 1 and 29 December 1914; 5, 6, 7, 11 January 1915, NAACP Papers, Special Correspondence, Reel 24; Mary White Ovington, *The Walls Came Tumbling Down* (1947; New York: Arno Press and the New York Times Press, 1969), 23.

10. Ovington, *Walls*, 23; W. E. B. Du Bois to Butler Roland Wilson (hereafter BRW), 16 July 1915, W. E. B. Du Bois Papers, microfilm edition viewed at Boston Public Library, Reel 5; BRW to AHG, 12 November 1915, AHG Papers.

11. Mark A. De Wolfe Howe, *Portrait of an Independent: Moorfield Storey, 1845–1929* (Boston: Houghton Mifflin, 1932); Ann Louise Leger, "Moorfield Storey: An Intellectual Biography," (Ph.D. diss., University of Iowa, 1968); William B. Hixson, *Moorfield Storey and the Abolitionist Tradition* (New York: Oxford University Press, 1972).

12. Moorfield Storey to Oswald Garrison Villard (hereafter OGV), 11 September 1913, NAACP Papers, Special Correspondence, Reel 24.

13. *BTW Papers*, 5:449; Albert E. Pillsbury to BTW, *BTW Papers*, 30 July 1901, vol. 6; Albert E. Pillsbury to Mary White Ovington (hereafter MWO), 11 January 1912, NAACP Papers C-73, Microfilm Reel 8; Albert E. Pillsbury to AHG, 24 April 1917, AHG Papers.

14. Clarence G. Contee, "Morgan, Clement G.," in *Dictionary of American Negro Biography*, 452.

15. May Childs Nerney to AHG, 7 December 1914, AHG Papers; Du Bois, *Autobiography*, 138–39; Lewis, *Du Bois*, 105–6.

16. *New York Evening Post*, 16 December 1916, in OGV Papers, File 1453, Houghton Library, Harvard University; BTW Papers, 5:n. 94.

17. Kellogg, *NAACP*, 80–83; Francis Jackson Garrison (hereafter FJG) to OGV, 25 and 26 March 1911; *Boston Globe*, 31 March 1911, 4; 1 and 3 April; *The Crisis* (May 1911).

18. "Report of the Committee on Organization of the Boston Branch," Box G-88, File "Boston, Ma. 1912–1920," NAACP Papers-LC.

19. FJG to OGV, 1 December 1911; *Boston Globe* (evening ed.), 29 November 1911, 6.

20. *The Crisis*, August 1911, 160–62; Minutes, Board of Directors, 6 February 1912, NAACP Microfilm Papers, Part I, Reel 8; FJG to OGV, 20 January 1912, OGV Papers; Kellogg, *NAACP*, 120; *The Crisis* (March 1912): 203. *The Crisis* probably erroneously lists George G. Garrison as treasurer.

21. Kellogg, *NAACP*, 199–200.

22. American Bar Association Circular Letter, 8 August 1912; Butler Wilson to May Childs Nerney, 23 August 1912, NAACP Microfilm Papers, Part 11, Reel 1.

23. William R. Morris to May Childs Nerney, 5 September 1912; Butler Wilson to May Childs Nerney, 3 September 1912; Moorfield Storey to May Childs Nerney, 20 February 1913; NAACP Microfilm Papers, Part 11, Reel 1.

24. *The Crisis* (August 1913): 191.

25. *Boston Globe*, 2 January 1913, 2.

26. *Boston Globe*, 13 February 1913, 11; David Donald, *Lincoln Reconsidered: Essays on the Civil War Era* (New York: Vintage Books, 1961), 3, 20.

27. Link, *Woodrow Wilson*, 64–66.

28. Villard, *Fighting Years*, 216–35; Du Bois, *Autobiography*, 263–64; FJG to OGV, 6 and 11 August; 6 and 31 October 1912, OGV Papers; Butler Wilson to AHG, 12 November 1915, AHG Papers; Moorfield Storey to OGV, 11 September 1913, Special Correspondence Microfilm, NAACP Papers; Howe, *Storey*, 260–61.

29. Kellogg, *NAACP*, 159–65.

30. Moorfield Storey letter in Howe, *Storey*, 262; Fox, 168–79.

31. *Boston Globe*, 21 October 1913, 9; *The Crisis* (December 1913): 89; FJG to OGV, 24 October 1913, OGV Papers.

32. FJG to OGV, 6 and 9 November 1913, OGV Papers; *The Crisis* (January 1914): 141.

33. Fox, *Trotter*, 168–87.

34. FJG to OGV, 29 October, 4 and 5 November 1913, OGV Papers; Butler Wilson, "The Growth of Race Prejudice in New England and How We Are Meeting It," NAACP Papers, Microfilm Part 1, Reel 8.

35. NAACP Annual Report, 1914, 46; NAACP Papers-LC.

36. *Boston Globe*, 16 February 1916, 2.

37. *Boston Herald*, 13 November 1914, 13; FJG to OGV, 13 November 1914, OGV Papers; *The Crisis*, (January 1915): 136, and (April 1915): 300.

38. FJG to OGV, 16 and 24 January 1915, OGV Papers.

39. FJG to OGV, 1 February 1915; *Boston Herald*, 8 March 1915, 11; Kellogg, *NAACP*, 181.

40. FJG to OGV, 9 March 1915, OGV Papers.

41. *The Crisis*, (December 1917): 91; (January 1918): 136–37; (April 1918): 283–84.

42. Storey to AHG, 10 October 1918, includes "Confidential Statement of Dr. Barry, YMCA Secretary at Ft. Devens"; Storey to AHG, 18 November 1918, AHG Papers.

43. Howard W. Coleman to John Shillady, received 13 January 1919; Nelson Dukes to NAACP, 16 March 1919, Box G-88, "Fort Devens" File, NAACP Papers-LC.

44. Butler Wilson to John Shillady, 7 April 1919; Boston Branch Bulletin, January 1920, Box G-88, NAACP Papers-LC.

45. Lewis, *Du Bois*, 506–9.

46. Butler Wilson to May Childs Nerney, 1 April 1915; Nerney to Wilson, 5 April 1915; NAACP circular letter, 7 April 1915; NAACP Papers Microfilm Part 11, Series A, Reel 32. Future NAACP *Birth of a Nation* correspondence is from this reel.

47. Jack Beatty, *The Rascal King: The Life and Times of James Michael Curley (1874–1958)* (Reading, Mass.: Addison-Wesley, 1992), 172–75.

48. MWO to Joel Spingarn, 9 April 1915, NAACP Papers; Beatty, *Curley*, 180–81; MWO, *Walls*, 128–29.

49. *Boston Globe*, 19 April 1915, 1; *Boston Post*, 18 April 1915, 1; Beatty, *Curley*, 181–84.

50. *Boston Globe*, 19 April 1915 (evening ed.), 1 and 12; 21 April 1915, 1 and 4; 22 April 1915, 1; 23 April 1915, 18; 24 April 1915, 16.

51. *Boston Globe*, 21 April 1915, 4; 24 April 1915, 16.

52. Advertisement in *Boston Globe*, 27 April 1915, 4; *Boston Globe*, 27 April 1915, 12; *The Congregationalist and Christian World*, 22 April 1915, in NAACP Papers.

53. *Boston Globe* 26 April 1915, (evening ed.), 1; Moorfield Storey letter to *Boston Herald*, in NAACP Papers.

54. Joseph Prince Loud to May Childs Nerney, 23 and 29 April 1915, enclosed

articles in *Boston Post*, 11 April 1915, and *Boston Traveller*, 23 and 27 April 1915, NAACP Papers.

55. *Boston Globe*, 26 April 1915, 9.

56. *The Crisis* (June 1915): 88; *Boston Globe*, 3 May 1915, 1; *Boston Herald*, 3 May 1915, 1.

57. *Boston Globe*, 3 May 1915, 1; *Boston Herald*, 3 May 1915, 1; William Brigham to W. E. B. Du Bois, 26 May 1915; Du Bois to Brigham, 5 June 1915, Du Bois Papers, Reel 5.

58. Beatty, *Curley*, 184–86.

59. Kellogg, *NAACP*, 107–16; Lewis, *Du Bois*, 466–500.

60. Bruce, *Archibald Grimké*, 185–213.

61. For example, May Childs Nerney to AHG, 21 October 1914, AHG Papers.

62. Butler Wilson to AHG, 24 December 1914, AHG Papers.

63. May Childs Nerney to AHG, 7 December 1914, AHG Papers; Du Bois, *Autobiography*, 139–40; FJG to OGV, 8 April 1915, File 1453, OGV Papers.

64. Kellogg, *NAACP*, 107; Butler Wilson to W. E. B. Du Bois, 6 January 1916; Du Bois to Wilson, 12 January 1916, Du Bois Papers, Reel 5.

65. George G. Bradford (hereafter GGB) to AHG, 20 April 1915, AHG Papers.

66. GGB to James Weldon Johnson, 21 March 1918, Box G-38, "Financial Matters" File, NAACP Papers-LC.

67. James Weldon Johnson to GGB, 27 March 1918, Box G-38, "Financial Matters" File, NAACP Papers-LC.

68. GGB to Du Bois, 23 April 1919, in AHG Papers, 1919 Correspondence File.

69. GGB to John Shillady, received 24 April 1919; 29 April 1919, Box G-38, "Financial Matters" File, NAACP Papers.

70. *The Crisis*, December 1918, 71.

71. FJG to OGV, 2 January 1913, 11 October 1913, File 1451, OGV Papers.

72. Kellogg, *NAACP*, 31, 45 n; FJG to OGV, 19 October 1909; 18 January 1914, File 1452, OGV Papers.

73. Butler Wilson to AHG, 12 November 1915, Mary Wilson to AHG, November [no day] 1915, January [no day] 1915, AHG Papers; Mary Wilson to May Childs Nerney letters, marked "received" 29 October, 1 and 29 December 1914; 5, 7, 11, 31 January 1915, in Mary Wilson file, NAACP Papers Microfilm ed.

74. NAACP Branch Bulletin, February 1918, on microfilm at LC; Boston Branch Bulletin, 20 May 1920, Box G-88, "Boston, Ma. 1912–1920" File, NAACP Papers-LC.

75. Boston Branch Bulletin, 20 May 1920, Box G-88, "Boston, Ma. 1912–1920" File, NAACP Papers-LC.

76. NAACP Branch Bulletin, June–July 1918 on microfilm at LC; Hayden, "Faith, Culture and Leadership," 8, 24–26, 38–39.

234 Notes to Pages 163–169

CHAPTER SIX: THE LEGACY OF JOHN BOYLE O'REILLY

1. Noel Ignatiev, *How the Irish Became White* (New York: Routledge, 1995) discusses African- and Irish-American relations in nineteenth-century Philadelphia; Thomas H. O'Connor, *The Boston Irish: A Political History* (Boston: Northeastern University Press, 1995); Roger Daniels, *Coming to America: A History of Immigration and Ethnicity in American Life* (New York: Harper, 1991), 121–45; Oscar Handlin, *Boston's Immigrants, 1790–1880: A Study in Acculturation,* (1941; Cambridge: The Belknap Press of Harvard University Press, 1979).

2. George Potter, *To the Golden Door: The Story of the Irish in Ireland and America* (Boston: Little, Brown, 1960), 102–9.

3. Benjamin Quarles, *Black Abolitionists* (1969; New York: Da Capo Press, 1991), 131–33; *BET,* 7 August 1875.

4. Potter, *Golden Door,* 371–87; William V. Shannon, *The American Irish* (New York: Macmillan, 1963); the classic statement of this case is Handlin, *Boston's Immigrants.*

5. Potter, *Golden Door,* 372–77; Francis Robert Walsh, "The Boston Pilot: A Newspaper for the Irish Immigrant, 1829–1908" (Ph.D. diss., Boston University, 1969), 118, 277.

6. Walsh, "Pilot," 118–39; Dennis P. Ryan, *Beyond the Ballot Box: A Social History of the Boston Irish, 1845–1917* (Rutherford: Fairleigh Dickinson University Press, 1983), 130–32.

7. Walsh, "Pilot," 147–76; Alan Lupo, *Liberty's Chosen Home: The Politics of Violence in Boston* (1977; Boston: Beacon, 1988), 19–44.

8. Walsh, "Pilot," 176–85.

9. Thomas N. Brown, *Irish-American Nationalism, 1870–1890* (Philadelphia: J. B. Lippincott, 1966), 1–15.

10. James Jeffrey Roche, *Life of John Boyle O'Reilly* (New York: Cassell, 1891), 1–103.

11. Ibid., 101–21.

12. Brown, *Irish-American Nationalism,* 85–100.

13. *BET,* 7 August 1875, 2 and 4; *Boston Herald,* 7 August 1875, 2; Roche, *O'Reilly,* 142, 152–54, 481–86.

14. Arthur Mann, *Yankee Reformers,* 27–44.

15. *BET,* 7 December 1885; *Boston Herald,* 8 December 1885.

16. Roche, *O'Reilly,* 738–42.

17. *BET,* 13 April 1886, 2; *Boston Herald,* 13 April 1886, 2. Roche, *O'Reilly,* confuses this speech with the December 1885 speech.

18. *BET,* 14 November 1888; O'Reilly, "Crispus Attucks," in Roche, *O'Reilly,* 408–14.

19. *Boston Pilot,* 18 January 1890, 1 and 4; 1 February 1890, 4; 8 February 1890, 4; 5 July 1890, 19 July 1890.

20. Roche, *O'Reilly,* 333–89.

21. The omitted journal is *Donahoe's Magazine*; a good case could be made for discussing Martin Lomasney, Patrick Maguire as politician, or Patrick Collins. All but Maguire have biographers. For Collins, M. P. Curran, *Life of Patrick A. Collins* (Norwood, Mass.: Norwood, 1906); for Curley, Beatty, *Rascal King*; for Fitzgerald, John Henry Cutler, *"Honey Fitz"*; for Lomasney, Leslie G. Ainley, *Boston Mahatma* (Boston: Bruce Humphries, 1949). The silence of these writers on race relations suggests how far the question was from the minds of all the protagonists.

22. Mann, *Yankee Reformers*, 44–51, reprises Roche's life and wider views.

23. *Boston Pilot*, 1 and 4 November 1890; 8 and 4 November 1890; 27 February 1892, 4.

24. *Boston Pilot*, 17 January 1891; 24 January 1891; 31 January 1891.

25. *Boston Pilot*, 22 January 1898, 4; 25 August 1900, 4.

26. *Boston Pilot*, 11 August 1900, 4; 25 August 1900, 4; 26 October 1901, 4; 8 August 1903, 4.

27. Brown, *Irish-American Nationalism*, 181.

28. *Boston Globe*, 29 November 1896, 1; 30 November 1896, 1; Blodgett, *Gentle Reformers*, 59, 141–44, 158–60, 165–70; Cutler, *"Honey Fitz,"* 68–71.

29. *Republic*, 15 February 1890, 4; Blodgett, *Massachusetts Democrats*, 97–98, 146, 151–54.

30. *Republic*, editorials of 25 January, 4 February, 22 March, 19 April 1890.

31. *Republic*, 16 August 1890.

32. Doris Kearns Goodwin, *The Fitzgeralds and the Kennedys* (New York: St. Martin's, 1987); O'Connor, *Boston Irish*.

33. Goodwin, *Fitzgeralds*, 112–14.

34. Logan, *Negro*, 94–96; *Congressional Record*, 8 January 1901, 739–41.

35. *Boston Globe*, 6 January 1910; unidentified clipping, 7 January 1910, Box 1, Packet 3; unidentified clipping, 23 April 1910, Box 2, John F. Fitzgerald Scrapbooks, Holy Cross University Library; *Boston Globe*, 5 July 1910.

36. Unidentified clipping, 21 July 1910, Box 2, Packet 4, Fitzgerald notebooks; *Boston Globe*, 23 April 1904, 2; 29 August 1907, 3; 4 December 1907, 14; 31 March 1911, 4. For Trotter on Fitzgerald, and his use of the Irish revolution as an example for African-Americans, see the *Guardian*, 23 November 1907, 2 December 1911, 20 May 1916, 1; 28 April 1917, 1; 14 June 1919.

37. Beatty, *Curley*, 178, 184–85; *Boston Post*, 29 March 1917, 7; See NAACP chapter for *Birth of a Nation*.

38. See Richard A. Ballou, "Even in 'Freedom's Birthplace'!"

39. Blodgett, *Gentle Reformers*, 204–39.

40. Ralph M. Goldman, *Dilemma and Destiny: The Democratic Party in America* (Lanham, Md.: Madison Books, 1986), 88–103; Beatty, *Curley*, 124–29.

41. Blodgett, *Gentle Reformers*, 262–83.

42. Based on sampled readings of *Republic*, 1892–96; 1900–1904.

43. Shannon, *American Irish*, 114–30.

44. The Reverend Mother Augustine [Eulalia Tuckerman], "Life of Archbishop Williams," typescript, Archdiocese of Boston; Robert H. Lord, et al., *History of the Archdiocese of Boston in the Various Stages of Its Development, 1604–1943* (Boston: Pilot, 1944), 3:101–37, 161–83.

45. Harlan, *Wizard*, 82; *Pilot*, 17 January 1891, 2; 1 September 1900, 4.

46. James M. O'Toole, *From Generation to Generation: Stories in Catholic History From the Archives of the Archdiocese of Boston* (Boston: Daughters of St. Paul, 1983), 80–84; *Pilot*, 4 August 1900, 1; Guide to Williams Papers, Archdiocese of Boston, 26.

47. Mother Augustine, "Williams," 643; *Pilot*, 18 August 1906, 4; James M. O'Toole, *Militant and Triumphant: William Henry O'Connell and the Catholic Church in Boston, 1859–1944* (Notre Dame: University of Notre Dame Press, 1992), 168.

48. O'Toole, *Militant*, 75–78. O'Toole describes O'Connell's securing of the bishopric as "the decisive nail in the Americanist coffin."

49. Walsh, "Pilot," 276–77; *Pilot*, 21 April 1906, 4; 9 September 1906, 4.

50. *Pilot*, 27 March 1915, 4; 3, 10, 17, 24 April 1915.

51. O'Toole, *Militant*, 167–68; the Reverend Richard J. Cushing, "Mother Katherine Drexel and the Sisters of the Blessed Sacrament Golden Jubilee, 1891–1941" (pamphlet); Sister Mary Leo to C. J. Sullivan, 15 September 1914; Sullivan to Sister Mary Leo, 16 September 1914; C. J. Sullivan to Sister Mary Katherine Drexel, 16 December 1914, all in Convent of the Blessed Sacrament File SI-109, Archives of Archdiocese of Boston.

52. *Pilot*, 15 January 1916, 1.

53. Green and Donahue, *Boston's Workers*, 75–93.

54. Mann, *Yankee Reformers*, 175–200.

55. Logan, *Nadir*, 140–56; a recent discussion of racial exclusion in the labor movement is Eric Arnesen, " 'Like Banquo's Ghost, It Will Not Down': The Race Question and the American Railroad Brotherhoods, 1880–1920," *American Historical Review* 99, no. 5 (December 1994): 1601–33.

56. Ethel M. Johnson, "Labor," in *Fifty Years of Boston: A Memorial Volume Issued in Commemoration of the Tercentenary of 1930*, ed. Elizabeth M. Herlihy (Boston: Subcommittee on Memorial History of Boston Tercentenary Committee, 1932), 216–18; Robert D. Leiter, *The Teamsters Union: A Study of Its Economic Impact* (New York: Bookman Associates, 1957).

57. *Labor Leader*, 26 December 1891, 1; 13 June 1891, 1; 11 June 1892, 2; and 1887–97 for general coverage.

58. Daniels, *In Freedom's Birthplace*, 328, 333, 343–78. By 1920, there were still only 9,584 African-American workers out of 350,207, less than 3 percent of the total, according to *Census*, Table 13, 4:368.

59. *Boston Herald*, 21 February 1894, 1; photo in Green, *Boston's Workers*, 82.

CHAPTER SEVEN: THE CASES OF HOLMES, LEWIS, AND STOREY

1. Oliver Wendell Holmes, *The Common Law* (1881; Boston: Little, Brown, 1951), 1.

2. Charles A. Lofgren, *The Plessy Decision: A Legal-Historical Interpretation* (New York: Oxford University Press, 1987); *Boston Globe, Herald, Transcript,* and *Post,* checked for 19 and 20 May 1896.

3. Liva Baker, *The Justice From Beacon Hill: The Life and Times of Oliver Wendell Holmes* (New York: HarperCollins, 1991); Sheldon M. Novick, *Honorable Justice: The Life of Oliver Wendell Holmes* (Boston: Little, Brown, 1989), 198–99 for Foster.

4. *Giles v. Harris* 189 U.S. 479 (1903); *Bailey v. Alabama* 219 U.S. 219 (1911). Holmes found for a Washington-sponsored plaintiff in *Rogers v. Alabama* 192 U.S. 226 (1904).

5. Baker, *Justice,* 105–53; Novick, *Honorable Justice,* 35–89; Oliver Wendell Holmes to Amelia Holmes, 17 and 19 November 1862, in Mark A. De Wolfe Howe, ed., *Touched With Fire: Civil War Letters and Diary of Oliver Wendell Holmes* (Cambridge: Harvard University Press, 1947), 71 and 73.

6. Baker, *Justice,* 163–245; Novick, *Honorable Justice,* 93–135.

7. Baker, *Justice,* 246–70; Novick, *Honorable Justice,* 135–60; direct quote is Baker's summary, 257.

8. Holmes, *Common Law,* I, 41.

9. Baker, *Justice,* 273–356; Novick, *Honorable Justice,* 163–77, 228–37.

10. Baker, *Justice,* 339–57; Novick, *Honorable Justice,* 267–73.

11. *Brownfield v. South Carolina* 189 U.S. 426 (1903).

12. *State v. Brownfield* 60 South Carolina 509.

13. J. C. May [Wilford H. Smith] to R. C. Black [Emmet J. Scott] 15 July 1903, in *BTW Papers,* 8:207.

14. *Rogers v. Alabama* 192 U.S. 226 (1904).

15. *Giles v. Harris* 189 U.S. 475 (1903).

16. Harlan, *Wizard,* 244–47.

17. *Giles v. Harris* 189 U.S. 475 (1903).

18. Ibid.

19. Harlan, *Wizard,* 247; Novick, *Honorable Justice,* n. 459.

20. Baker, *Justice,* 431–32; *U.S. v. Shipp* 203 U.S. 563 (1906); *U.S. v. Shipp* 214 U.S. 386 (1909).

21. Baker, *Justice,* 467–71; 478–81; *Frank v. Mangum* 237 U.S. 309 (1915).

22. Baker, *Justice,* 573–74.

23. Harlan, *Wizard,* 250–51; *Bailey v. Alabama* 211 U.S. 452 (1908); *Bailey v. Alabama* 219 U.S. 219 (1911).

24. *Bailey v. Alabama* 211 U.S. 452 (1908).

25. *Bailey v. Alabama* 219 U.S. 219 (1911).

26. Ibid.

27. Pete Daniel, "Up From Slavery and Down to Peonage: The Alonzo Bailey Case," *Journal of American History* 57 (December 1970): 654–70; BTW to Charles Dyer Norton, 6 January 1911, 10:534–35; William Howard Taft to BTW, 8 January 1911, 10:539, *BTW Papers.*

28. Baker, *Justice,* 471; *U.S. v. Broughton* 235 U.S. 133 (1914); *U.S. v. Reynolds* 235 U.S. 133 (1914).

29. Baker, *Justice*, 473–75; *McCabe v. Atchison, Topeka and Sante Fe Railway* 235 U.S. 151 (1914).

30. Baker, *Justice*, 498–500; *Buchanan v. Warley* 254 U.S. 60 (1917).

31. *U.S. v. Mosley* 238 U.S. 383 (1915).

32. Baker, *Justice*, 595–97.

33. For Morris and Rock, Daniels, *In Freedom's Birthplace*, 61–62, 70, 73, 448–53; for Walker, Charles Sumner Brown, "Genesis of the Negro Lawyer in New England," *Negro History Bulletin* (April 1959); for Ruffin, *Dictionary of Negro Biography*, 535.

34. For Morris, William H. Ferris, *The African Abroad; or, His Evolution in Western Civilization: Tracing His Development Under Caucasian Milieu* (New Haven: Tuttle, Morehouse and Taylor, 1913), xiii; for Benjamin, *Black Biographical Dictionaries*, microfiche from *Who's Who in Colored America*, 281–82; for Wilson and Morgan, see chapter 5; for Grimké, see Bruce, *Archibald Grimké*.

35. Ferris, *African Abroad*, 767.

36. Stephen R. Fox, *The Guardian of Boston: William Monroe Trotter*, 160; Peter Shriver Jr., "Lewis, William Henry," in *Dictionary of American Biography* (*DAB*), supp. 4, 492–94; Clarence G. Contee Sr., "Lewis, William Henry," in *Dictionary of American Negro Biography*, 396–97, in clipping file, Cambridge Public Library; Harlan, *Wizard*, 16.

37. *Boston Globe*, 26 May 1893, 4, in clipping file, CPL; Daniels, *Birthplace*, 95–96, 275; Fox, *Trotter*, 26.

38. William Henry Lewis (hereafter WHL) to BTW, 29 December 1902, *BTW Papers*, 6:614.

39. Fox, *Trotter*, 45; Harlan, *Wizard*, 16–17, 32–69; WHL to BTW, 16 September 1903, *BTW Papers*, 7:285.

40. "Lewis, William Henry," in *DAB*; quoted in Fox, *Trotter*, 159–60.

41. WHL to BTW, 2 July 1909, 10:141; 14 June 1911, 11:216; 10 December 1911, 10:406; BTW to WHL, 20 December 1911, 11:412, *BTW Papers*.

42. *Boston Globe*, 27 August 1912; *Boston Herald*, 28 August 1912.

43. WHL to BTW, 7 March 1913, 134; 27 March 1913, 148, vol. 11, *BTW Papers*.

44. Fox, *Trotter*, 108; BTW to WHL, 9 November 1908, 11:689; 19 June 1912, 11:551, *BTW Papers*.

45. Ferris, *African Abroad*, 797.

46. *Boston Globe*, 13 February 1913, CPL clipping file; Fox, *Trotter*, 192–97.

47. Hixson, *Moorfield Storey*, 191–205; Leger, "Moorfield Storey," 346–53.

48. Hixson, *Abolitionist*, 6–10; Leger, "Moorfield Storey," 9–17.

49. Hixson, *Abolitionist*, 11–15; Leger, "Moorfield Storey," 27–33.

50. Moorfield Storey (MS) to William Monroe Trotter (WMT), 12 January 1911, in Letterbook 11, Moorfield Storey Papers, Massachusetts Historical Society.

51. MS to Susan Storey, 27 November 1867, quoted in Howe, *Portrait*, 43–44.

52. *Boston Common*, 17 December 1910, in Scrapbook; MS to Charles Francis Adams, 19 November 1908, 1 December 1908, 3 March 1909, in Letterbook 10,

Storey Papers are random examples of correspondence showing friendly disagreement on the race question; "To the Voters of Massachusetts," (1892), in Scrapbook 5, Storey Papers; Leger, "Moorfield Storey," 50–89.

53. *Boston Herald*, 2 January 1910, 1; handbill for 7 January 1910 meeting; *Boston Evening Transcript*, 31 March 1911, Scrapbook 3, Storey Papers.

54. *Boston Evening Transcript*, 11 November 1911, in Scrapbook 3, Storey Papers for auto club.

55. Hixson, *Abolitionist*, 45–97, direct quote, 59.

56. Moorfield Storey, "Negro Suffrage Is Not a Failure," *Colored American Magazine* (December 1903): 909–11.

57. MS to Horace Bumstead, 27 January 1911, MS to WMT, 12 January and 16 March 1911, Letterbook 12; MS to WMT, 11 March 1909, 18 March 1909, Letterbook 10; 23 April 1912, Letterbook 13 in Storey Papers; 16 September 1913, in Howe, *Independent*, 261; *Boston Guardian*, 23 February 1918; *Guardian*, n.d., Scrapbook 5, Storey Papers.

58. *Springfield Republican*, 30 June 1907, Scrapbook 3, Storey Papers.

59. Baker, *Justice*, 482–83; Hixson, *Abolitionist*, 136–37; MS to Joel Spingarn, 12 July 1915, Letterbook 17, Storey Papers.

60. MS to May Childs Nerney, 6 August 1915, Letterbook 17, Storey Papers.

61. MS to Turner K. Hackman, 20 September 1916, Letterbook 18, Storey Papers; Logan, *Negro*, 94–96.

62. MS to James Weldon Johnson, 18 December 1919, in Special Correspondence, Part I, Reel 24, microfilm papers of the NAACP.

63. Hixson, *Abolitionist*, 139–42.

64. MS to Robert L. O'Brien, 6 November 1917; MS to OGV, 6 November 1917, Letterbook 20, Storey Papers.

65. Hixson, *Abolitionist*, 142–44.

66. Robert L. Zangrando, *The NAACP Crusade Against Lynching, 1909–1950* (Philadelphia: Temple University Press, 1980), 28–29.

67. MS to Roy Nash, 16 October 1916, Letterbook 18, Storey Papers.

68. Hixson, *Abolitionist*, 163.

69. MS to Walter White, 11 July 1918, Special Correspondence, Part I, reel 24, microfilm NAACP Papers; 16 July 1918 to John R. Shillady, Letterbook 20, Storey Papers.

70. MS to John R. Shillady, 29 March 1919, Letterbook 20 in Storey Papers; *New York Evening Post* and *New York Times*, undated, Scrapbook 5, Storey Papers.

71. Program, National Conference on Lynching; Conference Address to Nation, Scrapbook 5, Storey papers.

72. *Boston Chronicle*, 10 May 1919; typescript MS speech to Detroit NAACP, 26 June 1921 or 1922(?).

73. *Congressional Record*, 10 January 1922, Scrapbook 5, Storey Papers.

74. *Boston Herald*, 23 and 24 April 1922, Scrapbook 5; Hixson, *Abolitionist*, 165–75.

75. Hixson, *Abolitionist*, 181–84; Baker, *Justice*, 574.

Selected Bibliography

PRIMARY SOURCES

Manuscript Collections

Archives of the Archdiocese of Boston
Blackwell Family Papers, Schlesinger Library, Radcliffe College
W. E. B. Du Bois Papers, microfilm edition, Boston Public Library
John F. Fitzgerald Scrapbooks, Library of the College of the Holy Cross
Francis Jackson Garrison Papers, Schomburg Collection, New York Public
    Library
Archibald H. Grimké Papers, Moorland-Spingarn Room, Howard University
George Frisbie Hoar Papers, Massachusetts Historical Society
Oliver Wendell Holmes Papers, Harvard University Law School
League of Women for Community Service Collection, Schlesinger Library, Rad-
    cliffe College
National Association for the Advancement of Colored People Papers, microfilm
    edition
NAACP Papers, Manuscript Division, Library of Congress
Cora V. Reid (MacKerrow) Papers, Schlesinger Library, Radcliffe College
Alfred Russell Papers, Mugar Library, Boston University
William E. Russell Papers, Massachusetts Historical Society
Moorfield Storey Papers, Massachusetts Historical Society
William Monroe Trotter Papers, Mugar Library, Boston University
Oswald Garrison Villard Papers, Houghton Library, Harvard University

Cases

Bailey v. Alabama 211 U.S. 452 (1908)
Bailey v. Alabama 219 U.S. 219 (1911)
Brownfield v. South Carolina 189 U.S. 426 (1903)
Giles v. Harris 189 U.S. 479 (1903)
McCabe v. Atchison, Topeka and Santa Fe Railway 235 U.S. 151 (1914)

Rogers v. Alabama 192 U.S. 226 (1904)
State v. Brownfield 60 South Carolina 509
U.S. v. Broughton and U.S. v. Reynolds 235 U.S. 133 (1914)

SECONDARY SOURCES

Books

Abrams, Richard M. *Conservatism in A Progressive Era: Massachusetts Politics, 1900–1912.* Cambridge: Harvard University Press, 1985.
Ainley, Leslie G. *Boston Mahatma.* Boston: Bruce Humphries, 1949.
Amory, Cleveland. *The Proper Bostonians.* New York: Dutton, 1947.
Anderson, Jervis. *A. Philip Randolph: A Biographical Portrait.* 1972. Reprint, Berkeley and Los Angeles: University of California Press, 1986.
Anthony, Susan B., and Ida Husted Harper, eds. *History of Woman Suffrage.* Vols. 4 and 5. Reprint, Salem, N.H.: Ayer, 1985.
Ayers, Edward L. *The Promise of the New South: Life After Reconstruction.* New York: Oxford University Press, 1992.
Baker, Liva. *The Justice From Beacon Hill: The Life and Times of Oliver Wendell Holmes.* New York: HarperCollins, 1991.
Baker, Ray Stannard. *Following the Color Line: American Negro Citizenship in the Progressive Era.* 1908. Reprint, New York: Harper Torchbooks, 1964.
Barnes, Gilbert Hobbs. *The Anti-Slavery Impulse, 1830–1844.* 1933. Reprint, New York: Harcourt, Brace and World, 1964.
Bartlett, Irving H. *Wendell Phillips: Brahmin Radical.* Westport, Conn.: Greenwood, 1961.
Beatty, Jack. *The Rascal King: The Life and Times of James Michael Curley (1874–1958).* Reading, Mass.: Addison-Wesley, 1992.
Beisner, Robert L. *Twelve Against Empire: The Anti-Imperialists, 1898–1900.* 1968. Reprint, New York: McGraw-Hill, 1971.
Blackwell, Alice Stone. *Lucy Stone.* Boston: Little, Brown, 1930; Kraus Reprint, 1971.
Blodgett, Geoffrey. *The Gentle Reformers: Massachusetts Democrats in the Cleveland Era.* Cambridge: Harvard University Press, 1966.
Bontemps, Arna. *One Hundred Years of Negro Freedom.* New York: Dodd, Mead, 1961.
Broderick, Francis L. *W. E. B. Du Bois: Negro Leader in a Time of Crisis.* Stanford: Stanford University Press, 1959.
Brown, Thomas N. *Irish-American Nationalism, 1870–1890.* Philadelphia: J. B. Lippincott, 1966.
Bruce, Dickson D. Jr. *Archibald Grimké: Portrait of a Black Independent.* Baton Rouge: Louisiana State University Press, 1993.
Brundage, W. Fitzhugh. *Lynching in the New South: Georgia and Virginia, 1880–1930.* Urbana: University of Illinois Press, 1993.

Chamberlain, Joseph Edgar. *The Boston Transcript: A History of Its First Hundred Years*. Boston: Houghton Mifflin, 1930.

Cromwell, Adelaide M. *The Other Brahmins: Boston's Black Upper Class, 1750–1950*. Fayetteville: University of Arkansas Press, 1994.

Cronon, Edmund David. *Black Moses: The Story of Marcus Garvey and the Universal Negro Improvement Association*. Madison: University of Wisconsin Press, 1968.

Curran, M. P. *Life of Patrick A. Collins*. Norwood, Mass.: Norwood, 1906.

Cutler, John Henry. *"Honey Fitz": Three Steps to the White House: The Life and Times of John F. (Honey Fitz) Fitzgerald*. New York: Bobbs-Merrill, 1962.

Daniels, John. *In Freedom's Birthplace: A Study of the Boston Negroes*. 1914. Reprint, New York: Negro Universities Press, 1968.

Daniels, Roger. *Coming to America: A History of Immigration and Ethnicity in American Life*. New York: HarperCollins, 1990.

Donald, David. *Lincoln Reconsidered: Essays on the Civil War Era*. New York: Vintage Books, 1961.

———. *Charles Sumner and the Coming of the Civil War*. 1960. Reprint, New York: Fawcett Columbine, 1989.

Du Bois, William Edward Burghardt. *The Autobiography of W. E. B. Du Bois: A Soliloquy on Viewing My Life from the Last Decade of Its First Century*. New York: International Publishers, 1968.

Edelstein, Tilden G. *Strange Enthusiasm: A Life of Thomas Wentworth Higginson*. New Haven: Yale University Press, 1968.

Emilio, Luis F. *A Brave Black Regiment: History of the Fifty-Fourth Regiment of Massachusetts Volunteer Infantry, 1863–1865*. 1894. Reprint, New York: Bantam Books, 1992.

Epstein, Abraham. *The Negro Migrant in Pittsburgh*. 1918. Reprint, New York: Arno and New York Times Press, 1969.

Ferris, William H. *The African Abroad; or, His Evolution in Western Civilization: Tracing His Development Under Caucasian Milieu*. New Haven: Tuttle, Morehouse and Taylor, 1913.

Filler, Louis. *The Crusade Against Slavery, 1830–1860*. New York: Harper Torchbooks, 1960.

Flexner, Eleanor. *Century of Struggle: The Women's Movement in the United States*. 1969. Reprint, Cambridge: The Belknap Press of Harvard University Press, 1975.

Foner, Eric. *Free Soil, Free Labor, Free Men: The Ideology of the Republican Party Before the Civil War*. London: Oxford University Press, 1973.

Formisano, Ronald P., and Constance K. Burns, eds. *Boston, 1700–1980: The Evolution of Urban Politics*. Westport, Conn.: Greenwood, 1984.

Fox, Stephen R. *The Guardian of Boston: William Monroe Trotter*. New York: Atheneum, 1970.

Franklin, John Hope. *From Slavery to Freedom: A History of Negro Americans*. 3d ed. New York: Knopf, 1967.

Fredrickson, George M. *The Black Image in the White Mind: The Debate on Afro-American Character and Destiny, 1817–1914.* 1971. Reprint, Hanover, N.H.: Wesleyan University Press, 1987.

Garraty, John A. *Henry Cabot Lodge: A Biography.* New York: Knopf, 1953.

Gatewood, Willard B. *Aristocrats of Color: The Black Elite, 1880–1920.* Bloomington: Indiana University Press, 1990.

Giddings, Paula. *When and Where I Enter: The Impact of Black Women on Race and Sex in America.* New York: William Morrow, 1984.

Gilmore, Al-Tony. *Bad Nigger! The National Impact of Jack Johnson.* Port Washington, N.Y.: National University Publications, Kennikat Press, n.d.

Goldman, Ralph M. *Dilemma and Destiny: The Democratic Party in America.* Lanham, Md.: Madison Books, 1986.

Goodwin, Doris Kearns. *The Fitzgeralds and the Kennedys.* New York: St. Martin's, 1987.

Green, James, and Hugh Carter Donahue. *Boston's Workers: A Labor History.* Boston: Trustees of the Public Library of the City of Boston, 1979.

Grimké, Archibald H. *William Lloyd Garrison: The Abolitionist.* 1891. Reprint, New York: Negro Universities Press, 1969.

Handlin, Oscar. *Boston's Immigrants, 1790–1880: A Study in Acculturation.* 1941. Reprint, Cambridge: The Belknap Press of Harvard University Press, 1979.

Harlan, Louis R. *Booker T. Washington: The Making of a Black Leader, 1856–1901.* London: Oxford University Press, 1975.

———. *Booker T. Washington: The Wizard of Tuskegee, 1901–1915.* New York: Oxford University Press, 1986.

———. *Booker T. Washington in Perspective: Essays of Louis R. Harlan.* Edited by Raymond W. Smock. Jackson: University Press of Mississippi, 1988.

———, ed. *The Booker T. Washington Papers.* 14 vols. Urbana: University of Illinois Press, 1972.

Hennessy, Michael E. *Four Decades of Massachusetts Politics, 1890–1935.* Norwood, Mass.: Norwood Press, 1935.

Henri, Florette. *Black Migration: Movement North, 1900–1920; The Road From Myth to Man.* Garden City, N.Y.: Anchor Books, 1976.

Herlihy, Elizabeth M., ed. *Fifty Years of Boston: A Memorial Volume Issued in Commemoration of the Tercentenary of 1930.* Boston: Subcommittee on Memorial History of Boston Tercentenary Committee, 1932.

Hicks, John D. *The Populist Revolt: A History of the Farmers' Alliance and the People's Party.* Lincoln: University of Nebraska Press, 1961.

Higginson, Mary Thacher, ed. *Letters and Journals of Thomas Wentworth Higginson, 1846–1906.* Boston: Houghton Mifflin, 1921.

Higginson, Thomas Wentworth. *Army Life in a Black Regiment.* 1869. Reprint, Boston: Beacon, 1970.

Higham, John. *Strangers in the Land: Patterns of American Nativism, 1860–1925.* New York: Atheneum, 1963.

Hirshson, Stanley P. *Farewell to the Bloody Shirt: Northern Republicans and the Southern Negro, 1877–1893.* 1962. Reprint, Chicago: Quadrangle Paperbacks, 1968.

Hixson, William B. *Moorfield Storey and the Abolitionist Tradition.* New York: Oxford University Press, 1972.

Hofstadter, Richard. *The Age of Reform: From Bryan to F.D.R.* New York: Vintage Books, 1955.

Holloran, Peter C. *Boston's Wayward Children: Social Services for Homeless Children, 1830–1930.* Boston: Northeastern University Press, 1994.

Holmes, Oliver Wendell Jr. *The Common Law.* 1881. Reprint, Boston: Little, Brown, 1951.

Horton, James Oliver, and Lois E. Horton. *Black Bostonians: Family Life and Community Struggle in the Antebellum North.* New York: Holmes and Meier, 1979.

Hopkins, Pauline. *Contending Forces: A Romance Illustrative of Negro Life North and South.* Boston: Colored Co-operative Publishing, 1900.

Howe, Mark A. De Wolfe. *Portrait of an Independent: Moorfield Storey, 1845–1929.* Boston: Houghton Mifflin, 1932.

———, ed. *Touched With Fire: Civil War Letters and Diary of Oliver Wendell Holmes.* Cambridge: Harvard University Press, 1947.

Hughes, Langston. *Fight for Freedom: The Story of the NAACP.* New York: Norton, 1962.

Ignatiev, Noel. *How the Irish Became White.* New York: Routledge, 1995.

Jacobs, Donald Martin, ed. *Courage and Conscience: Black and White Abolitionists in Boston.* Bloomington: Published for the Boston Atheneum by Indiana University Press, 1993.

James, Edward T., ed. *Notable American Women, 1607–1950: A Biographical Dictionary.* Cambridge: The Belknap Press of Harvard University Press, 1971.

Johnson, James Weldon. *Along This Way: The Autobiography of James Weldon Johnson.* 1933. Reprint, New York: Viking, 1968.

Kellogg, Charles Flint. *NAACP: A History of the National Association for the Advancement of Colored People.* Vol. 1, 1909–1920. Baltimore: Johns Hopkins University Press, 1967.

Korngold, Ralph. *Two Friends of Man: The Story of William Lloyd Garrison and Wendell Phillips and their Relationship with Abraham Lincoln.* Boston: Little, Brown, 1950.

Kornweibel, Theodore Jr. *No Crystal Stair: Black Life and the Messenger, 1917–1928.* Westport, Conn.: Greenwood, 1975.

Kraditor, Aileen S. *Means and Ends in American Abolitionism: Garrison and His Critics on Strategy and Tactics, 1834–1850.* New York: Pantheon Books, 1969.

———. *The Ideas of the Woman Suffrage Movement, 1890–1920.* 1965. Reprint, New York: Norton, 1981.

Kusmer, Kenneth L. *A Ghetto Takes Shape: Black Cleveland, 1870–1930.* Urbana: University of Illinois Press, 1976.

Lader, Lawrence. *The Bold Brahmins: New England's War Against Slavery, 1831–1863.* 1961. Reprint, Westport, Conn.: Greenwood, 1973.

Lane, Ann J. *The Brownsville Affair: National Crisis and Black Reaction.* Port Washington, N.Y.: National University Publications, Kennikat Press, 1971.

Leiter, Robert D. *The Teamsters Union: A Study of Its Economic Impact.* New York: Bookman Associates, 1957.

Lerner, Gerda. *The Grimké Sisters From South Carolina: Rebels Against Slavery.* Boston: Houghton Mifflin, 1967.

Levy, Leonard W. *The Law of the Commonwealth and Chief Justice Shaw.* New York: Oxford University Press, 1957.

Lewis, David Levering. *W. E. B. Du Bois: Biography of a Race, 1868–1919.* New York: Henry Holt, 1993.

Link, Arthur S. *Woodrow Wilson and the Progressive Era, 1910–1917.* 1954. Reprint, New York: Harper and Row, 1963.

Lofgren, Charles A. *The Plessy Case: A Legal-Historical Interpretation.* New York: Oxford University Press, 1987.

Logan, Rayford W. *The Negro in American Life and Thought: The Nadir, 1877–1901.* New York: Dial, 1954.

Logan, Rayford W., and Michael R. Winston, eds. *Dictionary of American Biography.* New York: Norton, 1982.

Lord, Robert H., John E. Sexton, and Edward Harrington. *History of the Archdiocese of Boston in the Various Stages of Its Development, 1604–1943.* Boston: Pilot Publishing, 1944.

Lupo, Alan. *Liberty's Chosen Home: The Politics of Violence in Boston.* 1977. Reprint, Boston: Beacon, 1988.

Mann, Arthur. *Yankee Reformers in the Urban Age.* Cambridge: The Belknap Press of Harvard University Press, 1954.

Marke, Julius J., ed. *The Holmes Reader.* New York: Oceana's Docket Books, 1955.

McFeely, William S. *Frederick Douglass.* New York: Norton, 1991.

McPherson, James M. *The Struggle for Equality: Abolitionists and the Negro in the Civil War and Reconstruction.* Princeton: Princeton University Press, 1964.

———. *The Abolitionist Legacy: From Reconstruction to the NAACP.* Princeton: Princeton University Press, 1975.

Meier, August. *Negro Thought in America, 1880–1915: Racial Ideologies in the Age of Booker T. Washington.* 1963. Reprint, Ann Arbor: University of Michigan Press, 1968.

Miller, Perry. *Errand Into the Wilderness.* Cambridge: The Belknap Press of Harvard University Press, 1978.

Miller, William Lee. *Arguing About Slavery: The Great Battle in the United States Congress.* New York: Knopf, 1996.

Mowry, George E. *The Era of Theodore Roosevelt and the Birth of Modern America, 1900–1912.* New York: Harper Torchbooks, 1962.

Morgan, Edmund. *Visible Saints: The History of a Puritan Idea.* New York: New York University Press, 1963.

Novick, Sheldon M. *Honorable Justice: The Life of Oliver Wendell Holmes*. Boston: Little, Brown, 1989.

O'Connor, Thomas H. *Lords of the Loom: The Cotton Whigs and the Coming of the Civil War*. New York: Scribner's, 1968.

———. *Bibles, Brahmins, and Bosses: A Short History of Boston*. 3d rev. ed. Boston: Trustees of the Public Library of the City of Boston, 1991.

———. *The Boston Irish: A Political History*. Boston: Northeastern University Press, 1995.

O'Connor, Thomas H., and Alan Rogers. *This Momentous Affair: Massachusetts and the Ratification of the Constitution of the United States*. Boston: Boston Public Library, 1987.

Osofsky, Gilbert. *Harlem: The Making of a Ghetto, Negro New York; 1890–1930*. New York: Harper and Row, 1966.

O'Toole, James M. *From Generation to Generation: Stories in Catholic History From the Archives of the Archdiocese of Boston*. Boston: Daughters of St. Paul, 1983.

———. *Militant and Triumphant: William Henry O'Connell and the Catholic Church in Boston, 1859–1944*. Notre Dame: University of Notre Dame Press, 1992.

Ottley, Roi. *The Lonely Warrior: The Life and Times of Robert S. Abbott*. Chicago: Henry Regnery, 1955.

Ovington, Mary White. *The Walls Came Tumbling Down*. New York: Arno Press and the New York Times Press, 1969.

Pleck, Elizabeth Hafkin. *Black Migration and Poverty: Boston, 1865–1900*. New York: Academic Press, 1979.

Potter, George. *To the Golden Door: The Story of the Irish in Ireland and America*. Boston: Little, Brown, 1960.

Quarles, Benjamin. *Black Abolitionists*. 1969. Reprint, New York: Da Capo, 1991.

Ransom, Reverdy. *The Pilgrimmage of Harriet Ransom's Son*. Nashville, Tenn.: Sunday School Union, n.d.

Renehan, Edward J. *The Secret Six: The True Tale of the Men Who Conspired with John Brown*. New York: Crown, 1995.

Roche, James Jeffrey. *Life of John Boyle O'Reilly*. New York: Cassell, 1891.

Ross, B. Joyce. *J. E. Spingarn and the Rise of the NAACP, 1911–1939*. New York: Atheneum, 1972.

Ruchames, Louis. *The Abolitionists: A Collection of Their Writings*. New York: Capricorn Books, 1963.

Rutman, Darret. *Winthrop's Boston: Portrait of a Puritan Town*. Chapel Hill: University of North Carolina Press, 1965.

Ryan, Dennis P. *Beyond the Ballot Box: A Social History of the Boston Irish, 1845–1917*. Rutherford: Fairleigh Dickinson University Press, 1983.

St. James, Warren D. *The National Association for the Advancement of Colored People: A Case Study in Pressure Groups*. New York: Exposition Press, 1958.

Schirmer, Daniel B. *Republic or Empire: American Resistance to the Philippine War.* Rochester, Vt.: Schenkman Books, n.d.

Schriftgiesser, Karl. *The Gentleman From Massachusetts: Henry Cabot Lodge.* Boston: Little, Brown, 1944.

Shannon, William V. *The American Irish.* New York: Macmillan, 1963.

Solomon, Barbara Miller. *Ancestors and Immigrants: A Changing New England Tradition.* New York: John Wiley and Sons, 1965.

Spear, Allan H. *Black Chicago: The Making of a Negro Ghetto, 1890–1920.* Chicago: University of Chicago Press, 1967.

Stevens, Walter J. *Chip On My Shoulder.* Boston: Meador, 1946.

Taylor, Susie King. *Reminiscences of My Life in Camp.* New York: Arno Press and the New York Times, 1968.

Thernstrom, Stephan. *The Other Bostonians: Poverty and Progress in the American Metropolis, 1880–1970.* Cambridge: Harvard University Press, 1973.

Thornbrough, Emma Lou. *T. Thomas Fortune: Militant Journalist.* Chicago: University of Chicago Press, 1972.

Three Negro Classics: Up From Slavery. The Souls of Black Folk. The Autobiography of an Ex-Colored Man. With an Introduction by John Hope Franklin. New York: Avon, 1965.

Tindall, George Brown. *The Emergence of the New South, 1913–1945.* Baton Rouge: Louisiana State University Press, 1967.

Trotter, Joe William Jr. *The Great Migration in Historical Perspective.* Bloomington: Indiana University Press, 1991.

Villard, Oswald Garrison. *Fighting Years: Memoirs of a Liberal Editor.* New York: Harcourt, Brace, 1939.

Welch, Richard E. Jr. *George Frisbie Hoar and the Half-Breed Republicans.* Cambridge: Harvard University Press, 1971.

Wells-Barnett, Ida B. *Crusade for Justice: The Autobiography of Ida B. Wells.* Edited by Alfreda M. Duster. Chicago: University of Chicago Press, 1970.

West, Dorothy. *The Living Is Easy.* Old Westbury, N.Y.: Feminist Press, 1982.

Wood, Gordon S. *The Radicalism of the American Revolution.* New York: Knopf, 1992.

Woods, Robert A., ed. *The City Wilderness: A Settlement Study.* 1898. Reprint, New York: Garrett, 1970.

Woodward, C. Vann. *Origins of the New South, 1877–1913.* Baton Rouge: Louisiana State University Press, 1951.

———. *Reunion and Reaction: The Compromise of 1877 and the End of Reconstruction.* 1951. Reprint, Boston: Little, Brown, 1966.

———. *The Strange Career of Jim Crow.* 3d rev. ed. 1955. Reprint, New York: Oxford University Press, 1974.

Zangrando, Robert L. *The NAACP Crusade Against Lynching, 1909–1950.* Philadelphia: Temple University Press, 1980.

Pamphlets and Unpublished Manuscripts

The Reverend Mother Augustine [Eulalia Tuckerman]. "Life of Archbishop Williams." Archdiocese of Boston.

Ballou, Richard A. "Even in 'Freedom's Birthplace'! The Development of Boston's Black Ghetto, 1900–1940." Ph.D. diss., University of Michigan, 1984.

Burrows, John Howard. "The Necessity of Myth: A History of the National Negro Business League, 1900–1945." Ph.D. diss., Auburn University, 1977.

Harmond, Richard Peter. "Tradition and Change in the Gilded Age: A Political History of Massachusetts, 1878–1893." Ph.D. diss., Columbia University, 1966.

Hayden, Robert C. "Boston's NAACP History, 1910–1982." Pamphlet published by Boston Branch, NAACP, 1982.

———. "Faith, Culture and Leadership: A History of the Black Church in Boston." Pamphlet published by Boston Branch, NAACP, and Robert C. Hayden, 1983.

Hill, Adelaide Cromwell. "The Negro Upper Class in Boston: Its Development and Present Structure." Ph.D. diss., Radcliffe College, 1952.

Jacobs, Donald Martin. "A History of the Boston Negro from the Revolution to the Civil War." Ph.D. diss., Boston University, 1968.

Johnson, Violet Mary-Ann. "The Migration Experience: Social and Economic Adjustment of British West Indian Immigrants in Boston, 1915–1950." Ph.D. diss., Boston College, 1992.

Leger, Ann Louise. "Moorfield Storey: An Intellectual Biography." Ph.D. diss., University of Iowa, 1968.

Salem, Dorothy C. "To Better Our World: Black Women in Organized Reform, 1890–1920." Ph.D. diss., Kent State University, 1986.

Terborg-Penn, Rosalyn Marian. "Afro-Americans in the Struggle for Woman Suffrage." Ph.D. diss., Howard University, 1977.

Walsh, Francis Robert. "The Boston Pilot: A Newspaper for the Irish Immigrant, 1829–1908." Ph.D. diss., Boston University, 1969.

Articles

Arnesen, Eric. " 'Like Banquo's Ghost, It Will Not Down': The Race Question and the American Railroad Brotherhoods, 1880–1920." *American Historical Review* 99, no. 5 (December 1994): 1601–33.

Baldwin, Maria. "The Changing Idea of Progress." *Southern Workman* (January 1900): 15–16.

Blodgett, Geoffrey. "The Mind of the Boston Mugwump." *Mississippi Historical Review* 48, no. 4 (March 1962): 614–34.

Brown, Charles Sumner. "Genesis of the Negro Lawyer in New England." *Negro History Bulletin* (April 1959).

Bushee, Frederic. "Ethnic Factors in the Population of Boston." Publications of the American Economic Association 4 (2 May 1903, microfiche ed.).

Daniel, Pete. "Up From Slavery and Down to Peonage: The Alonzo Bailey Case." *Journal of American History* 57 (December 1970): 654–70.

Mabee, Carleton. "A Negro Boycott to Integrate Boston Schools." *New England Quarterly* 41 (September 1968).

Meier, August. "Booker T. Washington and the Negro Press, With Special Reference to the *Colored American Magazine*." *Journal of Negro History* 38 (January 1953): 67–90.

Robboy, Stanley J., and Anita W. Robboy. "Lewis Hayden: From Fugitive Slave to Statesman." *New England Quarterly* 46 (December 1973): 591–613.

Ruchames, Louis. "Race, Marriage and Abolition in Massachusetts." *Journal of American Negro History* 40 (1955): 250–73.

———. "Jim Crow Railroads in Massachusetts." *American Quarterly* 8 (1956): 61–75.

Schockley, Ann Allen. "Pauline Elizabeth Hopkins: A Biographical Excursion Into Obscurity." *Phylon* 33, no. 1 (Spring 1972): 22–26.

Smith, Robert P. "William Cooper Nell: Crusading Black Abolitionist." *Journal of Negro History* 55 (1970): 182–99.

Thornbrough, Emma Lou. "The National Afro-American League, 1887–1908." *Journal of Southern History* (November 1961): 494–512.

Welch, Richard E. "Opponents and Colleagues: George Frisbie Hoar and Henry Cabot Lodge, 1898–1904." *New England Quarterly* (June 1966): 182–209.

Whyte, William Foote. "Race Conflicts in the North End." *New England Quarterly* 5 (1939).

Wood, Gordon S. "The Massachusetts Mugwumps." *New England Quarterly* (December 1960): 435–51.

Index

252 Index

Civil rights (*cont.*)
  Catholic Church and, 177–81; William
    Howard Taft and, 69, 72; women's suf-
    frage and, 89, 91
Civil War: Massachusetts blacks in, 14–15
Clansman, The (Dixon), 147
Clapp, W. W., 36
Clark, Albert, 41
Clement, Edward Henry, 47–49, 54, 68
Cleveland, Grover, 24
Clifford, J. R., 119
Cobleigh, Rolfe, 139, 150, 151
Cole, J. Will, 67
Coleman, Harold W., 147
Collins, Patrick, 173
Colored American Magazine, 7, 62–67,
    100
Colored National League, 38
Colored Patriots of the Revolution (Nell),
    13
Colored Women's League, 96
Common Law, The (Holmes), 187, 189
Conway, Katherine, 178, 180
Corrigan v. Buckley, 209
Cotton Whigs, 18
Courtney, Samuel F., 75
Crafts, Ellen, 14
Crafts, William, 14
Crane, Winthrop Murray, 114, 126
Crawford, George W., 114
Crime, 11–12
Crisis, 118, 134
Crothers, Samuel M., 61
Crummell, Alexander, 37, 97
Crumpacker, Edgar D., 174
Cummings, Edward, 110
Cuney, Maud, 50
Curley, James Michael, 20, 21, 173; *The
    Birth of a Nation* and, 148–49, 152, 175
Curtis, Benjamin, 35

D'Alessandro, Dominic, 181
Daniels, John: on African-American
  women's club movement, 94–95; at
  Alexander's Magazine, 67–68; on black

economic demographics, 74, 183; on
  Boston's urban conditions, 10–12; *In
  Freedom's Birthplace* and, 183; on race
  relations, 7; on southern migrants, 9
Davidson, Olivia A., 59
Davis, Jefferson, 7
Debt law, 194–95
Democratic party: in Boston, 173; civil
  rights and, 43, 176; election of 1890
  and, 50; Federal Elections bill and,
  42–43; John O'Reilly and, 167; racism
  in, 176
Disfranchisement (*see also* Voting rights);
  in Alabama, 191–92; Booker T. Washington and, 79, 191; Henry Blackwell
  on, 91–92; of southern blacks, 25; Supreme Court on, 191–92; in Texas,
  196–97; William Lloyd Garrison II
  on, 92
Dixon, Thomas, 147, 151
Douglass, Frederick, 13, 18, 19, 36, 40, 88
Downing, George T., 40, 116
Du Bois, W. E. B.: *Alexander's Magazine*
  on, 68, 70; Booker T. Washington
  and, 79–80, 81, 98; on Maria Baldwin,
  103–4; NAACP and, 134, 153–54; *Souls
  of Black Folk*, ix, 66, 68; on voting
  rights, 51; William Monroe Trotter
  and, 111, 113–16, 151–52
Dukes, Nelson, 147
Dunbar, Paul Lawrence, 61
Dupree, William H., 15, 37, 53, 63
Dutton, Henry Worthington, 47
Dyer, Leonidas C., 210–11
Dyer antilynching bill, 210–11

Education (*see also* Literacy); blacks in
  Boston and, 11; Blair bill and, 33, 38
Eliot, Charles W., 46, 61, 76, 77
Emilio, Luis F., 14–15
Everett, Edward, 18
Everett, William, 49

Fairlie, John A., 110
Faneuil Hall, 6, 38, 115, 127–28

Wendell, Barrett, 61
Wendell Phillips Club, 61
West, Dorothy, 60
West Indians: in Boston, 10
Whaley, A. W., 119
White supremacy: in Gilded Age, 23; in
  Progressive Era, 24; women's suffrage
  and, 22, 83, 86, 87
Whittier, John Greenleaf, 126
Wickersham, George W., 201
Wilkins, Fred ("Shadrach"), 14
Willard, Francis, 96
Williams, George Fred, 49, 176
Williams, John J., 178, 179
Williams v. Mississippi, 25
Wilson, Butler, 128; army racism and,
  147; as attorney, 117, 198; NAACP and,
  136–37, 144, 147, 153–54
Wilson, Mary Evans, 136–37, 158
Wilson, Woodrow, 24; federal segrega-
  tion and, 142–44; William Monroe
  Trotter and, 120
Winthrop, John, 3
Winthrop, Robert C., 18
Wolff, James H., 6, 14, 198–99

Woman's Era, 96, 97, 98, 99–100, 102
Woman's Era Club, 12, 19, 94, 99, 104
Woman's Journal: abolitionist tradition
  and, 89–90; closing of, 93; Henry
  Blackwell and, 83, 85; NAWSA and,
  86, 91; on southern race relations,
  90–91; on white supremacy, 87
Women's suffrage: antislavery movement
  and, 86; black women and, 84, 93–94;
  civil rights and, 89, 91; Josephine St.
  Pierre Ruffin on, 99–100; linkage to
  literacy, 87–89; Maria Baldwin and,
  105; in Massachusetts, 93; national associations, 85, 86; Pauline Hopkins on,
  100; racism and, 83, 85–86, 91; social
  class and, 89; white supremacy and, 22,
  83, 86, 87; whiteness of, 86–87; William Lloyd Garrison II and, 19; *Woman's Era* on, 99–100
World War I: black support of, 121–22;
  effects on blacks, 177; effects on Irish-
  Americans, 177; racism during, 24–25

YMCA, 144

Zueblein, Charles, 116